Strangers Always

Strangers Always

A Jewish Family
in Wartime Shanghai

Rena Krasno

Pacific View Press
Berkeley, California

Photo credits: Palace Hotel, Whangpoo River, and Shanghai
Waterfront from the album of Dr. Amadeua Baldi, courtesy of Marilyn
M. Baldi; Bet Aharon and Cathedral Church from *Shanghai of To-day*
(Kelly & Walsh, Shanghai, 1928)

Map: *Shanghai,* by Ellen Thorbecke (North China Daily News and
Herald: Shanghai, 1938)

Cover design by Rob Hugel

Library of Congress Catalog Card Number: 92-61320
ISBN 1-881896-02-1

Printed in the United States of America

In memory of my parents,
David and Aida Rabinovich

Contents

List of Illustrations   *viii*

Foreword   *ix*

Preface   *xiii*

1942   1

1943   45

1944   99

1945   153

Epilogue   205

Index   209

List of Illustrations

Map   xvi–xvii

Wedding picture of parents, David and Aida Rabinovich

Parents, aunt, and uncle of author

Mother's sister in Chinese wheelbarrow

Yorifumi Enoki, Japanese friend

David Rabinovich at his writing

Anti-Semitic Russian newspapers

Mussolini's resignation announced in code

Boris Topas, Jewish leader and torture victim

Palace Hotel

Whangpoo River

Bet Aharon, Sephardi synagogue

Cathay Hotel

Cathedral Church

Trade advertising sheet from Honkew ghetto

Ashkenazi Jewish Communal Association Letterhead

Masthead of *Nasha Jizn* (Our Life)

Rabindranath Tagore's dedication

Parents' permits for immigration to Israel

Max Scheidlinger and friend

Board of the Shanghai Jewish Club

Shanghai's Waterfront

Foreword

What I saw of Shanghai in 1977, on my first trip to mainland China, made a lasting impression. The disheartening lethargy and drabness in the other cities I saw contrasted sharply with the scene on Shanghai's main street, Nanjing Road, with its vast number of people, filling the sidewalks and spilling out into the street, moving with purpose and energy. Another strong impression came from the distinctive architecture of the city, drawn from every sort of European style of the last century or so, giving evidence of its cosmopolitanism and harking back to its history as a meeting place of East and West.

Since then I have been back to Shanghai many times, and that same sense of vitality has only increased. By now, also, there is an additional layer of modern hotels, catering to the tourists, and on a par with the best anywhere in the world. The city, it is true, suffers from the general neglect of its physical plant which the leveling of class distinctions brings in its wake. One no longer finds corpses of starving fugitives of famines, such as are described in this book, but by the same token, there are no longer the wealthy, tended by their hosts of servants, to occupy the mansions and clubs of the past. Only the tourists and a growing number of foreign businessmen are reviving in faint measure that life of luxury and frivolity and worse that gave Shanghai its wicked image in the pre-World War II days, so well captured by Marlene Dietrich in the film *Shanghai*.

To recount the historical events that produced the city of Shanghai is to trace the history of China over the last century and a half. The Opium War, brought on by the

Chinese attempt to stop the flow of opium into their country, was the pretext used by the Western nations to force the Chinese to open their ports to foreign trade. Part of the peace arrangements included the provision that certain areas of Shanghai were to be administered by the foreign powers—Chinese administration and law could not extend to those who lived within the borders of these extraterritorial enclaves. Foreign communities in China as far back as one can go had always been held responsible for their own administration, but they were accountable, through an appointed headman, to the Chinese government; such group responsibility did not differ in principle from the way all of China was administered, and the *danwei* or units to which everyone in present-day China is attached, are a continuation of just such a system. The Westerners, (one includes here the Japanese) carried it much further, however, for they removed their enclaves, and the land these occupied, from the purview of the Chinese state, and in effect made of these extraterritorial colonies a kind of no-man's land. Even the Chinese who lived within these borders were protected from the reach of the Chinese authorities, and so these areas became a shelter for those who plotted against the state and a distribution point for seditious literature and movements. The system of extraterritoriality, deeply resented by the Chinese, came to include a broad array of special privileges for the foreigners, including even the right of their governments to maintain their own military forces for the protection of their nationals. It was during World War II, in which China was an ally, that the Allied powers began to give up these concessions, and by 1947 the last vestige was withdrawn.*

Shanghai was only one of a number of ports open to settlements of foreigners, but its size and location made it the most important. The variety and heterogeneity of its inhabitants may not have differed much from such cities as New York, but these people did not give their

---

*On extraterritoriality, see Wesley R. Fishel, *The End of Extraterritoriality in China* (Berkeley, Calif.: University of California Press, 1952).

allegiance to the country in which they lived. Brought together thus, the society was an extremely complex one. Over the past years there were many books written by sojourners there, emphasizing the bizarre and exotic. These rather superficial accounts have in more recent times come to be replaced by scholarly studies—the labor unions, literary societies, educational institutions, clandestine political movements, and other facets of Chinese society have attracted attention and provided a series of doctoral dissertations and books. What we have lacked is the voice of those who lived in Shanghai during its international heyday, those years before and during World War II. Such are now beginning to appear—one thinks of Nien Cheng's recent *Life and Death in Shanghai* or Francizka Taussig's *Shanghai-Passage* (Vienna: Verlag für Gesellschaftskritik, 1987)—and this is in good time, because when those survivors are gone, there will be no way of recapturing the sense of firsthand participation. It is thus our good fortune to have this record of Rena Krasno's experiences under the Japanese occupation of Shanghai during the war.

I have had the pleasure during the last few years to have come to know Rena through our participation in the work of the Sino-Judaic Institute, where she is in charge of public relations. She is a person of many interests, with a sense of curiosity and an intelligence and an enthusiasm for the life about her that makes any conversation with her so fascinating and stimulating. Since the years depicted in this book, she has lived in Japan, Korea, the Philippines, and Israel and now, the United States, constantly expanding her horizons and linguistic accomplishments. It is interesting to see in this book those same characteristics of personality already evident in her younger years, and it is just these which lend such charm and perception to her account. Cast in the form of a diary of her experiences (because her account is based on such diaries), one finds here much that has the freshness of immediate experience, but also much more, for she is able to provide a much wider canvas on which to depict a time and a society which have disappeared forever. Rena belonged to only one portion of this multifaceted society, but she did not limit herself to that one community, and in her writing we can find an engrossing and evocative account of a wide array of peoples and experiences, and as we accompany her, and through her eyes, we can see that world for ourselves.

Albert E. Dien
Asian Languages Department
Stanford University

Preface

Shanghai before Pearl Harbor and the Japanese Occupation was a vibrant, multifaceted city with clearly defined social stratifications. Among foreigners, the highest echelon was comprised of representatives of the Great Powers: the United States, Great Britain, France. Then came the Germans, who had lost some of their privileges after the defeat of their country in World War I, followed by citizens of "lesser" nations: Greeks, Turks, Spaniards, Italians, Iraqis, Syrians.

Below these proud passport-bearing nationals were the stateless, mainly White Russians, who had fled the 1917 Revolution, and Russian Jews who had escaped from both civil disorder and anti-Semitic pogroms. Although officially classified as a single entity, they represented two very distinct communities. Moreover, the Jewish community was subdivided into two ethnic groups: the Sephardis (of Middle Eastern rather than Spanish origin) and the Ashkenazis (of European origin). Later, a third category of newcomers was included—refugees from Hitler's Holocaust.

The next social stratum consisted of Eurasians, or "half-castes" who had the misfortune of being despised by the whites as well as the Chinese and lived in a social "no-man's land," often with devastating psychological results.

And the Chinese? They were the huge, massive, subdued background. Foreigners' relations with them were usually limited to business and daily dealings with servants and shopkeepers. Most whites had never been invited to a Chinese house, nor had they entertained Chinese guests in their own homes.

Pearl Harbor changed the face of Shanghai forever. Although after 1933, during an undeclared war on China (euphemistically named by Japan "The China Incident"), the Japanese had grabbed some 10,000 square miles of land outside Shanghai, they had been forced to respect the neutrality of the French Concession and the International Settlement. The attack on Pearl Harbor and the resulting Pacific War removed the last obstacle to the Japanese conquest of the entire city. The victorious invaders incarcerated "enemy nationals" in internment camps, while the stateless remained trapped in the city at the total mercy of the occupying forces. I belonged to the latter category—a Russian Jew without nationality.

Throughout the war period (from December 1941 to August 1945) I kept detailed diaries and clipped newspaper items that aroused my interest, amusement, or—in most cases—ire. In spite of wars, disruptions, and moving from country to country, they are still in my possession today, more than half a century later. Ah, those diaries! The first of several was given to me by my mother on my eighth birthday: a thick red book that could be locked with a key. Later I bought hardcovered notebooks (my favorite a polka-dotted red one) at the Japanese Gohdo Stationery Store to which I would rush whenever I was in the neighborhood. I had inherited my father's attraction to all objects connected with writing: paper, envelopes, "Aquarella" colors, "Faber" pencils, pens, and nibs.

For the past many years I have been avidly reading literature about Shanghai, searching in vain for encompassing firsthand reports on this critical point in history which sounded the death knell of colonialism. The paucity of material turned me back again and again to these diaries and the various documents I saved along with them, finally inspiring me to gather them together and publish them in the form of this journal, in the hope of recapturing those momentous days and sharing them with others.

This account is entirely factual, at least as I saw it from my personal perspective: Shanghai's diverse reality was perceived from a different angle by each one of its multimillion inhabitants. Some names have been changed for obvious reasons.

The purpose of the footnotes is to clarify historical facts and events perhaps unfamiliar to the general public and to provide information about the fate of some of the people and places after the War.

My thanks are due to my editor at Pacific View Press, Bob Schildgen, for his enthusiasm and moral support.

Rena Krasno
Mountain View, California

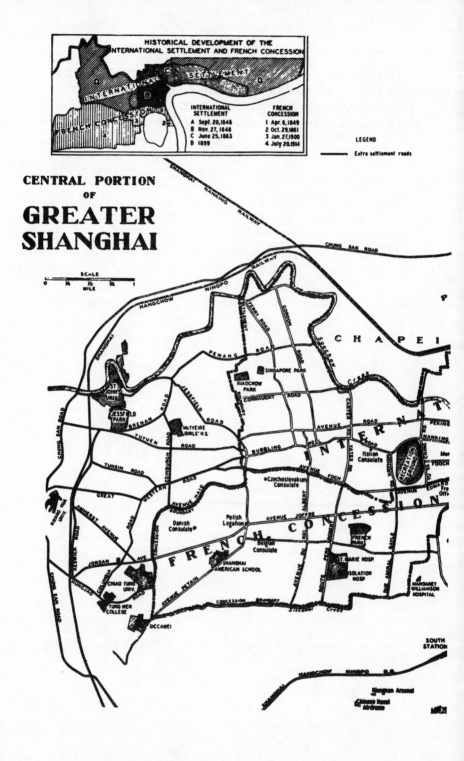

HISTORICAL DEVELOPMENT OF THE
INTERNATIONAL SETTLEMENT AND FRENCH CONCESSION

INTERNATIONAL SETTLEMENT	FRENCH CONCESSION
A Sept. 20, 1846	1 Apr. 6, 1849
B Nov. 27, 1848	2 Oct. 29, 1861
C June 25, 1863	3 Jan. 27, 1900
D 1899	4 July 20, 1914

LEGEND
——— Extra settlement roads

CENTRAL PORTION
OF
GREATER
SHANGHAI

SCALE
0   ¼   ½   ¾   1
MILE

1942

Isolation weighs like a heavy mantle on the shards of Shanghai's foreign population. Gone are the absolute monarchs of the foreign concessions, gone their privileges, their extraterritorial rights.

In 1842, at the end of the Opium War, the Treaty of Nanking had forced a vanquished and humiliated China to open five ports—among them Shanghai—to Western trade. Threats and intimidation led to the extraction by Great Britain of "most favored nation" status. This meant that any privileges or immunities granted thereafter to any other foreign power would immediately and automatically apply to all British subjects in China. Jealous of England's domination, the United States in 1844 and France in 1846 succeeded in obtaining the same conditions. Germany and Russia also bullied China for their piece of the pie.

In the very heart of Shanghai, "miniature countries" were created: the British, Americans, and French organized their own tax systems, courts, defense forces, and schools.

The Chinese, in their own homeland, moved down to the lowest stratum of the social structure.

A month ago, Pearl Harbor twisted and changed a state of affairs that had seemed permanently entrenched in Shanghai. Today, all-powerful, all-feared, bayonet-armed Japanese soldiers occupy our city. Greeks, Iraqis, Syrians, stateless Russians, and Jews, reinforced by refugees from Hitler's horrors are but droplets in a sea of Chinese—unwanted, unneeded, alone. France, defeated by Germany in 1940, is tolerated by the Japanese, but many Frenchmen have left for safer shores, some to join De Gaulle's Free French Forces. Germans—Japan's allies—have become the foreign elite and the Nazi flag, sporting its black Swastika, flutters arrogantly above the Kaiser Wilhelm Schule.[1]

---

[1] Kaiser Wilhelm Schule was attended by German children only. After the War, U.S. forces used its premises for an officers' club.

Every day the streets become filthier. Popular British double-decker buses have vanished, diesel oil and gasoline are unavailable, and scarce single-decker buses run on smoky charcoal. They do look strange, with a stovelike contraption in the front and a pipe belching dark smoke. The French call them *gazogènes*, and have converted the limousines of their high-ranking officers to this system. Electric tramcars with clanging bells supply the main means of transportation. Clumsy wheelbarrows block the thoroughfares, their enormous single wheel turning in a wooden cage, carrying people, small farmyard animals, and utensils. Carts drawn by emaciated horses slow down the traffic, and ever-present rickshaws dart between all these vehicles cutting a crooked path through chaotic crowds.

Since the Japanese occupation, prices have risen: one grape costs 30 cents, one egg 40 cents, a pair of shoes $800–$900, and a short rickshaw ride $15. The new currency is called CRB (Central Reserve Bank) and has replaced the old Fa Pi. Beggars huddle on sidewalks searching for lice in their tattered rags. This morning, I saw a wasted Chinese boy with long, tousled hair and ulcered legs grab a parcel from a White Russian woman as she came out of a butchery. He shredded off the newspaper wrapping as he dashed away gnawing at the contents—a chunk of raw meat. Blood dripped down his face as the woman screamed.

The Japanese have named the Pacific War "Greater East Asia War," a war whose ultimate goal is to "liberate 1,000,000,000 Asians from Western colonization and exploitation." We now live in the "Greater Asia Co-Prosperity Sphere" and are urged to "chop up Anglo-Saxon Devils," to "butcher the U.S. and Britain."

Increasing misery and provocative Japanese slogans demanding "Asia for the Asiatics" bring to the fore long-hidden Chinese resentment against the "Europeans," i.e., the whites. Hostility and anger are openly demonstrated on the streets of Shanghai. As I ride my bicycle Chinese urchins brush against me shouting taunts and curses and, several days ago, the tram conductor refused to hand me my change. When I stubbornly insisted, he flung the coins at my feet where they were snatched away instantly by anonymous hands. This afternoon a Chinese grocer would not serve me, saying mockingly: "Missee come back when eyes no blue!"

Amah removed the dishes from the table after dinner, Mama retired to her bedroom exhausted after an arduous day, my younger sister—five years my junior—sat cutting out paper dolls on the sofa. Papa and I remained seated while he sipped his strong deep-amber tea sweetened with three lumps of sugar. Papa, in the Russian manner, never drinks tea from a cup but from a solid glass set in a silver holder with a handle. He looked at me with irritation and grumbled angrily:
"Stop wrinkling your forehead!"
I suppressed a furious reply. This was a habit I had picked up from him! Then immediately regretting his short temper Papa said:
"This terrible war is making me very nervous. The thought that Jews in Europe are being systematically destroyed obsesses me night and day. How can we save our people, their wonderful culture, their traditions? The Nazis are flinging Jewish books into bonfires, burning 'degenerate' art, extinguishing every creative breath that diverges from their party ideology—a fierce ideology contrary to all natural, humane feelings."
He took off his glasses, set them on the table and rubbed his forehead.
Then he affectionately patted my hand, still guilty about having upset me, and continued. "Do you know what my dearest hope is? To create a center of Jewish culture here in distant China, far from Europe, from Hitler, from the German Reich."
As a first step, Papa and a group of like-thinking friends have founded The Jewish Book Publication Society. They translate and publish Russian versions of English and Yiddish novels and short stories written by beloved Jewish authors: Mendele Mocher Sfarim, Sholem Aleichem, Israel Joshua Singer, and others.

Papa took it upon himself to translate into Russian the American Ludwig Lewisohn's *The Island Within.*

Apart from the Jewish Publication Society (popularly called The Jewish Book), Papa is involved as editor and main writer of the Russian-language magazine, *Nasha Jizn (Our Life),* "Shanghai's National Independent Democratic Organ of Jewish Thought." It prints articles on the daily life of Shanghai Jews, Jewish culture and general news affecting Jews both in China and abroad. Politics are scrupulously avoided.

This month, an entire page appeared in English in *Nasha Jizn* in response to persistent complaints from European refugee would-be readers who know no Russian. The editorial board is also discussing the inclusion of a Yiddish supplement.[2]

As editor responsible for the magazine's policy, Papa must contend with the strangling presence of Japanese censorship and the possibility of nefarious repercussions on the Jewish Community. This is a permanent source of worry and soul-searching: he refuses to lie or flatter the Japanese occupiers, yet is forced to express only partial facts.

Before the first issue of *Nasha Jizn* finally appeared on May 2 last year, its "founding fathers" would meet frequently in our living room and loud arguments would erupt. All—like Papa—are liberals of uncompromising integrity and . . . quick tempers! Today, since Lithuanian, Latvian, and Polish refugees participate in the editorial board, discussions have become somewhat more subdued in deference to the "newcomers"—much to my sister's and my disappointment since we loved to giggle listening to passionate outbursts on the other side of our bedroom wall:

"*Nikogda!*" (Never!) . . . "*Vozmutitelno!*" (Outrageous!) . . . "*Idiotstvo!*" (Idiocy!)

Although Mama claims I am *papina dochka* (father's daughter) and always defend him hotly against the slightest hint of criticism, I too have come to resent the

---

[2]Entire English and Yiddish sections were later added to the magazine so that it became, in effect, trilingual.

constant demands on his time by his publications and social work in the Jewish Community, so I rudely broke his train of thought by bursting into a wild tirade— which I immediately regretted—about being "deprived of a father by those books, that magazine, and all those endless refugees from Europe." Then, pausing for breath, I braced myself to withstand a furious onslaught, but surprisingly Papa did not shout a reply. He merely looked dejected and finally spoke:

"Yes, it is true that *Nasha Jizn,* "The Jewish Book," and various committees on which I serve cost me hard work and many, many sleepless nights. But don't you understand that in these disastrous times we all must make sacrifices? Actually it is thanks to your mother bearing the burden of family breadwinner that I can dedicate all my time to causes that I consider urgent and imperative. Don't you see that we are now at a point in history where the very survival of the Jewish people is at stake? We are doomed if we don't keep up a collective spirit to overcome today's dangers."

He paused, sipped some tea and raised his voice in fury:

"I don't believe that the Allies are anxious to deliver us from the Nazis! The United States and Britain set up all kinds of obstacles to the immigration of Jews from Europe. Some refugees are even sent back to a frightening fate."

Papa and I are both hotheaded and often pounce at each other, but I love him more than any other being in the world.

Papa arrived in Shanghai in 1921 from Vladivostok, on his way to Palestine, together with several other fiery but penniless Zionists. They shared an attic room in a Jewish boarding house. Since they could not afford to pay for regular meals, they drank innumerable glasses of scalding tea from the constantly simmering samovar on the dining room table and devoured thick chunks of bread the kindhearted landlady provided free of charge.

In preparation for *halutz* (pioneer) lives, Papa's companions took lessons in shoemaking and basketweaving
from skilled Chinese, while my disappointed father lay
immobilized with an acute attack of appendicitis. As his
friends proceeded on their convoluted journey to the
Holy Land, Papa underwent surgery and remained in
Shanghai.

Shortly after, he met and married my mother.[3]

In 1921, there were some 500 Russian Jews living in
Shanghai. Who were they and how had they reached
this distant city?

The first Russian Jewish settler in Shanghai to become a permanent resident was a man named
Haimovich, who arrived in 1887. Others followed after
the Russo-Japanese War (1904–1905) when a number of
Russian Jewish soldiers decided not to return to their
anti-Semitic homeland, stayed in North China, and
gradually trickled into Shanghai. In 1907, the first
Ashkenazi (Russian Jewish) synagogue was inaugurated
and a congregation founded.

After the Great War of 1914–1918, Russian Jewish soldiers again trekked to China, their numbers swollen by
civilians escaping the atrocities of the Russian
Revolution.

A nucleus of Russian Jews arrived in Harbin during
the construction of the Chinese Eastern Railroad. In 1896
China had signed a treaty with the Russians ensuring
mutual assistance against any future Japanese aggression. One of the terms of the treaty was China's
agreement to Russia building a railroad (later known as
the Chinese Eastern Railroad) across Manchuria up to
Vladivostok. Russia also obtained extraterritorial rights
in a strip extending two-and-a-half miles on each side of
the railroad, meaning that Russian law would apply
fully in this five-mile-wide area. Thus, part of
Manchuria became in effect an extension of Siberia, but

---

[3]One of my father's companions, M. A. Novomeysky, became the
founder of the Dead Sea Potash Works, and another, Evzeroff,
initiated the construction of Binyanei Hauma, a great convention and
concert hall at the entrance of Jerusalem.

a freer Siberia, a kind of liberated "Wild West" with its own rules and regulations. It was natural that Russian Jews should gravitate toward such a region, which was almost persecution-free, mainly because Russia did not want to show the Chinese that any white man—even a Jew—could ever be treated as inferior to an Asian!

As railway construction proceeded in 1901, Jews fleeing terror and pogroms immigrated to Harbin—a key point in the railway between Vladivostok in the east and Chita in the west. Some flourished, opened stores, breweries, refineries, paint factories, and hotels. Others, seeking a more secure future in international Shanghai, drifted south. By 1924, the number of Russian Jews in Shanghai reached 800, most having settled in Wayside in the International Settlement. Later, in the late 1920s, they started to move to the French Concession.

More Jews left Harbin for Shanghai in 1928. On this date the Soviet government returned the Chinese Eastern Railroad to China and foreign business enterprises were adversely affected by the opening of the economy to Chinese participation.

In the meantime, anti-Semitism persisted and grew in Russia, with a pogrom in Ukraine resulting in:

500 Jews slaughtered—
200 Jews burned and buried alive—
40,000 Jews dead as a result of neglected wounds—
20,000 Jewish women raped.

No wonder more and more panic-stricken Jews fled by rail, sea, and even on foot to reach the relative safety of China.

In 1931, the Japanese invaded Manchuria, kidnapped the last Manchu emperor in Tientsin, and made him the figurehead ruler of Manchuria, which they renamed Manchukuo. Terror and extortion became the order of the day. In Harbin, the Japanese Military Police (Kempeitai), aided and abetted by White Russian Fascists, blamed the Jews for starting the Russian Revolution, raided a Jewish hospital, a synagogue, and an old people's home, confiscating money and documents and terrorizing their victims. The result: hundreds of Jews sought the haven of Shanghai.

Following these upheavals, Shanghai today has some 1,000 Russian Jewish families, totalling over 4,000 persons—a solid community!

At first, the Jews were considered in Shanghai as part and parcel of the White Russian Community (i.e., non-Soviet) but in 1937 the Shanghai Municipal Council recognized the Jews as a distinct communal association which operated under the umbrella of the White Russians. . . .

It was getting late. My sister gathered her things and went into the bedroom we share. Papa and I sat quietly and after a while he resumed the conversation:

"You know very well we stateless people have no embassy, no consulate, no official representatives whatsoever. In fact, we had to create our own administration to take care of all the needs of Jews from birth to death."

"Don't the hospitals issue birth certificates?" I asked.

"Yes, but we supply our own. Boys receive one only after their Brit Milah (circumcision). This confirms their Jewish identity."[4]

Papa moved to an armchair to read today's paper and I decided to call my friend Genny for one of our prolonged chats.

February 1942

My mother is now in the children's toy and fashion business. Since the Japanese took over the British firm where my father worked as provision department manager he has been unable to find suitable employment, especially since he refuses to consider a job even remotely connected with the Japanese Occupying Forces. Thus, my mother has become the family's sole source of income—a cause of concern as the general economic situation deteriorates.

---

[4]This proved to be of great importance after the establishment of the State of Israel. Only those able to prove their Jewish origin were admitted automatically as immigrants.

Some time ago, Mama opened a children's dress salon and toy shop on Avenue Joffre—the French Concession's main artery. A Chinese "couturier" creates children's garments for her, mainly out of fabric remnants. Old movie magazines with photos of Shirley Temple serve as Mama's main inspiration for clothing designs. As for toys, two White Russian ladies supply delightful, one-of-a-kind handmade stuffed animals, while a Chinese carpenter transfers to reality Mama's dreams of dolls' cribs, rocking chairs, miniature kitchens and bedroom furniture sets. Thus Mama's store named "Peter Pan" not only contributes to the survival of our family but also puts food on the table of a little group of talented and dedicated workers.

To our great amusement, many customers have never heard the story of Peter Pan and assume the business had been called after its Chinese owner! Some even address my mother as Mrs. Pan and ask, "Is your husband Chinese?"

Mama leaves early in the morning and returns late in the evening. She bought a secondhand 21-inch children's bicycle and although she had never ridden before in her life, calmly perched on the seat and took off undauntedly. She covers many miles from one end of Shanghai to the other in search of pre-War stocks of fabrics and toys. When successful, she returns in triumph, a tiny woman with a pile of boxes tied to the back of her small bicycle. She unearthed last month a huge roll of grey plush which the Russian ladies have used for manufacturing whimsical elephants, floppy-eared puppies and . . . a long flannel-lined jacket for me which I detest![5]

Neither the bombs nor the Japanese dampen Mama's *joie de vivre*. A humorous, vivid raconteuse, she regales us with stories about her customers, one of whom was Emily Hahn, the famous U.S. journalist/writer.[6] Emily Hahn, an eccentric, bright young woman arrived in Shanghai before the War in 1935, sporting a short bob

[5]It kept me warm throughout the War.
[6]Author of *The Soong Sisters, China to Me*, etc.

hairstyle, a novelty in our city at the time. She landed a job with the venerable British *North China Daily News*[7] writing feature stories and interviewing members of Shanghai's variegated society. She adored garden parties, arriving in floating dresses and large floppy hats, but her prim appearance belied her sometimes shocking speech and behavior. She had—contrary to local mores—many Chinese friends, and it was rumored she had even married a Chinese.[8] She hated discrimination and fulminated against those who "feel about Eurasians as our Southerners do about mulattoes." She ranted when the Columbia American Club, which excluded Chinese members and guests, did not permit famous Chinese Hollywood actress Anna May Wong to bowl in their alley—at a time when crowds mobbed the Grand Theatre to see a popular film in which she starred!

Emily Hahn became Mama's customer because of her Singapore Gibbon, Mr. Mills. He had beige fur, a black face and, according to my mother "wise, wise eyes that noticed everything." Actually, it was not Miss Hahn but Mr. Mills who was Mama's client: the children's salon created made-to-order outfits for him. Since Miss Hahn insisted he accompany her to elegant cocktail parties and receptions, she required him to be appropriately dressed!

Once when one of Mr. Mills' suits was ready, Mama decided to deliver it personally to Miss Hahn's home. Mama steadfastly denied that curiosity rather than the need for special service had propelled her, in spite of my sister's and my accusations to the contrary. Be that as it may, when Mama arrived, she was calmly received by a stark naked Emily Hahn and a fully clad monkey. As my mother tried to control her laughter at the unusual sight, Miss Hahn explained that nudity to her meant total freedom.

A reluctant Mr. Mills was compelled to undress and try on his new suit, which fit perfectly, to my mother's relief. Emily Hahn mentioned that Mr. Mills was very

[7]Founded in 1864.
[8]The marriage, according to Chinese law, was a formality to disguise Chinese ownership of a printing press from the Japanese.

sensitive to cold, contrary to herself, and in reply to my mother's questions as to his food preferences, she said: "Oh, he eats fruit and cake but what he REALLY does love are worms—the kind the Chinese feed their birds." My squeamish mother shuddered. Miss Hahn also related that, worried about Mr. Mills' love life she had bought him a female gibbon, Mrs. Mills. However, to her disappointment, Mrs. Mills showed no passionate interest in her intended and "acted like a bored grandmother."

March 1942

Two years of intensive studies for the French baccalaureate, the upheaval of the Japanese Occupation, and the chilling war news from Europe appear to have sapped my desire for further education—at least for the present. Murky forebodings darken the future and my moods swing from gloom to hope, from despondence to spontaneous joy. Is this what youth is meant to be?

Contradictory and overwhelming feelings surge within me: no desire to study but the hunger to learn; hatred for violence but the wish to exterminate the Nazis; the physical need for passionate love but the moral obligation to pursue the ideal of chastity.

The beginning of this year found me uncertain and confused. Now, after much soul-searching, I accepted a teaching position at the Shanghai Jewish School, simply as a stop-gap solution.

The Shanghai Jewish School stands at the corner of two busy streets. In 1931 I. M. Perry, a rich Sephardi Jewish resident, died leaving in his will 50,000 silver taels (about 36,000 Mexican dollars) for the construction of a school for Sephardi Jewish children. However, his testament stipulated that this money would only be available on the condition that the local Jewish Sephardi Community donated an equivalent sum. Fortunately, millionaire Elly Kadoorie came to the rescue, making good the difference. A modern school was eventually built: it had large windows, well-lit classrooms, a spacious central court, and faucets with filtered drinking water—a new-fangled convenience at the time.

At first, the Shanghai Jewish School was intended only for Sephardi children from families with serious financial problems. Its aim was to provide traditional Jewish education and safeguard youth from the rootless cosmopolitanism pervasive in Shanghai. Gradually, however, as Russian Jewish children fleeing pogroms trickled into Shanghai they too were welcomed kindly by the school committee which, besides providing free education, saw to it that they were fed and clothed. An Educational Aid Society was founded to raise money for the school. Then, as more and more Jews poured into Shanghai to escape from Hitler, an additional fund was created so as to enable the school to absorb numerous new pupils. Today the school suffers from a serious lack of funds and is struggling very hard to maintain acceptable standards. One of the results of this difficult situation is that teachers are very badly paid and the salary offered to me is laughable.

The character of the school has also changed. The Sephardi children no longer represent a majority and are by far outnumbered by pupils from European families. Parents are clamoring for standards of education compatible with those abroad so that when peace arrives one day their offspring will be able to pursue university education in other countries.

A young engineer, graduate of a Belgian university, has been appointed headmaster. A soft-spoken, serious, and dedicated man, he is striving to develop a curriculum based on the requirements of the London Cambridge examination.

When I started teaching on a Monday morning, I was told to go to the Assembly Hall where, according to school tradition, the entire student body and teachers gather to review important events of the past week. A short prayer is jointly recited:

"Hear O Israel: the Lord thy God, the Lord is One. And thou shalt love the Lord thy God with all thy heart and all thy soul and all thy might. Teach us, O God, to be good and kind to each other. Help us to love our parents, brothers, and sisters and to obey our teachers. Amen."

My emotion upon hearing these words rather surprised me. I am not religious at all and know very little about Judaism. God is never discussed in our home, although we do celebrate important Jewish holidays such as Passover and Yom Kippur—but this appears to result from national and not religious tradition. I find it difficult to explain to outsiders (and to myself!) why my family so passionately identifies with Jews. There is no doubt in my mind that I am part of the Jewish people, want to remain part of them and will never abandon them. Logically inexplicable but emotionally a fact!

At first my heart thumped with apprehension at the thought of facing a classroom of children for the first time but, fortunately, the pupils seemed to respond warmly to my spontaneous affection. During recess Erica—a pale Polish refugee girl wearing a balding fur strapped with a string around her waist—offered me a gift: a shell with the words "Tel Aviv" carved on its surface. She made me lean down and pressed the shell to my ear asking eagerly:

"Can you hear the waves? Can you hear the sea?"

When I nodded, she cried excitedly:

"It's the beach in Palestine!"

Her voice carried so much love and optimism that I could not but hug her.

Nowadays, I often remain after school to coach Klaus, a German refugee boy who appears to own only one pair of shorts: green "Lederhosen" that grow tighter and tighter on his rather chubby body. Klaus pronounces "s" like "sh": shtar, shtory, shtorm. It is most difficult for him to break the habit of German pronunciation. Today, at about four-thirty, three Japanese soldiers suddenly opened the door, stared into the classroom, then left without uttering a word, and Klaus froze into catatonic rigidity. His terror clearly reflected some traumatic past experience with the military and brought vividly to me the reality of Nazi horror.

Last week Estelle, a Sephardi girl from a destitute family, arrived to class wearing, as usual, filthy clothes and tattered tennis shoes. The teacher in charge of the entire lower school insisted that I send her home, but can a child of seven be responsible for such neglect? Should she be humiliated in front of all her classmates?

"Estelle, why aren't you wearing socks?"

"Because my mother is washing them."

As I spoke to my superior I tried to control the angry trembling of my voice and assured her that if she permitted Estelle to remain in class today, I would personally visit her home and speak to her parents. After some hesitation she agreed to my request.

Estelle's family lives in one room in a dark terrace house at the end of a narrow lane. All their neighbors are Chinese. Her mother, a grey-faced woman with an immense swollen belly, is dying of cancer. The family greeted me with warm smiles and grasped my hands. Feeling young, helpless, embarrassed, I explained the reason for my intrusion and they promised to wash Estelle in the mornings and provide her with clean clothing.

After the visit I pedaled my bike home as fast as I could, dashed into the flat, and was delighted to find Mama at home going through some bills. Most of the time she is out at her store or trying to find merchandise. I poured out the story of Estelle, giving vent to my fury and frustration. Mama, who is very kindhearted, appeared to be just as upset as I and quickly handed me two cans of Quaker Oats from her declining reserves, as well as money to buy the girl an extra pair of socks. Back on my bike, first to a haberdashery and then to Estelle's home . . . a 45-minute ride! Ooph!

Tonight we all listened glumly to the news on the radio. The Japanese have renamed Singapore Shonan ("Sho" being the first syllable of "Showa"—Emperor Hirohito's reign—and "nan" meaning south). It is clear they wish to eradicate past history! I thought of Shanghai becoming increasingly confined and oppressive, of the growing poverty and hunger. My only consolation was Erica's trust and her dream of Palestine.

April 1942

Walking alongside Eric, a 19-year-old Viennese refugee, I stealthily glance at his Barrymore profile, thick eyelashes, and lean, slightly concave cheeks. His simple elegance and courtesy reflect shades of a European culture obliterated in that Fascist-ravaged continent.

Eric was 15 on the night of November 9–10, 1938, later named "Kristallnacht," when Fascists smashed the glass of windows of Jewish homes and businesses. This wanton destruction unleashed an anti-Semitic tidal wave in Germany, Austria, and Sudentenland: 200 synagogues were set afire, 7,500 shops and small businesses destroyed, and thousands of Jews humiliated, beaten, arrested. Soon after, Eric's Jewish mathematics teacher was flung out of a second-story classroom to his death by mocking Nazi students, and his father disappeared.[9]

In the deepening gloom one ray of hope had appeared from a distant part of the world: the Open Ports of China, of which Shanghai was the most important one. All that the Open Ports authorities required from anyone seeking entry was proof of the possession of US$400. But here again Nazi intransigence intervened: no Jew was permitted to leave with more than ten Reichsmarks, which is less than US$3.

By this time, Jews in the United States began to understand the catastrophe that faced European Jewry, and great efforts were exerted to save those caught in the Nazi mesh. Arrangements were made to transfer sums of money to the Shanghai branch of the Chase Manhattan Bank to ensure the issuance of "landing passes" to Jewish refugees. Copies of these permits with lists of names of those seeking entry were then handed by the bank to representatives of Italian steamship companies. They in turn forwarded this information to their Italian head offices, which issued travel tickets to the Jews. The transportation costs were also financed by

---

[9]In some manner unknown to me his father later escaped and actually reached Shanghai.

American Jews in cases when refugees were unable to
pay for them in Reichmarks.

Thus Eric, his mother, and his older brother were
saved from almost certain death by U.S. Jews unknown
to them. They are only three among some 18,000
European Jewish refugees flooding Shanghai during
these past few years.

Eric and his family live in a tiny room in the French
Concession. They are among the more fortunate 4,000
refugees. Since housing is limited and well beyond the
means of destitute Europeans, most have been forced by
necessity to seek accommodation in a less prosperous
area: part of some 1,000 square miles occupied by Japan
after the so-called Undeclared War (the Sino-Japanese
hostilities terminated by Japanese victory). Much of this
territory is still in ruins, and refugees live among rubble
in "lane housing" along narrow, filth-strewn roads.
Others, in even more desperate straits, have been located in communal *Heime* (homes) supported by public
donations from Shanghai residents and ever-generous
U.S. Jews. Of course, since Pearl Harbor this complex situation has deteriorated further and nobody can guess
what Japan's next move will be as far as Jews are concerned. After all, the Germans are their allies and since
the total occupation of Shanghai by the Japanese the
gates of our city have been closed to Jewish refugees.

In spite of difficulties and uncertainties, Eric retains
an admirable Viennese *joie de vivre* and works cheerfully
many long hours as a waiter in a little Austrian restaurant famous for its Wienerschnitzel and Apfelstrudel.
Un-fortunately, I have never tasted the food about
which Eric rhapsodizes because he swore he would
"accidentally" spill some sauce on me should I appear
with another beau!

The owners of the restaurant—once prosperous
Viennese entrepreneurs—now rise daily before dawn,
ride rickshaws to the Chinese market in search of food
products, and have learned to bargain like natives. No
mean feat! Although they speak no Chinese they did
memorize numbers in that language, and this knowledge accompanied by much gesturing, feigned anger,

shock, and disgust serves them in good stead when purchasing meat and vegetables. One of the restaurant proprietors had always enjoyed gourmet cooking and
evolved into the perfect chef—a role to whose glamor
he adds by donning a high, starched, snow-white muf-
fin-shaped chapeau. The other, a theater and opera fan,
wears a borrowed tuxedo and acts as host, manager, and
accountant. He greets each incoming guest with charming courtesy and makes every woman feel like a queen.
Ah me! I must miss all that and only listen to Eric's accounts! In this artificial worldsplendor he accompanies
me to dances, swirling in graceful circles to the Blue
Danube Waltz, never tired, never dizzy, holding my
waist with firm masculinity.

Last Sunday morning we went to the Koukaza
("French") Park, sat on an octagonal bench surrounding
a tree-trunk, and Eric described in accented English life
in Vienna before the *Anschluss:* the coffee-shops, the op-
erettas, the Prater, the pretty girls (I didn't like that!), the
pastry that melted in one's mouth . . . Then he re-
counted a story he had heard from a Polish refugee. It
appears that a group of Yeshiva bochers—students of a
Jewish religious college—were riding the tram in the
French Concession, no doubt attracting gazes by their
side-locks, skull-caps, and black suits, never seen in
Shanghai before the War. Being recent newcomers the
young Jews were confused by their surroundings and
puzzled where to get off. There they stood hanging on to
the leather straps dangling from the ceiling of the tram
discussing what to do next. Imagine their stupefaction
when the Chinese tram conductor approached them and
offered directions in fluent, colloquial Yiddish! He explained that he had worked for many years at the home
of an old Jewish lady who spoke no English nor, of
course, Chinese. All she knew was Yiddish and he had
no choice but to pick up her dialect. After his employer
died he managed to get a job as a tram conductor
through a relative who had "pull." Eric and I laughingly
agreed that surely in all the world there could exist no
city more curious than Shanghai, where the remarkable
became routine!

When we returned home, Mama happened to be looking out the window and caught us holding hands. When I entered the apartment she asked me contemptuously:

"Do you have to cling to him? Are you afraid to fall if you walk alone?"

I paid her no heed and floated to my bedroom on a little cloud of happiness. However, at dinner her bad mood persisted and we soon found out the reason:

"Can you believe it? That nice German customer of mine, Mrs. Thiele, came to the shop today and told me that her husband does not permit her to continue buying in Jewish shops. The dirty, filthy Nazi! She looked so upset! I am sure he is a tyrant and that she is afraid of him. Poor woman!"

It is amazing what the mind does. It was as if a switch had clicked when I heard the word "German," and I was transported in space and time to Karatsu, Japan, two years before the start of the War. Karatsu was a seaside resort where my mother, my sister and I had spent two months' summer vacation at a simple but comfortable hotel. Our hotel manager, an outstandingly handsome Japanese with doelike eyes and brows in the shape of open birds' wings, delighted all his young guests by having delicious snacks wrapped up for them to take along to the beach or on hikes. A particularly endearing touch of his was to name dishes on the menu after us kids. I carefully saved the farewell menu in honor of my family when hotel guests were regaled on:

"Cordon Soup a la Alla" (my sister) and "Fried Fish a la Ira" (a Russian diminutive of my name).

At meals, all the youngsters ate together at one table apart from the adults. We were a noisy, laughing, chattering group of kids from Shanghai and Tientsin: Jewish, White Russian, Swiss, Scottish, English, and Iraqi. The only exceptions were two German boys obliged to sit at a table for four with their parents. Helmut, a blond, stone-faced, "Aryan" type masticated his food in silence and kept a ramrod straight posture throughout dinner. Hartmut, a roly-poly 10-year-old, cast occasional longing glances in our direction as we

loudly planned bonfires, picnics, and exploration of outlying villages. The four Germans wore plus-fours and
must have bathed in some hidden nook of the beach because, apart from meals, we never encountered them
anywhere. The German boys were obviously forbidden
to speak with any of us children.

I could understand Mama's sympathy for Mrs. Thiele
when I remembered Hartmut and almost said aloud:
"Sometimes I'm sorry for the Germans." But I was reluctant to start what would surely turn into a furious
discussion.

May 1942

A new word has been introduced into our vocabulary:
"Ersatz," meaning "substitute": "Ersatz" butter—a waxy
spread; "Ersatz" meat—soya bean; "Ersatz" porridge—
cracked wheat. Some of today's prices are:

Sugar—$8.00 a pound—

A small chicken—$200-$300—

Black market butter—$140 a pound.

Many Chinese can no longer afford to buy rice and
stoically eat a sticky dough of mysterious content. So
much for our "Greater Co-Prosperity Sphere"!

To escape Shanghai's tightening trap—at least mentally—I plunge into intensive reading. The need to reach
levels above and beyond the one where I exist has become almost obsessive. In discussions with friends I
quote, I fear pompously, the Chinese saying:

"To realize that our knowledge is ignorance is a noble
insight."

After much brooding I resolved not to return to
teaching this autumn and instead to enroll in the first
year of the Faculty of Medicine at the Jesuit Université
de l'Aurore, to which my baccalaureate diploma entitles
me. This decision is in some measure the result of my
friendship with a French classmate of mine who early in
high school decided to become a Jesuit priest. During
our prolonged walks in the Koukaza (French) Park we
discuss our widely differing philosophy and aims in life.
Although we appear to disagree on almost everything,
we both admire moral and intellectual ideals—a pursuit

from which I, alas, occasionally stray because to tell the
truth I love frivolous pastimes such as dancing and flir-
tation. [10]

Be that as it may, the Jesuits and their extraordinary
intellectual achievements fascinate me. The story of the
first Jesuit to break through the barrier of isolationism
in China, Father Matteo Ricci, is one I enjoy hearing repeated, a theme on which my friend waxes lyrical.

Father Ricci, an outstanding mathematician and lin-
guist as well an expert in the making of maps, clocks,
and spheres, was officially invited in 1583 by the governor of Shiuhing, China, to settle in that province and
teach the Chinese his skills. He convinced his Chinese
hosts of the importance of the principles of geometry,
which he insisted every army officer should master,
since "otherwise his wisdom and bravery would be exer-
cised in vain." Ricci's breadth of intellect was supported
by his most unusual visual memory: he could memorize at a glance a page covered with 500 random Chinese
characters.

It was also Father Ricci who, in 1605, wrote a long
memorandum to Rome about the existence of a Jewish
congregation in Kaifeng, Honan Province, after a chance
encounter with a Chinese Jew named Ai T'ien. Even today, over 400 years later, this is a subject that fascinates
Jews around the world. In Shanghai, there have been
some efforts to help this remote Jewish community to
survive, and a "Society for the Rescue of Chinese Jews"
was formed. All this to no avail since the Shanghai Jews
have had to contend throughout their history with sufficient problems of their own.

My French friend admires in particular Matteo Ricci's
understanding of Chinese culture—for which the Jesuit
developed a profound respect soon after realizing that
the Chinese would never reject the teachings of
Confucius and abandon traditional rites. As a result of
this inner conviction, Ricci believed that the only way to
success on his part (his main aim, of course, being the

[10]My friend's youthful dream came true and he became a very well-
known Jesuit priest.

spread of Christianity) would be to point out similarities rather than differences between Eastern and Western attitudes. He started wearing Chinese clothing and adopting Chinese manners. Not surprisingly, ultraconservative Rome disagreed entirely with Ricci and a great dispute developed, the so-called "Chinese Rites Controversy." It culminated after Ricci's death in 1704 when Pope Clement XI forbade the participation of Chinese Christians in rites honoring Confucius and their ancestors.

Yesterday in the park, my friend angrily brought up once again the subject of the historical dissension within the Church, furious at the myopic view of the Roman clergy.

"Can you imagine?" he cried indignantly, raising his usually soft voice. "It is only a few years ago in 1939 that Rome reversed this decision! *C'est ridicule!* For centuries the Jesuits in China had to struggle not only to overcome obstacles and dangers from the part of the Chinese, but also to battle against hurdles put up by their own church in Rome!"

It was a Chinese disciple of Father Ricci's who eventually moved to Shanghai, and gradually more and more Jesuits settled in our city, especially after the Treaty of Nanking in 1842. When foreign powers obtained extraterritorial rights in the city ports they were able to protect all their citizens, including, of course, missionaries, a fact that led to the establishment of new missions. However, the widespread resentment of the Chinese against the "Unfair Treaty" reflected on Christians, and Monsignor Celso Constani of Rome was to declare somewhat bitterly:

"Three hundred years of labor in China won the Missions only the stigma of 'imperialist aggressor' and 'foreign devil.' "

The Université de l'Aurore was established by the Jesuits in 1876 in the heart of the French Concession near the Cimetière des Soeurs. Today, its spacious grounds extend on both sides of Avenue Dubail, a wide and busy thoroughfare. Intended at first only for male students, its policy was later liberalized to include

women. I spoke to the incredibly handsome Jesuit Père
de Breuverie regarding my admission, which he welcomed. He suggested that I buy a skeleton now from a
former medical student who no longer needs it. Owning
a skeleton is a requirement for our osteology class and,
later, when the semester starts I would most probably
have to pay more. My parents gladly gave me the necessary money and I brought home "Oscar," complete with
"coffin," a rather nice hinged wooden case which rests
under my bed—a silent, friendly presence at night!

Due to the increasing number of deaths in the streets
of Shanghai, skeletons are readily available. On the university grounds I saw coolies roll wheelbarrows in the
direction of the Salle de Dissection with chemically
treated corpses piled topsy-turvy. By the way, Oscar's
former owner—who had named him after Oscar
Wilde!—explained that students were assigned in pairs
to each cadaver and he also suggested that I always select
a male for dissection. He told me that no matter how
emaciated a woman may be there always remains a thin
layer of fat that complicates dissecting.

June 1942

I don't feel too guilty towards my pupils in the Shanghai
Jewish School for my decision to enter the university
next fall. In any case, they would move to an upper class
and have a new teacher. I do love them though and
hope they reciprocate my feelings.

The first Sunday of this month a very popular end-of-
school event was held: Sportsday. I don't know how this
tradition started, but suspect it originated in the British
educational system. Before the War, I was invited several times on Sportsday to the English Shanghai Public
School, where several of my cousins studied. It was the
highlight of the scholastic year and as such treated very
seriously. My student Estelle, propelled by my enthusiastic support, ran like a flash, jumped over hurdles and
won first prize in the obstacle race—a moment of pure

joy in her sordid life—and an additional ray of happiness in mine.

When I was at the French Municipal College, most French teachers would disdainfully look down their nose when sports were mentioned, saying through tight lips:

"Only uncultured Americans waste time on such vain pursuits as athletics!"

I myself always loved walking and dancing but detested gymnastics—in which I was quite hopeless. In fact, throughout my school life I had participated actively only once in Sportsday, and not at the French School but at an event planned for Jewish children by Horace Kadoorie on the elegant grounds of his family residence, Marble Hall. I must have been 13 years old or so.

Sportsday at Marble Hall marked the closing of a "Summer Club" Horace Kadoorie had generously organized for children unable to escape the heat (often over 100 degrees!) and humidity of Shanghai. From conversations my mother held with other ladies in a specially formed committee to assist Mr. Kadoorie, I learnt that in actual fact a summer camp had been anticipated but that this venture did not materialize. Thus, the "Club" was a compromise solution, but nonetheless one that brought great joy to more than 200 participating children. The children were divided into groups according to their ages (8 to 18) and interests. Most meetings were held on the premises of the Shanghai Jewish School where exotic kosher meals were served: "Chinese Chow," Indian curry, and elaborate Iraqi and Syrian dishes I had never tasted before.

The invitation to Marble Hall climaxed a very happy and successful summer season—one which most participants would probably never forget.

The Ladies' Auxiliary Committee outdid itself. There were donkey rides, coconut shies, Hoop-La, Lucky Dips, Skittles, Chutes, and a mysterious fortuneteller. Partially concealed in flowing chiffon scarves she predicted to each and every child a life of glorious adventure and fabulous riches.

We were all treated like honored guests. Smiling Chinese servants dressed in crisp white cotton served apparently inexhaustible supplies of lemonade, orangeade, sandwiches, and iced cakes. Excited boys and girls took part in obstacle races, potato races, three-legged races, long jumps, and high jumps. All the girls were forced to wear rather horrid blue bloomers with tight rubber bands, in case their skirts flew up immodestly. I must admit that, till today, adults' attitudes in such matters bewilder me. Once when my baccalaureate class (most aged 18 and over) was climbing up the staircase to the second-floor auditorium, a French teacher ordered the boys to precede the girls. The reason: boys standing below might be tempted to peak under the girls' skirts! This exciting prospect had not entered anyone's mind, but now a new idea burgeoned!

At Marble Hall no records were broken but certainly happy memories were engraved in youthful minds. Horace Kadoorie, our host on this memorable occasion, is the scion of an aristocratic Sephardi family whose name is linked in the Far East—as well as in other parts of the world—with philanthropy, especially in the fields of education and health. Horace's father, Sir Elly (Eleazar Silas) Kadoorie, is an Iraqi Jew who arrived in China in 1880 to work as a clerk. Like so many Iraqi Jews who prospered in China, he started his career as a clerk at the Sassoon Company. Being an intelligent, if somewhat headstrong young man, he soon parted ways with his authoritarian employers and set up his own brokerage business. He eventually went to London where, in 1897, he married Laura Mocatta, the daughter of a prominent Spanish Jewish family. The Mocattas, like tens of thousands of other Jews, had fled the Inquisition, reached Holland, and later settled in England where they founded the firm Mocatta & Goldsmid Ltd. (1684). Its reputation for decency was such that they were appointed official brokers to the Bank of England in 1696.

In 1899 a son[11] was born to Laura and Elly

----

[11]Lord Lawrence Kadoorie, C.B.E., J.P., a leading figure in Hongkong, known for his business acumen and philanthropy.

Kadoorie.They named him Lawrence. In 1902 a second son, Horace, was born.

After living in London and Hongkong, Elly Kadoorie returned to Shanghai where his brokerage business developed with remarkable success. In spite of his rapidly increasing fortune, Elly Kadoorie often repeated a favorite dictum to which he adhered:

"Wealth is but a sacred trust to be administered for the welfare of society." Thus, Elly Kadoorie founded a T.B. sanatorium and the Dermatological Section of the Sun Yat-sen Hospital, for which he was awarded Honorary Tables and the Gold Medal by the Chinese government. For his generous contributions to Chinese educational institutions he received the coveted Order of the Brilliant Jade. Many other countries recognize his philanthropic work.[12]

In 1919, a great tragedy struck the Kadoorie family in Shanghai when their home was destroyed in a raging fire. Laura Kadoorie bravely rushed back into the flames in an attempt to save her children's governess and perished. After this terrible incident Elly Kadoorie entrusted some of his business and personal responsibilities to his two sons, who proved very successful in their own right. The death of Mrs. Kadoorie was an emotional blow from which her survivors had some difficulty to recover. The three gentlemen left Shanghai and Elly Kadoorie commissioned an English architect to build a new residence. Unfortunately, it turned out that the man was a drunkard and the more gin he imbibed the grander became his plans for the house. Finally, he deviated almost completely from the original concept and built a huge mansion which included an immense ballroom 65 feet high, 80 feet long and 50 feet wide, as well as a magnificent veranda stretching an entire 225 feet! All other rooms were also huge. It must be said, however, that once the Kadoories recovered from their first shock at the sight of their new abode they settled in

---

[12]Great Britain made him Knight Commander of the British Empire and France gave him the Légion d'Honneur, this being but two among many decorations.

very comfortably and all their visitors remarked on its agreeable ambiance of warmth, comfort, and quiet beauty. No doubt the characters of the Kadoories added to this atmosphere: all were soft-spoken, courteous, and considerate. The father, a pious man, could be seen every morning standing deep in prayer on the second-floor balcony of his bedroom. Decked in a Jewish prayer shawl, he bent back and forth as he prayed in the traditional manner.

Laura Mocatta was never forgotten. The family built in her name a Jewish synagogue in Oporto, Portugal. The synagogue, a symbol of the revival of Judaism among Portuguese *conversos*, was consecrated on January 16, 1938.[13]

Marble Hall, where we children spent that delightful Sportsday, had seen many important visitors before our loud "invasion." Rabindranath Tagore, the first Asian winner of the Nobel Prize for Literature arrived with a small group of supporters, and their warm words as well as sketches can be seen today in the guest book of the Kadoories. As a result of this visit, Elly Kadoorie financed the building of a much-needed well in Tagore's home village. Many other luminaries accepted the kind hospitality of the Kadoorie family in Marble Hall.[14]

After Pearl Harbor when Japanese troups invaded Shanghai, a group of blue-clad marines arrived to take over Marble Hall. All the shutters in the residence went down and neighbors wondered what would happen to the beautiful, shining marble floors. Would hob-nailed boots destroy them? Later we heard through the grapevine that Japanese soldiers brought into the house wooden planks on which they stepped in an effort to preserve the marble! The rumor is that the Japanese intend to use the Kadoorie residence as their military

---

[13]For the occasion palm trees were brought into the courtyard and flowers planted in the shape of the Magen David (Star of David). All the dignitaries of Oporto attended the reception that followed the official dedication ceremony.

[14]Today in the People's Republic Marble Hall is a "Children's Palace" where various courses in the arts are offered.

headquarters or as the official home of their puppet governor, Wang Ching-Wei.

Who knows what is happening now to the Kadoorie family?[15]

July 1942

The weather is muggy, temperatures rise to 103 degrees while electric fans stand dusty and idle due to power shortages. Nights bring no relief as we toss sleeplessly in sheets damp from perspiration.

Feeling limp, exhausted, dejected, I spent all day at home reading and listening to the radio. It was really quite funny to hear Shanghai's pompous fashion pundit refer to the *dernier cri* in summer outfits: shirt cut down from an old cotton dress, pants with wide elastic waist, straw "coolie" (conical) hat, shoes with linoleum tops and car-tire or cork soles. Every attempt is being made to use rubber tires far too worn to put on vehicle wheels. Cork is very light, very popular, but not durable, especially when worn in the rain. Still, I do long for cork-soled white sandals—far too expensive at $30,000!

Ah, the pre-War days when ladies purchased diaphanous silk blouses on Yates Road and ordered dresses, suits, coats from skillful Chinese tailors who copied French haute couture with unrivalled speed and dexterity! And the lingerie! Undies made from lush satin, sensuous georgette or crêpe-de-Chine, hand-embroidered and trimmed with delicate lace in pastel shades! An American lady once told my mother that her

---

[15]In December 1941, when Hongkong fell, Lawrence Kadoorie, his wife, and children were taken by the Japanese to the infamous Stanley Camp. Sir Elly, who happened to be on a visit in Hongkong was likewise interned. Horace Kadoorie had to vacate Marble Hall but remained relatively free in Shanghai. For some reason Lawrence was classified as a "Canadian journalist" and after five months of captivity was transferred with his family to Chapei Camp outside Shanghai. Sir Elly, who had become seriously ill, was placed in his son Horace's care. Towards the end of 1944 the Japanese permitted Lawrence to visit his father outside of the camp. Shortly after this Sir Elly died. Then, in an extraordinary development, the Kadoories were placed under house arrest in the servant's quarters of Marble Hall.

laundry in Chicago refused to wash her Shanghai Yates Road nightgowns, claiming they were elaborate evening dresses requiring expensive dry-cleaning and pressing whose cost would far surpass their purchase price.[16]

"I did so miss my amah," she said, "who washed all my undies by hand, quickly and uncomplainingly!"

Today, the heat is really stupefying. On the radio, the weatherman predicts a heavy storm. Hopefully it will break this suffocating temperature. Eugene, who once coached me in algebra, told me that all the information we hear on weather originates from the Zi-Ka-Wei Observatory. He even pointed the buildings out to me last week when we went for a very long bike ride. He explained that Zi-Ka-Wei had been founded by Jesuit fathers in 1872 and had become a center of typhoon forecasting. In fact, the Chinese government officially adopted the code of signals established by the Jesuits as far back as 1898, and they are in use until today.

Eugene had actually visited the Zi-Ka-Wei Observatory together with some French naval officers whose ship was anchored just outside Shanghai. They were all amazed at the outstanding work done by the Jesuit fathers. At two o'clock in the afternoon they witnessed how telegraphic information arrived from 24 stations in Manchuria, Korea, Japan, Formosa, and Indochina, as well as posts throughout China. Such data was assembled twice a day, at 10:00 a.m. and 2:00 p.m. The fathers published regular monograms, bulletins, and weather maps, signaled all meteorological information to the Port of Shanghai, and saved ships from foundering.

Who knows what the situation is today? Armed Japanese are on guard outside the observatory and it is strictly off limits except to those in possession of special permits. Gone are the days of open house and incomparable Jesuit hospitality! Lightning and booming thunder cut the electricity and silence the radio. Heavy rain

---

[16]Yates Road was a street in the International Settlement with many shops specializing in underwear, blouses, Mandarin coats, and objets d'art.

pours down as if from giant buckets. Immediately the air cools. I open the window. It is dark outside and somehow comforting. The streets are empty, empty of worried Shanghailanders, empty of Japanese, even empty of starving beggars. I love the rain.

August 1942

Why oh why didn't the world listen to warning voices a decade ago? In 1935 Professor Taid O'Conroy had written a book called *The Menace of Japan*, which Papa advised me to read.

"O'Conroy's conclusions are very convincing," Papa said, "but—as usual—the world pays no attention!"

Irish born O'Conroy married a Japanese aristocrat, taught in the prestigious Keio University in Tokyo, and lived almost exclusively in the Japanese style, hobnobbing both with intellectuals as well as high-ranking officers. His book, a tough indictment of Japan, ends with a powerful chapter entitled: "J'accuse!" (the title of Emile Zola's article in the famous Dreyfus Case). His call rang out: "I SAY JAPAN WANTS WAR."

Alas, the United States, Britain, and France remained unconcerned as Japan committed flagrant acts of aggression with fearless insolence, always convinced that "the Emperor's divine destiny will assure victory . . ."

Ah! the price the Allies have to pay for bloated self-confidence!

Today, we feel somewhat cheered because rumors reached us that U.S. marines landed in Guadalcanal. My elation is tinged with fear for all these young inexperienced Americans violently plunged into what must surely be a modern version of hell. There is a tight ball in the area of my stomach (or is it heart?). And, to tell the truth, neither can I help but worry about Japanese students I had become friendly with during a summer vacation in Inokuchi (Japan). My favorite one was Yorifumi, a medical student, a clean cut, serious youth who always wore a high-collared blue Hiroshima University uniform, similar to that of my father's when he studied engineering in Vladivostok. Yorifumi's family lived in the village where my mother, my sister and I spent July and August before the War. Mama had rented one room in a cottage belonging to the Japanese Noritaki agent in Shanghai with whom she had had some business dealings. He had spent many years in Canada, spoke fluent English, and was a warm, communicative person whom all our family liked.[17]

Mama, my sister, and I slept on the *tatami* (straw matting) floor on thick *futon* (flat mattresses) under an enormous mosquito net tied by strings to four hooks in the ceiling corners of the room. The white net had blue stripes around its edges and kept not only the mosquitoes out but also, unfortunately, the sea breeze. Another disadvantage was that the cottage was located near a railway line and it took us a while to get used at night to the rumblings and whistles of trains whose vibrations shook the house like minor earthquakes.

Our landlord's mother, wife and children occupied the rest of the cottage. My sister and I stifled giggles when we had to cross their room to leave the house because the grandmother would always be shuffling around clad only in a brownish skirt and completely bare from her waist up. Her thin pendulous breasts would swing as she moved.

Cooking was not Mama's forte since we always had excellent Chinese cooks in Shanghai, so our menu was mainly limited to fried fish, boiled giant crabs, and delicious fruit: large purple figs and flattish pink-white peaches, all of which we loved.[18]

Early in the morning as we awoke we would hear outside the tap-tap of wooden *geta* (Japanese-style sandals), a soothing, comforting sound. During the day, however, the quiet would be disturbed by the very loud music and staccato speeches on the radio of our neigh-

---

[17]His entire family was killed by the atomic bomb in Hiroshima. He survived because he was in Shanghai at the time.

[18]I saw similar flat peaches for the first time again in Jaca, Spain, in 1984. When I lived in Japan after the War and rhapsodized about the peaches in Inokuchi nobody appeared to know what I was talking about!

bor. He was the only owner of a radio on the street and probably wanted to share the programs with everyone. Only later did I realize that the music was always martial and the words war-inciting harangues.

Yorifumi, a gentle, poetic boy, once complained to me about his forced participation in strenuous physical exercises, the purpose of which was to "make him strong for the Emperor." He disliked—and I suspected feared—his instructor in military discipline, an army martinet who arrogantly terrorized not only the student body but the entire academic and administrative staff. Most probably Yorifumi regretted his confession in a moment of weakness, since he never mentioned the subject again and neither did I refer to it. Somehow I instinctively felt we were on dangerous ground.

When I returned to Shanghai, Yorifumi sent me frequent letters from Japan written on delicate, almost transparent paper, decorated with faintly visible, soft-colored landscapes. His handwriting was very neat and he quoted Japanese poems about the waves, the seafoam, the pearl sky, and the pines. Once he mentioned that when maple leaves rustled they whispered my name. I wondered if this indicated a romantic interest—I certainly hoped so! Since Pearl Harbor there has been no news from him.[19]

Yes, it was a lovely, lovely vacation that summer in Japan, the last days of peacetime innocence. My family was the only foreign group in the village, perhaps the only ones who had ever lived there. No doubt our presence aroused curiosity, perhaps hostility, but the innate courtesy of the Japanese made us—at least me—totally unaware of this fact. I very quickly made friends, enjoying the comradeship of children with whom in most cases I had no common language. Hungrily, I inhaled the bracing sea air, the pervading smell of pines and exotic foods. My sister and I explored village lanes, small open stores, the rocks on the beach, and the paths leading through wooded areas.

---

[19] I never heard from him again.

One fragrant evening, we sprawled on the sand listening to the slapping of waves when several Japanese children joined us. We had seen them before but this was the first time that they, a group of six kids aged 8 to 15 or so, approached us. Chiyoko, who introduced herself in English as a high school student who had studied in Hawaii, served as interpreter. We chatted as the sun sank in a flaming red ball into the darkening sea and Chiyoko reminisced about her life in Honolulu. She admitted she hated her school in Japan and longed to return to Hawaii. The other Japanese children sat mute, expressionless, obviously not understanding a word of English.

"Do you know," Chiyoko said, "that I have to watch everything I say in class? We kids have been ordered to spy on one another and even on our parents and friends! We must report to our teachers lack of 'thought purity.' "

I stared in puzzlement, so Chiyoko clarified:

"Well, they say there are many subversive organizations now in Japan—mostly Communists and other enemies of our country and the Thought Police must be informed about them.[20] In every street block there is the *Tonari Gumi* (Neighborhood Association) and they also keep track of everything people do and say . . . Snoopers! snoopers! snoopers!"

Chiyoko bent her head. With her broad, flat, round face she looked like a broken wooden Kokeshi doll.

"We never, never have any fun!" she mumbled.

Chiyoko fell silent and we watched the waves gently splash on the sand. I thought our conversation—or rather her monolog—had ended, but apparently she had only paused and felt an irresistible urge to pour out her feelings.

"Every morning at school," she continued "we have to bow in the direction of the Imperial Palace in Tokyo and recite by heart a long, long speech about our duties

---

[20]"Thought Police"are not to be confused with the Kempeitai, another distinct (but interlocking) section of the Japanese police. The Thought Section of the Criminal Affairs Bureau was founded in 1927.

to the Japanese nation. Then we all sing the Japanese anthem. All this is so hard for me!"

The following afternoon an unknown visitor who turned out to be Chiyoko's grandfather came to speak to Mama. Bowing deeply he explained in halting English that he wished to apologize for his granddaughter's "shameful behavior and lies" the previous night. He explained that she now had left the village in disgrace. Which one of the other Japanese children had understood English and reported Chiyoko to the authorities? We never saw Chiyoko again and nowadays I often think of her, wishing she knew how close I feel to her and how I inwardly weep for her.

September 1942

My daily ride to the university is an obstacle race! This morning, I pedaled for several yards when I heard a clanging sound and the wheels stopped suddenly. I fell off abruptly, feeling very foolish. The chain of my bike had come off and the oil left a large black smear on my leg.

Dragged the bike to the nearest repair shop where a Chinese apprentice with smudged face and greasy hands chatted leisurely with his companion. He insolently disregarded me and finally started fumbling with the chain while I begged him to hurry: "Chop! Chop!" ("Quick! Quick!" in Pidgin English). To no avail. He moved with deliberate slowness as I simmered in silent fury. Finally, got back on my bike riding in desperate haste when . . . a block away from the university a warning bell started ringing, indicating that a "blockade" (road-block) was about to be set up. Darn! Traffic came to an immediate standstill, the crossroad was roped off as rickshaws, wheelbarrows, and bicycles stood crowded tightly together. We waited in morose silence, and after some 30 minutes a large black car with curtained windows whirred past us with an escort of armed Japanese motorcyclists. Coolies leaned upon me and I suddenly felt an insect bite—most probably a louse. Ugh! Tension mounted and a young Chinese standing beside me holding his bike whispered in English in my ear,

"Wang Ching-Wei."

Wang Ching-Wei, formerly a national government official, had deserted his colleagues in Chungking to join ranks with the Japanese. In December 1939, after a young officer tried to kill him (Wang's aide was killed), he openly allied himself with Germany and Japan. As a young man Wang had studied in Germany, admired that country, and later had the occasion to meet Adolf Hitler privately. While the Chungking government angrily rebuffed Japan's proposal for China's "rebirth" as part of a New Economic Order—the much touted "Greater East Asia Co-Prosperity Sphere"—Wang maintained that China's resistance would result in national suicide. Surely he had not expected that the Japanese would eventually mock him and treat him like a puppet whose strings they pulled at will, nor that the Chinese masses would hate him for his treachery.

We always know when members of the Japanese Imperial Family are here because armed Japanese soldiers will be posted at regular intervals along their route. As the cars whiz, the soldiers turn their backs to the road since Japanese tradition forbids anyone to look upon a member of the Imperial household.

After the car-and-motorcycle escort disappeared from view, ropes were removed, whistles blown to indicate permission for the resumption of traffic, and rickshaws, carts, bicycles, pedestrians moved toward their destinations in a disorderly melee—faster than the few cars trapped between them!

It was impossible to ride my bike so I walked, pulling it along. In a vacant lot I passed every day on the way to Aurora I noticed newly-stored barrels of gasoline and wooden cases marked with black skulls. Ominous! A high barbed wire fence had been erected overnight to keep the curious out. Arrived at the end of the histology class feeling flustered, irritated, humiliated.

At noon, on my way home, saw notices in English and Chinese posted on buildings stating:

Despite the fact that the deadline has passed for registration of forbidden A-type radio sets in accordance with the Proclamation issued by the Broadcasting Control Office and their purchase by authorities, there are still a number of such sets that have not yet been brought to the Official Purchasing Office located at 1133 Szechuan Road.

Notice is hereby given that those who were unable to bring their radio sets to the Purchasing Office owing to unavoidable circumstances, should report to this office and obtain special permission for this delay, while those who fail to bring their radio sets and use them without such permission WILL BE PUNISHED ACCORDING TO MILITARY REGULATIONS.

October 1942

In spite of gathering clouds, cultural activities continue in the Jewish Community, highlighted by the opening of a library of Hebrew and Yiddish books at the Shanghai Jewish Club. The core of the library is a private collection donated by our Chief Rabbi, Meir Ashkenazi.

Rabbi Ashkenazi is a Lubavicher Hassid, a member of a very pious sect who strictly observe Jewish laws and traditions. Their teachings are based on the three pillars of "Wisdom, Insight, and Knowledge." Meir Ashkenazi arrived in Siberia (Vladivostok) from Russia after having completed his rabbinical studies and got engaged in 1919 to the daughter of Rabbi Soloveichik, a venerable Jewish leader whose method of Talmudic study is still practiced today in many *yeshivot* (religious colleges). The young couple eventually married in Harbin (Manchuria) and later moved to Shanghai.

Rabbi Ashkenazi is a tall, handsome man while his wife is physically plain. However, the *rabinsha's* intelligence, kindness, and practical wisdom quickly earned her the position of First Lady in the hearts of Jewish Shanghailanders. Babushka, Papa's mother, idolizes her and often speaks to me about her generosity and understanding. In fact, Babushka told me that it is on the initiative of my grandfather (who passed away when I was three) that Meir Ashkenazi was invited in 1925 to Shanghai. At that time, the Jewish Community included only some 300 people and their synagogue was in a private home. Later, a building was rented on Wayside

Road in the International Settlement, its second floor removed, pillars erected to support the roof, and a mezzanine constructed since women prayed separately from men. The architect of this proud new synagogue was my father's twin brother, Gabriel.[21]

One of Rabbi Ashkenazi's achievements was to bridge differences between the Ashkenazi and Sephardi Jewish Communities. There was, for example, the serious matter of the Baikal Road Cemetery. The Sephardis buried their dead wrapped only in shrouds in the old traditional Jewish manner. The Ashkenazis, on the other hand, had adopted some European customs and interred the bodies in coffins. After some diplomatic negotiation, it was decided to organize two separate *hevrot kadisha* (burial committees) to supervise the performance of last rites. The cemetery was divided into two sections, each with a separate entrance, and throughout the years no problems arose. My grandmother said, however, that although the Sephardi Community adhered strictly to its traditions, the Ashkenazis almost unnoticeably took over some Sephardi customs. On the whole, at least as far as burial is concerned, the two communities function in great harmony.

Today, Rabbi Ashkenazi, his wife, and two friendly daughters live rather modestly. According to Babushka, Rabbi Ashkenazi also has a son in Jerusalem. In spite of the rabbi's limited income, his home is always open to those who seek advice, and the warm-hearted rabinsha sees to it that a large table is permanently set for unexpected visitors. The Ashkenazi family is loved and respected not only by the Ashkenazi Jews, but also by the Sephardis. Today, even the Japanese treat our rabbi with respect. According to Papa, Rabbi Ashkenazi manages often to spare our community much suffering. When I pressed Papa to clarify as to how this was achieved, he

---

[21]He later designed the Synagogue of Immigrants from China in Tel Aviv, Israel.

said:,"It's a very confidential matter. You don't have to know."[22]

Last year, in April 1941, a beautiful Ashkenazi Jewish synagogue—the first building constructed specifically for this purpose—was finally inaugurated on a plot of land purchased in the French Concession where most Russian Jews now reside, a fact which must have made our rabbi very happy.

Babushka often talks to me about my grandfather who, she claims, adored me (his only grandchild then) and would often crawl on the floor letting me ride on his back, in spite of the fact that he was by nature far from a playful man, and was deeply involved in the study of Judaism. In Siberia, she said, Meir Ashkenazi had been one of his closest friends, admiring him when, in Vladivostok, he worked round the clock to help Jews fleeing from pogroms in Russia. These pogroms had been mainly instigated by the vicious anti-Semite Simon Petlura. In 493 attacks, Petlura and another criminal, Denikine, encouraged mobs to invade Jewish homes, extort money, loot, rape, and murder helpless victims under the pretext of collecting "war requisitions." The terror lasted almost four years from December 1918 to April 1921: 20,000 Jews were killed and 100,000 wounded and mutilated. Thousands fled to Vladivostok looking for shelter and respite and were welcomed by Rabbi Ashkenazi.

In May 1926, shortly after Rabbi Ashkenazi reached Shanghai, following my grandfather's successful recommendation to the Jewish Community, Petlura was assassinated by a young Jew, Shalom Schwarzbard. Schwarzbard was brought to trial and acquitted in November 1927.

"Oh, how the Jews prayed that he would be spared!" Babushka would tell me. "God must have heard us be-

---

[22]In their book, *The Fugu Plan* (New York: Paddington Press, 1979), Marvin Tokayer and Mary Swartz note that Rabbi Ashkenazi helped save unruly Yeshiva students from arrest and possibly fatal imprisonment by the Japanese.

cause the jury concluded that . . . and I remember these words by heart since I had read them over and over:

" 'His action had been spurred by a sacred anger, a desire to bring to the eyes of the entire world a horror of the dreadful crimes committed by Petlura against Jews.' " Sadly, one of the first duties of Rabbi Ashkenazi in Shanghai was to conduct a funeral service for his longtime friend, my grandfather.[23]

November 1942

Japan now controls French Indochina, Thailand, Burma, Malaya, the whole of the Dutch East Indian Empire, the Philippines, various Pacific Isles, Manchuria, and parts of China. Australia next? The Japanese have coined a new slogan, *Ichioku ichigun* (100 million as one bullet), and cries of "DOWN WITH THE AMERICAN AND ENGLISH DEVILS" reach fever pitch. We hear about a consolidated "Patriotic Press Association" with a thousand members being organized.[24]

Nowadays, as we read the papers we try to guess the truth between lines of propaganda, often puzzled as to the purpose of certain published reports, such as:

MAN SNORED TOO LOUD. DISMISSED FROM U.S. ARMY AT FRESNO, CALIFORNIA
Because he snored too loud, Leonard Williams has been discharged from the U.S. Army at Fresno, California. Army authorities found it impossible to locate a sleeping place for Williams that was both within bounds and beyond earshot, it was reported in New York.

---

[23]Rabbi Ashkenazi immigrated to the United States after the War. His many difficulties had undermined his health and he died at the age of 62, to the great sorrow of all who knew him.
[24]It was formally established in December 1942.

Whispers, however, bring us the good news that British, American, and French armies have landed in North Africa and that De Gaulle established a "Free French" government in Algiers. The Japanese must have received reports of such talk, and today's paper published on its first page the following notice:

GENDARMERIE IN WESTERN SECTOR FORBIDS RUMORS

The Japanese General in the West Area has issued a Proclamation for the suppression of rumors to preserve Peace and Order in that Area.

OFFENDERS WILL BE SEVERELY PUNISHED.

There are also frequent threats to those who hoard gasoline, which is now in very short supply. One sees few cars on the streets except for khaki-colored Japanese military vehicles. Our main means of transportation has become the bicycle, and the number of licenses issued in the areas of the International Settlement and French Concession has risen by 16,000 after Pearl Harbor. Hundreds of bicycle repair shops have sprung up throughout the city. My bicycle has a clumsy, black frame and is hard to maneuver. Its brakes constantly come loose. My friend Genny is luckier: her bike shows off its light, glorious, sleek shape in shiny chrome!

December 1942

Returned from Aurora University in a totally exhausted state and collapsed on my bed. Neither my arms nor legs would move and perspiration drenched my body. As I lay inert, Papa walked in looking for his dictionary, which I had borrowed. He spoke and his voice reverberated loudly in my ears. Suddenly, Mama appeared beside me, her cool hand on my forehead. I saw my parents' lips move but could distinguish no words. I was floating, suffocating. Then, without transition, I lay like a collapsing bag of rice on my mother's lap in a rickshaw. I tried to explain to her that she was holding me too tight, that her fingers grasped my waist like steel pincers, but I

could utter no sound. It was raining. The folding roof of
the rickshaw was open, a green tarpaulin fluttered down
to protect us against the downpour. Its wet odor nause-
ated me . . .

I am now in the Jewish Hospital with typhus—no
doubt transmitted by a louse bite during one of our frequent "barricades" when we are herded together in a
compact group: beggars, coolies, farmers, students, anyone who happens to be on the street. In my delirium I
saw Wang Ching-Wei's long, black car with its curtained
windows assuming menacing proportions, decorated
with swastikas. The Japanese motorcycle escorts suddenly are transformed into Nazis with hate-filled faces. I
see my sister being dragged away and open my mouth
wide in a soundless scream![25]

Since the Japanese Occupation, epidemics have increased. Before Pearl Harbor, public health officials in
the International Settlement and French Concession
would work in shifts round the clock with hundreds of
assistants in an attempt to curb the scourge of infectious
diseases in Shanghai. They would enter homes of the
poor to instruct them how to combat infection and removed the sick and the dead from alleys to prevent the
spread of epidemics. Yes, this is one area in which the
foreign powers did show concern for the Chinese. True,
human life in Shanghai had always been rather cheap,
but today it appears to be totally worthless.

My hospital ward is large and airy with eight beds. My
neighbor, a gentle, white-haired Jewish woman, clearly
rejoiced when my crisis was over and my temperature
lowered. Thoroughly weak, unable even to feed myself,
I listen with rapt attention to her stories of "old time
Shanghai."

"Do you know that 20 years ago, in 1922, Albert
Einstein visited Shanghai?" she asked. "Yes, it was indeed a proud moment for the Jewish community! A
delegation went to the port to meet his ship and my

---

[25]When I later saw an exhibit of Edvard Munch's paintings in Oslo,
his famed work entitled *The Scream* brought back the nightmare of the
typhus delirium.

husband and I had the great honor to be among those who welcomed one of the most remarkable men in modern history. I can even remember what I wore: a dark emerald green dress and a small velvet hat that I had brought back from a trip to Paris—not that Einstein would have noticed such details! He was such a modest man, rather untidy, with hair flying in the wind—like an absent-minded professor in some university. His eyes drew my attention: so soft, so kind, so gentle, so clever. Of course, there were all kinds of people greeting Einstein besides the Jews: the British, the French, the Americans, the stateless Russians, and hundreds upon hundreds of Chinese officials. On the very day Einstein reached Shanghai, news flashed around the world that he had won the Nobel prize. That evening the Chinese gave a banquet in his honor—you know, the luxurious type that only the Chinese know how to offer guests of great standing—and Einstein was asked to say a few words. He reluctantly agreed and I must admit he was not an eloquent speaker, but this did not matter at all!

"After several days in Shanghai, Einstein went on to Japan and when he returned to China he gave four lectures at the University in Peking. Every Chinese scientist who could possibly manage to be there was present. There was a remarkable interpreter who translated all Einstein's words into Chinese and everyone admitted that his skill was quite extraordinary. Of course, the interpreter himself was a Chinese scientist of very high standing and he and Einstein got along very well together. Einstein did not appear to have any of the silly prejudices many foreigners have in Shanghai and responded very warmly to the Chinese.

"Oh! we did have many famous visitors! In 1930, I managed to catch a glimpse of Douglas Fairbanks— whom all the women were mad about—and Mary Pickford—America's sweetheart!"

Hepatitis has compounded the misery of my typhus and yellowed my entire body. However, "beauty is in the eyes of the beholder," and Stanley, a St. John's

University[26] student, exclaimed fondly during his visit today: "You look so exotic with your blue eyes and golden skin." Eric, who sat at my bedside, glared at him, but I felt my morale rise sharply!

---

[26]St. John's University was founded in 1879 by the American Episcopal Church. Today it houses the East China Institute of Politics and Law, the Chinese School of Hygiene, and the Graduate Cadres Institute of Health.

1943

Eric arrived early this afternoon bearing a gift: a shimmering bottle of cologne in the shape of a crown. Where did he unearth this relic of pre-War luxury? After gently squeezing my hand, Eric glanced stealthily around the crowded ward to ensure that nobody was listening and whispered very softly into my ear:

"They say the Japanese have arrested 'Two-Gun' Cohen in Hongkong!"

Morris "Two-Gun" Cohen is a flamboyant Jewish adventurer whose life arouses much curiosity—and some admiration—among Shanghailanders. Papa once had the opportunity to have a long conversation with him in connection with some Zionist affair, since Cohen throughout his life has been a supporter of the Zionist cause. Cohen must have taken a liking to Papa—as most people do—and started talking about his extraordinary life. He laughed as he told my father, "I was born in the last century, in 1887!"

The son of a poor London *gabai* (synagogue warden), he admitted he had been quite an impossible little boy getting constantly into scrapes. His parents feared he would become a criminal since he always sought out excitement and broke regulations, getting into more and more serious trouble when he became a teenager.

"My mother would often call me a hooligan, a gangster. Poor woman! How often I made her cry!" Cohen told Papa. "Finally, in despair, my father contacted some people he knew who had a farm in Canada and arranged to send me there. Me, the London city boy!"

Of course, the farm was not a place that could appeal to Cohen's restless and impatient nature and he left as soon as possible, drifting from job to job. In the course of his wanderings he developed a close friendship with a small group of Chinese revolutionaries whose cause he began to espouse.

"You see," he explained to Papa, "I like the Chinese. We Jews have many things in common with them. One of them is that we make good friends but damned bad enemies! Ha! Ha!"

It was through these Chinese revolutionaries that Cohen eventually met the man who was to become his idol, Dr. Sun Yat-sen. Dr. Sun had arrived in Canada on an arms purchasing mission, defying his political opponents who had put a price of $1 million on his head. His supporters, worried about their leader's safety, suggested that he employ Cohen as his bodyguard since Cohen was an excellent marksman, sincerely supported the Chinese revolutionary movement to which he had proved loyal on various occasions, and was utterly indifferent to his own personal safety. Besides, Papa told me, "Cohen has a memory anyone could envy. He remembers the slightest details and the most exact figures. He is like a walking filing cabinet. Surely this must have proved to be very useful to Dr. Sun Yat-sen at a time when it was politically very dangerous to keep in writing notes of any kind."

Towards the end of his trip in Canada (it lasted several months), Dr. Sun asked Cohen if he would be prepared to undertake secret shipments of arms and ammunition to China. Cohen readily agreed and succeeded in buying for the Chinese not only guns and bullets, but even a number of planes. His entire life now centered on the revolution in China and on Dr. Sun Yat-sen. In fact, he confided to Papa:

"I only cried twice in my life. Once when my own father died and once when Dr. Sun died on March 12, 1925. He had cancer of the liver, you know."

Three years before his death, in 1922, Dr. Sun instructed Cohen to negotiate a contract with the Northern Construction Company of Canada to lay 1,500 miles of railway lines linking Canton to Chungking. First Cohen had to complete negotiations in Canada with the suppliers of the necessary materials and techniques. Then he boarded the SS *Empress of Asia* on July 28, 1922 and sailed to Shanghai to conclude the deal. When all was settled, Cohen acceded to Dr. Sun's invitation and remained in China. Dr. Sun eventually appointed him his aide-de-camp with the rank of colonel and he was later promoted to general. The Chinese pronounced his name "Ma Kun," and later referred to him as "General Ma" (assuming Morris was his surname which, in Chinese, always precedes the given name).[1]

The Japanese viewed Cohen with suspicion and later hatred mainly for the following reason: during the Sino-Japanese War Japan was accused of using poison gas against the Chinese population, a fact they indignantly denied, but Cohen was able to get hold of a Japanese gas cylinder and prove the Japanese officials to be liars—something they never forgot nor forgave.

Later in the evening Papa dropped in to visit me at the hospital and confirmed that he too had heard the rumor about Cohen's arrest in Hongkong. When I asked Papa what would happen to him now, he said, "I don't know. Don't think about it. Just worry about getting well."

Still I insisted, asking him at least to explain why he was dubbed "Two-Gun" and to describe his appearance to me. Papa reluctantly agreed, probably because I was ill.

"When Cohen was young," Papa said, "he underwent superb military training in Canada. He is an excellent shot and loves guns. Since he tends to show off, he made a point of always carrying two pistols quite openly, so people started referring to him as "Two Gun," and the name stuck. As to his appearance . . . Well, he's short and stocky with disproportionately broad shoulders. The last time I saw him he was slightly balding. Not an attractive man but his eyes struck me: they are piercing, intelligent, analyzing. He speaks with a funny accent—I don't know if it is Cockney or Canadian or, perhaps, a mixture of both. Actually, he has had very little formal education and is sometimes very rude, but there is no doubt that he is a very gifted man."[2]

---

[1]The Chinese characters for "Ma" and "Kun" mean "horse" and "earth." It is interesting to note that in Chinese history there were several famous Moslem generals named Ma.

[2]We found out after the War that Cohen had gone to Hongkong to rescue Mme. Sun Yat-sen. Mrs. Sun had established in Hongkong the China Defence League, an umbrella organization for charitable, medical, and welfare programs. Cohen later said, "I felt this might be the last service I could do for Dr. Sun." The Japanese arrested him and sent him to a concentration camp, which he managed to survive.

February 1943

Finally returned home from the hospital after what
seems to be a long, long time. My hair has been cut very
short. They wanted to shave it off completely because—
otherwise—it would slowly fall out as a result of weeks
of high fever, at least so many people claim. I retorted
that I would not submit to old wives' tales and com-
promised by agreeing to a boyish hairstyle. Now my
head is covered with thick brown curls, I am very thin
and on the whole find my appearance rather romantic—
somewhat similar to that of a heroine languishing from
a debilitating disease!

When I went out for the first time, I found shop windows dark, empty, musty. Many Japanese soldiers stride
about arrogantly on Avenue Joffre, speed by in military
vehicles transporting arms and supplies, and occasionally trot along on horseback glancing down at the pedestrians, who carefully avoid their gaze, hoping to escape
attention and possible trouble. Pavements are pitted by
dug-outs, supposedly for protection against enemy air-
raids, but most are filled with garbage and filthy water—
an additional source of disease.

The Japanese are requisitioning more and more office
buildings, warehouses, private residences, and flats. A
group of Jewish ladies, including Mama, have organized
a committee to help members of our community who
may suddenly find themselves evicted and homeless.
The committee has asked some youngsters to visit
Jewish families and determine how many people they
would be prepared to shelter in case such an emergency
should arise. Accompanied by Fira, a close friend of
mine, and my sister, I dropped in to the flats of several
people living in King Albert Apartments. In spite of the
rather ominous character of our mission, we enjoyed
being offered warm Jewish hospitality and eating goodies. However, when I returned home utterly worn out—

He returned to England when the War ended and, in 1966, traveled
to Peking on the invitation of the Chinese government to attend the
centenary celebrations for Dr. Sun Yat-sen. He died in London at the
age of 81.

an annoying aftermath of my long illness—Mama declared I was too weak to go again.

The Japanese keep hammering propaganda at Shanghai's population but Shanghailanders are no fools: the Chinese in Shanghai have gained a reputation for shrewdness and quick business minds and most of the foreigners have been through too many upheavals to be tricked by words and slogans. Nevertheless, our occupiers are tireless in their efforts to persuade us of the unbeatable might of the Axis powers. They are now showing an old film of the 1936 Olympic games in Europe's "most wonderful capital, Berlin." Tickets at the Doumer Cinema are sold out daily, but not for the reason assumed by the Japanese. People throng to see the Stars and Stripes flutter on the screen and to cheer American athletes—strong, young, handsome Americans far different from the dejected and bowed prisoners shown in Japanese newsreels. The appearance of Jesse Owens is the signal for shouts of "Bravo!" and non-stop applause: a roaring, vibrating, one-hearted demonstration of anti-Japanese feeling. My girlfriends and I have seen the film three times since it started running, and leave the theater with the palms of our hands aching from wild clapping. Fortunately, these effusions of pro-American feelings are being completely misinterpreted by the Japanese. We laughed to read in yesterday's paper:

SECOND SECTION OF OLYMPIC GAMES
SHOWING AT DOUMER THEATER

Current at the Doumer Theater is the second part of the film record of the Olympic Games held in Berlin in 1936. Since the first part of the film Fest der Völker enjoyed a 15-day run, a rare case for a foreign film, the success of the second part is a foregone conclusion.

Other propaganda efforts on the part of the Japanese are far less amusing and considerably more worrying. Domei News Agency published this morning a report reading:

**FORMER ALLIED COMMANDERS LEAD NORMAL
PEACEFUL LIFE IN TAIWAN PRISONERS' CAMP**

A Taiwan War Prisoners' Camp, February 15 (Domei).
While most of them (American prisoners) are none too
willing to touch on the dismal defeats suffered, all
freely admitted that the treatment received has been
magnanimous, particularly General Wainwright, who
said he owed a debt of gratitude in a personal letter to
the Japanese authorities. . . .[3] The bill of fare consists
chiefly of vegetables but meat is added periodically,
despite the fact that even the Japanese are denying
themselves this item of food as much as possible. Since
the prisoners measure beyond the standard of an average
Japanese, ample sized beds with soft enough mattresses
are provided especially for the sake of comfort. . . . The
War Prisoners are allowed to buy cigarettes freely
which is a wartime luxury for anybody, while
phonograph concerts are held three times a week to
lighten the spirit which is prone to turn gloomy despite
the relatively favorable conditions of detention. The
easy yet systematic routine has enabled the men to gain
enormously in weight compared to the famished and
weary condition in which they were brought from the
fronts. . . . General Wainwright showing more composure
than the average American under the present
circumstances, still praised General MacArthur his
superior, despite the latter's escape from Corregidor
Island leaving behind General Wainwright and the
Filipino-American troops to their fate.

None of us believe Domei news items, but what is the
truth? What are they doing to those poor American
captives?

Hoping to relieve increasing worry, Mama invited
some refugee friends to a little party in the evening.

---

[3]General Jonathan Wainwright, hero of Bataan and Corregidor, replaced General Douglas MacArthur in the Philippines and was
taken prisoner together with his troops after a desperate battle on
May 6, 1942. U.S. forces rescued him from the Japanese in August
1945, in time to participate in the surrender ceremony aboard the
USS *Missouri*. He was emaciated after years of starvation and later
disclosed he had been severely beaten by Japanese guards on many
occasions.

Fritz and Otto, two musically endowed brothers immediately created a "European ambience": Fritz played the
piano, blending tune after tune, while Otto sang
German lieder in a pleasant baritone. Trudie, a 13-year-
old girl played the accordion. She wore a dark green
dirndl—an outfit popular among Alpine peasants—
which matched her slightly almond-shaped eyes. She
appeared to me to reflect a world of snowy mountain
peaks, edelweiss, and deer nibbling grass!

The living room had been cleared for dancing. Otto, a
slightly balding man, held his back ramrod straight,
clasping his partner—mostly my cousin Essie, who is
three years my senior—at a polite distance. In spite of his
stiff body, his movements were unexpectedly fluid and
rhythmic and Essie seemed to be enjoying herself.
Sounds of "Wien, Wien" carried us from the
Whangpoo to the Danube, to a pre-War Austria with no
Hitler, no marching boots, no cracking of leather whips
against shuddering bodies.

The morning after this jolly evening (February 18), a
new Japanese proclamation printed in all the newspapers and posted on public buildings burst upon the
Jewish Community with the force of an exploding
bomb!

**PROCLAMATION CONCERNING RESTRICTION
OF RESIDENCE AND BUSINESS
OF STATELESS REFUGEES**

1. Due to military necessity, place of residence and business of the stateless refugees in the Shanghai Area
shall hereafter be restricted to the under-mentioned
area in the International Settlement east of the line
connecting Chohoro, Mokairo and Todotsudo, west of
Yoyuho Creek, north of the line connecting Toshikobairo,
Makairo and Kaisanro, and south of the boundary of the
International Settlement. [The Occupation forces had
given Japanese names to streets and locations.]

2. The Stateless refugees at present residing and/or
carrying on business in the districts other than the above
area shall remove their places of residence and/or
business into the area designated above by May 18, 1943.
Permission must be obtained from the Japanese

authorities for the transfer, sale, purchase or lease of rooms, houses, shops or any other establishments which are situated outside the Designated Area and are now being used by the Stateless refugees.

3. Persons other than the Stateless refugees shall not re-move into the area mentioned in Article 1 without permission from the Japanese Authorities.
4. Persons who will have violated this Proclamation or obstructed its enforcement shall be liable to severe pun-ishment.

    —*Commander-in-Chief of the Imperial Japanese Army*
    in the Shanghai Area
    —*Commander-in-Chief of the Imperial Japanese Navy*
    in the Shanghai Area

My father made immediately several urgent phone calls and disappeared for the rest of the day, returning only late at night. He looked grey, shaken, and refused to answer any of our questions.[4]

Today, February 20, the Japanese published additional instructions:

The Imperial Japanese Army and Navy Authorities in a Joint Proclamation issued Wednesday announced the re-striction of residences and places of business of the Stateless refugees to a Designated Area comprising sec-tions of the Wayside and Yangzepoo Districts, as from May 18. By Stateless refugees are meant those European refugees who have arrived in Shanghai since 1937.[5]This measure is motivated by military necessity and is there-fore not an arbitrary action intended to oppress their le-gitimate occupation. It is even contemplated to safe-guard as far as possible their place of residence as well as their livelihood in the Designated area. Therefore the Stateless refugees to whom the Proclamation ap-plies must as a matter of course comply with it, while the public at large is also requested to comprehend its

---

[4]My father was in truth not as surprised at the Japanese announcements as we might have thought. For clarification see addendum at the end of this section, "Postscript" to "February 1943."
[5]I.e., Jews who had escaped from the Nazi Holocaust.

significance and to offer positive cooperation with the execution of the above measures. Persons who have violated or intentionally attempted to evade this Proclamation will be punished in accordance with Military Law, while persons who have obstructed the enforcement of this Proclamation by trying to take advantage of the removal and get illegitimate or unreasonable profits in connection with the purchase, sale or lease of land, houses, etc. are also liable to punishment.

Postscript to February 1943

After my father's death in 1979, I found among his papers copies of two letters he had written to Moshe Shilo, Director of Military Archives, Tel Aviv. In these letters my father cited the names of two Japanese officials who, he believed, deserved special gratitude for their efforts to help Jews during the Second World War. The first letter, dated January 2, 1968 states in part:

Mr. Shibota—Japanese Vice-Consul in Shanghai:
Risking his career, and perhaps his life, Mr. Shibota called in August 1942 a meeting of leaders of Shanghai Jewish communities in the private residence of Mr. Speelman and confidentially advised them that the Japanese authorities under pressure of the Germans, are contemplating segregation and isolation of German Jewish refugees on an island at the mouth of the Yangtze river and suggested that the Jewish communities organize themselves and take steps to prevent or at least soften the pending order.
The leak of information before an official announcement led to postponement of the restriction order till February 1943 and enabled the Jewish communities in China to intervene and make the necessary representations. The leader of the Jewish communities, Dr. Abraham Kaufman, proceeded to Tokyo and managed to meet there the highest Japanese authorities. As a result of all this some important changes were introduced in the orders which had been ready for publication. The most important change was that the segregation area was made within Shanghai city limits and thus it was possible to maintain contact

with those removed there and give them every possible
assistance.

All those who attended the above meeting—Mr. Ellis
Hayim, Mr. M. Speelman, Mr. B. Topas and Mr. J.
Bitker, as well as Mr. Shibota were arrested within 24
hours by the Japanese Gendarmerie. Mr. Shibota was
dismissed from his post and sent back to Japan. His fate
is unknown to me.[6] Though I was acting as Honorary
Secretary of the Shanghai Jewish Communal
Association—Ashkenazi—for some reason I could not
attend the meeting.

March 1943

Apprehensive about the welfare of our family, Ah Kwei
suddenly arrived on a surprise visit carrying a small
basket of mandarin oranges. She came into the living
room asking, "Evelibody alligh?" ("Everybody all
right?")

For the past 15 years Ah Kwei has taken care of various young children in our clan. Rather tall for a
Chinese, she combs her thin hair in a tight bun and
dresses immaculately: black, crisp, shiny pants and white
starched jacket with high collar. Her face is deeply
scarred with pock marks, her feet are flat and large. She
is one of the few Amahs I know whose feet had not been
broken according to the ancient custom. When Ah Kwei
was growing up, the feet of little girls from a very early
age would be swathed in long narrow bandages bound
tighter and tighter, causing agonizing pain for years. The
children had to endure this torture twice a day when
bandages would be changed, besides constant nagging
pain day and night. The end result: tiny crippled feet
four to five inches long which, when shod in satin slip-
pers, supposedly provoked an erotic reaction in Chinese
men! Poets referred to them as "golden lilies," rhap-
sodizing over the crippled women's tottering gait that
made them appear as if the slightest breeze would topple
them over: feeble, helpless, submissive creatures. Fang

---

[6]Mr. Shibota was located by the Jewish community in Tokyo after
the War. During Passover 1976 he was honored publicly by the Jews
in Japan. He died the following year.

Hsien, a Manchu dynasty poet wrote an entire book about the charm of bound feet, claiming, "You may appreciate the elegance only by the eye of the mind." I often wondered how Ah Kwei had escaped this torture and once asked:

"Why you no havee smallee feetee?"

Her dry reply: "No likee!"

She would divulge no more. Ah Kwei did tell me, however, that her limp (she drags her left foot in a curved movement) is the result of working long hours in flooded rice fields.

"Too much wata (water) spoilee feetee."

She has never married and next to the Japanese, whom she abhors, the human beings she hates most are men—with two possible exceptions: my father and her eldest nephew, whom she adores.

"Men belong (are) like dogee" is her frequent comment.

Ah Kwei intentionally mispronounces my boyfriends' names, calling Julius "Girafu" (giraffe) and Raymond "Lemon," and she openly rejoices at the end of each romance, mincing no words:

"Man no good. Why you likee? You stupid."

Although illiterate herself, she venerates education and dismisses my mother's frequent complaints about my studying too much and not sleeping enough with the enjoinder:

"Never mind she say. You do! You be number one!" (Pay no attention to what she says, keep working, be the best.)

Does Ah Kwei sometimes intimidate us? Yes! Do we love her? Yes, oh yes!

After a short visit Ah Kwei left, ordering me to be "Number One in Doctor School" and begging us to be careful because Japanese "he velly, velly bad man, make velly bad thing."

Well, it is indeed true that the Japanese grip is tightening on all Shanghailanders, especially the Jewish refugees. We open the paper daily with some fear, anticipating bad news and vexatious "Notifications." Today's orders read:

REFUGEES TO REPORT TO PAO CHIA
PRIOR TO CHANGING HOMES[7]

Referring to the Proclamation concerning restriction on residence and business of Stateless refugees promulgated on February 19 and with a view of facilitating the removal of such refugees to the Restricted Area, it is brought to notice, that every such person prior to changing his or her address is to report to the Foreign Section of the Police District concerned. Police Census Form and Resident Certificate should be brought along for verification.

Refugees able to prove that they have permanent jobs outside the ghetto may apply for a special pass to leave the restricted area from 7 a.m. to 7 p.m. The official responsible for issuing such passes is a sadist named Ghoya who dubs himself "The King of the Jews."[8] An erratic creature with abrupt changes of mood, Ghoya slaps, roughs up, and humiliates applicants at whim, granting or withholding permits for no logical reason. The refugees fear and hate him.

To enable the refugees to leave the ghetto, the Jewish Community is frantically searching for proof of jobs, attempting to obtain "employment certificates" from various established companies. Sympathetic Chinese, foreigners, and even in one case a German, support the desperate efforts of the Jewish community. To complicate matters, employment certificates are valid only for one month, after which time they must be re-examined by the Japanese, thus necessitating a compulsory visit to the dreaded Mr. Ghoya.

Papa's brow appears to be permanently wrinkled—a certain sign of deep worry—and he runs around trying somehow to obtain employment certificates outside the

[7]Pao Chia ("protect the home" in Chinese) was organized by the Japanese in 1942 as part of a "self-policing" plan in Shanghai.

[8]After the War, rumors circulated that Ghoya had actually been a U.S. agent and had behaved as he did to cover his activities. The fact is that in spite of his cruelty, he had never—to my knowledge—seriously harmed anyone and had always been gentle with children.

restricted area for his refugee friends: journalists and writers who are suffering both physical and mental degradation. This morning Papa was particularly upset when he read in the paper:

REFUGEE DIES AFTER TAKING NITRIC ACID
A Polish Jewish refugee committed suicide after taking nitric acid. The reasons for this decision are unknown.

April 1943

The osteology exam lasted four hours. Père Hernault, a Santa Claus look-alike, haphazardly plucked bones out of a wooden case, handed one to each student with instructions to identify it, describe it, sketch it, explain its structure and function. I got a vertebra. Good! Students claim that the Jesuit father judges papers not by content but by weight, so I scribbled at a furious pace filling 17 pages. Ooph!

When the bell rang, I staggered out stretching cramped fingers and found Gleb waiting for me in the hall. Gleb is a Russian émigré law student. He has dark hair, olive skin, and a tiny seductive beauty-spot at the left corner of his mouth. His smile is a flash of gleaming white.

Gleb invited me to a dance at the "Sokol" later that evening and I accepted eagerly, although I do feel ill at ease in this Russian Sports Club, whose lounge is dominated by an oil portrait of Czar Nicolai, the anti-Semitic ruler who had once declared:

"As long as I am Czar, the Jews of Russia will NOT receive equal rights."

Nor does Sokol's framed, patriotic, virile motto ease my anguish:
In our thoughts—OUR MOTHERLAND RUSSIA
In our muscles—STRENGTH
In our hearts—AUDACITY.

My father's mother, Babushka, often talks about Jewish suffering in Russia. She had to bribe—at great personal risk—university authorities so that her two gifted twin sons would be included in the very restricted

Jewish quota. The fact that my father had earned his high school's prestigious Gold Medal was of no help whatsoever.

But the wheels of fortune spin, and during the Russian Revolution the persecutors often became victims themselves, fleeing in terror from the Bolsheviks. Shanghailanders experienced directly the results of the murderous civil war in Russia when destitute Russian refugees began to appear on the streets of our city and— much to the annoyance of the colonial powers—lowered the high and mighty image of the white man among the Chinese masses! This trickle of frightened humanity soon gathered into a rushing stream. In November 1922, on the eve of the Bolshevik occupation of Vladivostok, a fleet of ships under the command of Admiral Stark sailed into Shanghai.[9] Huddled on board were soldiers, sailors, civilians—among them scores of women and children. The decks were piled high with armaments, pots, pans, baby cribs and baskets, while laundry tied to five-inch guns dried in the sun!

Shanghai's authorities categorically refused to permit disembarkation and stood their ground even as food rations in the ships petered out. Admiral Stark made desperate efforts to negotiate with representatives of Chinese and foreign powers but could not move them. The situation deteriorated and, in the black of the night, crews started helping refugees to make their way stealthily towards the banks of the Whangpoo River. Finally, Admiral Stark sailed his ships to Manila where his crews and remainder of passengers disembarked legally. The ships were eventually sold to help the Russian refugees survive in the Philippines.

In September 1923, three other ships arrived in our city from Russia: the *Ohotsk*, the *Zashchitnik*, and the *Mongunai* carrying General T. L. Gleboff, Commander of the Far Eastern Cossack Corps, and his loyal unit of Cossacks and their families. These were the vanguard of

---

[9]The ships were the *Baikal*, the *Paris*, the *Svir*, the *Batarea*, the *Vziravatel*, the *Ilia Murometz*, the *Patescal*, the *Dirmiud*, and the *Farvater*.

a flood of Russians that continued for more than a decade. The wave of refugees reached 13,000 by 1929, 20,000 by 1932, and it is said there are 50,000 White Russians in China today.

The Russians that poured into Shanghai included individuals ranging from nobles and high ranking officers to beggars, from the top "intelligentzia" to the lowliest, most ignorant *muzhiks* (the peasants in Czarist Russia who were regarded as minors with few rights under old Russian law and treated almost like beasts of burden). The economic situation of these Russians seemed hopeless, but they gradually entered the social structure of Shanghai—far below nationals of the Colonial Powers and slightly above the Chinese. Former Cossacks and army men became bouncers, bodyguards, watchmen, policemen. Russian women eked out a precarious living as seamstresses, cooks, manicurists, hairdressers, bar hostesses and, in more desperate cases, prostitutes. Shanghai was introduced to Russian food, which became very popular, and Russian restaurants named "Kavkaz," "Renaissance," "Balalaika" flourished.[10] Vodka flowed, caviar and sour cream were consumed by the pound, flaming *shashlik* (marinated skewered lamb) was served on gleaming swords by handsome youths clad in rather theatrical Cossack uniforms, while gypsies sang their haunting, heart-rending songs.

Slowly some Russians learnt English, opened specialty stores, obtained clerical jobs in British, American, and French firms although their salaries, no matter how high their position, were always far below those of their passport-bearing colleagues. Nor, of course, did they ever get all-expenses-paid home leave like the others. Engineers, doctors, teachers, musicians, actors, and artists began to practise their profession.

The dream of almost every stateless White Russian girl was and is to marry a foreigner who has a valid passport. However, colonial companies used to do everything in their power to prevent what they considered

[10]In Shanghai even today some Chinese restaurants still serve borscht!

a *mesalliance*. British firms, as well as some American
ones, wrote "marriage rules" into bachelors' contracts of
employment. Before being permitted to marry, they had
to serve their company three, five or even as long as ten
years! Besides, their superior would interview the
prospective bride to determine her "suitability as a
wife"! If a young man lost his head over a Russian
woman, he would be swiftly transferred to a post in another Chinese city or returned to England or the United
States. These rigid rules were bent only in the case of
British or American girls, many of whom arrived in
Shanghai ostensibly to visit family or friends but whose
real purpose was to "catch a husband." One must admit
that the French were far more liberal in regard to marriage of their nationals to Russian women.

Even today, especially since the Japanese Occupation,
the situation of White Russians in Shanghai remains
very difficult. Their humiliating economic and social
situation fans the fires of rightist fascist elements who
yearn for past true or imagined glories and long to return to a monarchist Russia whose excesses have been
forgotten and whose beauty has been idealized.

The dance to which Gleb took me was organized by
the Russian Emigrants Association. This association
handles the community's social, cultural, medical and
religious affairs—much in the way the Jewish
Community takes care of its own people. There is, of
course, no White Russian consul and only the Soviet
government is represented officially in Shanghai. To
cover expenses, the Russian Emigrants Association established an Annual Poll Tax (per capita fee) on each
member amounting to the equivalent of pre-War yuan
$3.00.[11] However, it is difficult to collect even this paltry
sum because of the deep poverty of an overwhelming
number of Russians. Tonight's dance is yet another effort to raise funds. I suspect Gleb invited me so late because he had to scrounge around to find money to buy

---

[11]In the 1920s the Chinese yuan dollar was worth US $2.00, but its
value began to drop sharply until it reached only US $0.30 at the
end of the 1930s.

entrance tickets and I would never dare insult him by offering to pay for myself. Gleb handed our tickets at the door to a thin elderly man who stood like a sentinel— probably a former officer in the Czarist army.

A wooden floor had been placed on the lawn surrounded by little round tables and rickety chairs. Many pretty girls moved gracefully with their partners to the rhythm of old polkas, tangos, foxtrots, waltzes. Gleb danced with elegant *fin de siècle* chivalry while my burgundy taffeta dress rustled enticingly—I hoped—as I twirled.

Sudden repeated shrieks of air-raid sirens brought the dance to an abrupt halt. The club manager, appearing to be on the verge of hysteria, shouted:

"Put out your cigarets! Immediately! This is a real attack!"

Japanese orders against smoking outdoors during air-raids (even drills) are strictly enforced. Disobedience leads to severe reprisals since the Occupation forces want to confuse "enemy" bombers by plunging Shanghai into total darkness.

Gleb and I, as well as everyone else on the dance floor, stood stock-still, momentarily paralyzed by shock. Distant booms of exploding bombs reverberated and people started to run to the building. For some reason, we all spoke in whispers waiting, waiting . . . As the raid continued, I pleaded with Gleb to try and make our way home since I was certain my parents would panic about my absence. All phone lines were dead and there was no way to reassure them. Against his better judgment Gleb finally agreed and we crept in the dark alongside the buildings, crouching in doorways whenever we heard the boots of approaching Japanese soldiers. The rustling of my dress was no longer "enticing," just a dangerous nuisance, except for its dark color, unnoticeable in the unlit streets, for which I was suddenly grateful. In one of the doorways we stumbled upon a beggar lying at our feet scratching, scratching, scratching. Lice!

When we arrived home my parents greeted us with relief at our safety and fury at our foolhardiness. In spite of my protests, Gleb gallantly assumed all blame and apologized. He remained with us until the all-clear and impressed my parents by his intelligence and good manners—to my great joy. Even my sister found him "ady" (our secret code word for "adorable").

May 1943

Papa is working on an article for his paper *Nasha Jizn* (*Our Life*) about the Sephardi Jewish Community in Shanghai who still adhere to their own Middle Eastern traditions in social and religious matters.[12] Their services are slightly different from ours and although I know very little about the Jewish religion, I must admit I find the way Sephardi Jews conduct their prayers more appealing than the Ashkenazi tradition. The reason may be their dignified comportment, their particular pronunciation of Hebrew words, and their music.[13]

The first Sephardi Jews arrived in Shanghai shortly after the opening of the five Chinese "Treaty Ports"[14] (1842) and the first permanent Jewish office in Shanghai was opened in 1850 by a gentleman named Elias Sassoon. Elias was the son of the famous *nasi* (president) of the Bombay Jewish Community, David Sassoon (originally from Baghdad), a man of such power and wealth that many dubbed him "The Rothschild of the Far East." Shortly after his arrival in India, David embarked on trade with Persian Gulf ports, dealing in commodities which he either sold directly or bartered. In 1838 when the failure of U.S. cotton crops caused panic in world markets, David shrewdly shipped Indian cotton in huge bulk to the British Isles. At the same time, he started importing English textile goods and sell-

---

[12]The word Sephardi originates from Sefarad, meaning "Spain" in Hebrew. The Sephardim are Jews from the Iberian Peninsula,while the term Ashkenazi applies to Jews from Germany and Eastern Europe. In Shanghai, we used the term Sephardi to describe the Middle Eastern Jews, who are actually a third distinct group .

[13]The Hebrew spoken today in Israel approximates the Sephardi pronunciation, not the Ashkenazi.

[14]Shanghai, Ningpo, Canton, Amoy, and Foochow.

ing them at considerable profit not only in India but also in the Middle East. He further increased his ever-growing wealth by wise investments in the Bombay Cotton Exchange. In 1843 David, who liked to supervise personally every aspect of his business, went to the post office himself to pick up some mail. He noticed that one of his British competitors had received voluminous correspondence from China and after this happened repeatedly, Sassoon made discreet enquiries. He soon found out that Britain was rapidly developing trade with China. Never one to miss a good opportunity, David Sassoon shipped his son Elias to Shanghai, and following several visits it was decided to open a branch office of David Sassoon & Sons here. Three Jewish clerks from Bombay soon joined Elias, thus planting the seed of the Sephardi Jewish Community in Shanghai. In the new Sassoon branch office, Elias followed his father's successful business practices, dealing in commodities not only directly for his firm but also as commission agent for other buyers. He rapidly established a high reputation for managing to obtain prime cargo space and competitive freight rates for his clients.

The first Sassoon clerks in Shanghai and all those who followed them from the head office were graduates of a special school David Sassoon had established in India in order to train future employees. Education and textbooks were provided free of charge and students were obliged to study four languages: English, Arabic, Hebrew, and Hindustani. Other subjects on the curriculum were geography, mathematics and, perhaps most important of all, accounting. Moreover, David Sassoon was strict about the religious education of the youths entrusted to him: all of them (like all male members of Sassoon's own family) were obliged to learn all the laws of *kashrut* (ritual fitness according to the Jewish faith, especially in the matter of diet) and learn how to slaughter chickens according to the Jewish ritual to enable them to eat meat should they find themselves in some distant outpost. To this end, Sassoon engaged the services of an expert *shohet* (slaughterer) who taught and tested his pupils with uncompromising rigidity.

To further emphasize the Jewish character of his head office and branches in various cities and countries, David Sassoon ordered letterheads and checks bearing both English and Hebrew lettering. Moreover, every Sassoon firm was closed on Saturdays (Sabbath) and important Jewish festivals.

It is Elias who, in 1862, purchased a plot of land in Mohawk Road (International Settlement) where the first Shanghai Jewish Cemetery was established.

As the years went by, three different groups of Sephardi Jews grew alongside each other in Shanghai: the very rich who owned sumptuous villas with tennis courts, croquet lawns, stables, horse-drawn carriages, and later luxurious cars driven by uniformed chauffeurs; the growing middle class of clerks, bank employees, teachers, salespeople and accountants, and finally, the indigent, many of whom had arrived in Shanghai claiming unproven relationship to one of the wealthy Sephardi families and hoping for a handout.

Most of the wealthier Sephardi Jews from Bombay bore British passports because India is part of the British Commonwealth. According to British law of the time, they could keep their British passport for three generations—even if two generations were born outside the British Empire. But these passports were not equivalent to "real" British passports and clearly stated "British Commonwealth." Nevertheless, in Shanghai they were once an important advantage and some of their bearers assumed English manners and pretensions! One English sport, for example, popular among the well-to-do Sephardi Jews was the "Paper Chase." On certain Sunday mornings a trail of colored paper was laid by the so-called "Trail Master" leading through the countryside, after which some 20 properly accoutered gentlemen on horseback would gather at the starting point. They would then ride following the paper trail, jumping over creeks, ditches, and fences, and whoever reached the final goal first would be awarded a prize. They enjoyed this expensive sport until the Occupation made it impossible. I have never heard of any of my Ashkenazi

Jewish friends and families ever participating in such pastimes!

As far as I am concerned, these wealthy Sephardi Jews could have been living on another planet and, the more Papa told me about their way of life, the more wondrous it appeared. It was hard for me to imagine owning one's own horses and stables. While I often visited the Race Course to watch men in sparkling white play cricket, lawn balls, and tennis, never had I seen an actual horse race. In May and November each year (before Pearl Harbor, of course) races would be held on Saturday, Monday, Tuesday, and Wednesday afternoons. Important races were considered as holidays and sometimes even banks and offices were closed. Among the crème de la crème of Shanghai who owned race horses were prominent Sephardi Jews. Little wonder that when rag-tag Russian Jewish refugees began to arrive the Sephardis regarded them with surprise, amusement, and perhaps disdain. By today, however, we Ashkenazis have become "Old China Hands" and the presence of the Japanese has turned all Shanghai's society topsy-turvy. Those wonderful British passports are now a disadvantage because their bearers can be interned in camps with other British nationals. Moreover, there is now a new wave of penniless Jews—the European refugees—so old-timers are brought closer together, not only due to the fact of being "veterans," but also in order to help more effectively the new arrivals who are experiencing such serious distress.

June 1943

Although my father works very hard for the good of the Jewish Community he receives no remuneration and cannot support his family—not a pleasant reality for him. It is my mother who keeps our heads above water with her shop, fortunately an occupation she loves and which satisfies her creative and imaginative talents. Prior to the War Papa was employed in the provision department of a venerable British trading firm established in 1858. His job lasted 23 years and ended abruptly when the Japanese requisitioned "enemy" businesses, i.e., British, American, and Dutch.[15]

I visited my father's office one single time when I happened to be in the vicinity. It was a lofty red brick building on Canton Road and, for some reason, the interior smelled of sawdust. As I entered the "Foreigners Only" elevator, a Chinese stepped in with me only to be haughtily waved away by the operator, Chinese himself! The poor man had no choice but to ride the back lift reserved for "natives." Silently, with pounding heart, I watched this humiliation.

The British usually treat the Chinese with disdainful condescension. Right up until the Occupation they led privileged lives while "local staff," both stateless foreigners and Chinese, struggled along. Those "first class citizens" enjoyed paid home leaves, fat bonuses, generous retirement plans, and other fringe benefits the rest could never hope to obtain. In general they showed no interest in Chinese culture or way of life. In fact, they created for themselves a miniature of their home country: an Anglican Church, English schools, annual parades on the King's birthday, St. Andrew's balls with bagpipes and haggis, cricket grounds, fox hunts.

My father never discussed these injustices when he was still working (I know his own salary was also insufficient), probably because there was nothing he could do to overcome them and he did not want to distress us. Sometimes when my mother would raise the subject he would respond with irritation and I would feel angry, embarrassed, and ashamed for him. The thought that he was not treated as an equal, that some small ignorant British clerk had privileges above and beyond any he could ever expect made my blood churn. I wish I could better control my emotions and accept situations I cannot change, but my very being rebels at all the indifference, cruelty, and arrogance I witness.

---

[15]The company's general manager, my father's superior, went straight to their offices on the day he was released from internment camp in 1945. He then ordered the Japanese to clear out within 48 hours!

My father, however, did sincerely like some of his British superiors, especially his last general manager who at Christmas time would send beautifully wrapped gifts to my sister and me. His private chauffeur would deliver them at the door and it was a most joyous occasion for us. Moreover, Papa also enjoyed his work, was impeccably loyal to his company, and took pride in many of its projects.

I remember him lecturing me, saying, "You are mistaken if you think that work in a large trading company is boring. You also are wrong if you think that we have not contributed anything to develop Asia. For example, in 1923, the year you were born, a terrible earthquake devastated Yokohama in Japan. The Japanese needed enormous quantities of wood to repair the damage, and we worked day and night to see to it that large shipments of Oregon pines be sent urgently by our Seattle office to Japan. Believe me, we—and I know this for a fact—were not only thinking of profits but also of helping the Japanese people." The successful outcome of this operation enhanced my father's company's reputation in the timber business, and Shanghai soon became an important customer. These Oregon pines were to play a vital role in the construction of some of the Bund's most impressive buildings: the Hongkong & Shanghai Bank, the Yokohama Specie Bank, the Chartered Bank, and the new Maritime Custom House.

"Those trees were just colossal," Papa said. "Real giants 80 to 130 feet long. When the cargo arrived on the Whangpoo River the lumber was flung overboard. We were never permitted to unload during the day because it would have disturbed all the river traffic, so once I went at night to see what was happening. It was an unforgettable sight, those huge trees tied together by chains into enormous rafts and towed to the embankment. All this done in semi-obscurity by men scrambling around, dwarfed by the pine trunks, like a scene from *Gulliver's Travels!*"

Once landed, the trees were dragged with thick ropes to construction sites where coolies sawed them to required lengths and then drove them very close together into Shanghai's muddy, mushy subsoil. Sometimes the earth was so wet, it was almost liquid. After the operation was completed an indestructible base had been raised on which a concrete foundation was poured.

"So," Papa smiled, "when we walk into these buildings on the Bund we can imagine that we are stepping into the United States!"

A couple of days ago Papa went to visit the manager of a large grocery store who, before Pearl Harbor, used to purchase large quantities of foodstuff imported by his British firm. He was pleased to meet there his former compradore who likewise had dropped in for a chat. Papa had not seen this gentleman since the Japanese takeover and was distressed at his appearance. The compradore was no longer the feisty, smiling man of pre-War times but a thin, rather shabbily dressed version of his former self. Even his large moon-face seemed to have narrowed. Aware of Papa's discomfort, the compradore mumbled soothingly: "Maskee! Maskee!"

As Papa wondered what the Occupation had done to the man, he could not help but think how different the word "maskee" now sounded. Before the War it reflected indestructible optimism. It meant "never mind" and indicated all would turn out well, things would somehow work out in our remarkable city where anything could and did happen. No longer. The compradore's resigned "maskee" was simply a sign of reassurance to a onetime colleague.

The word "compradore" comes from the Portuguese word *compra*, which means "buy." The Portuguese had been among the first foreign traders in China and had left their mark in more ways than one. A compradore was the Chinese middleman between foreign enterprises and the Chinese market; he initiated business, guaranteed accounts, collected debts. No large foreign trading company could exist without him, nor could he make a living without them. In short, it was a symbiotic relationship which in most cases worked to the advantage of both parties. Nevertheless, there was no socializing between compradores and their employers except for official banquets when important Chinese clients had to be entertained.

Many compradores—including the one in Papa's office—had become very wealthy making large commissions. Their word meant more than a signed contract. It symbolized old-fashioned Chinese merchant honor, a centuries-old tradition. All that was required of a compradore to finalize a business deal, no matter how important, was the compradore's "Can do!" while his "No can do" ended irrevocably all negotiations. In fact, it would have been construed as a personal insult were the compradore asked to stamp his *chop* (seal) on a written document after having reached verbal agreement.

On the rare ocasions when he came to see Papa at home, it amused me that Papa's powerful Chinese compradore spoke nothing remotely related to "King's English." His language in dealing with foreigners was "Pidgin," a word based on the Cantonese pronunciation of "business" (pi-ji-ness). Of course, few non-Chinese ever considered the necessity of studying Chinese themselves! I believe that the total Pidgin vocabulary of the compradore consisted of no more than a couple hundred words—a mixture of English and Portuguese. Few were recognizable except to experienced Shanghailanders' ears! Many foreign children raised by their amahs speak only Pidgin for the first few years of their life, especially if their mothers socialize actively, spending hours on mah-jong, tennis, and tea parties with very little time for their offspring. These children use terms like "savee" (know), "chop chop" (quick), "wallawalla" (shout, quarrel), and their special grammar turns "good, better, best" into "goodie, more betta, much more betta."[16]

In spite of past prejudices, I tend to believe Papa's compradore looks back to "the good old times" with sincere longing.

---

[16]Fifty years later, I automatically revert to Pidgin when visiting Hongkong or Taiwan.

July 1943

A photograph of Mussolini framed in asterisks was published in today's Russian paper. At first sight, the accompanying text is a strange, almost nonsensical poem which seems to be totally unconnected with the Italian dictator. However, when one reads the beginning letter of each line downwards—it appears in bold type—the following message can be deciphered:

"Mussolini Ushel V Otstavku" (Mussolini resigned).[17]

How could the Japanese censors have missed this little trick in communication?

Mussolini is far less remote to Shanghailanders than Hitler or Stalin because his favorite daughter Edda lived in our city 10 years ago (from 1930–1933) as the wife of the Italian consul (later chargé d'affaires) Count Galeazzo Ciano. Their smiling photographs often appeared in the Sunday edition of the *North China Daily News:*[18] both were dazzling, immaculately dressed, and hosted Shanghai's most exquisite dinners. This morning when I dropped into Mama's store one of her customers, Galina, a White Russian, sat in front of the counter chattering away. A gorgeous blonde, Galina had been much in demand in "High Society" before the War, in spite of being a mere stateless person, because of her lovely looks and amusing—often unintentionally—manner. She was reminiscing about the Cianos:

"He was the most enchanting diplomat in Shanghai. En-chant-ing! All the women were in love with him, including his wife! And his parties! He always managed to hire Shanghai's best cooks, sometimes stealing them from his best friends. But he did everything in such a charming way that everyone forgave him."

I wonder what is happening to the Cianos now?[19]

---

[17]A coup by King Victor Emmanuel and Marshal Badoglio forced Mussolini to resign on July 25, 1943.

[18]Commonly called N.C.D.N., a leading British organ outside Hongkong.

[19]On January 11, 1944, Count Ciano and five other top Italian politicians were shot by the Fascists with Mussolini's tacit approval. Edda Ciano in her book *My Truth* writes that since they

The general situation in Shanghai is becoming more
and more suffocating. Our reality is determined by
Japanese "Notifications" such as:

Notice is hereby given that the entire dockyards
located at 193 and 21 Kew Tchan Ka in Nantao
(including buildings, appurtenances, installations,
machineries and materials) as well as property and
effects connected with the management of the sale
enterprise have been requisitioned for the sole and
exclusive use of the Imperial Japanese Navy.

However, not only have the Japanese requisitioned
real estate of supposed military value, but they are also
taking over private residences among which, unfortunately, is our apartment located on the top floor of a
modern building called Tower Apartments. A couple of
weeks ago, a Japanese couple rang our bell, bowed
slightly as I opened the door, entered politely and made
us understand they wished to "inspect" our home. They
were young, rather shy, and the pretty woman wore a
delicate kimono. In spite of the fact that Mama well
knew we would be forced to give up our home without
any reimbursement whatsoever, she spoke in a friendly
manner to the visitors and showed them around, opening closets, explaining the use of the hot water boiler,
and even pointing out the view from our balcony. Her
behavior did not surprise me, because I assumed it was a
reflection of the famous "Siberian hospitality" in which
she (and we) were brought up. But my sister thought
that perhaps Mama was actually trying to avoid an unpleasant situation that she could not control. Having
found our residence to their satisfaction the Japanese
couple announced in broken English their intention to
move in within a week.

Mama treated them so politely it seemed as if she
were doing them a favor. "I hope you'll enjoy it," she

were executed as traitors they were forced to straddle chairs with
their backs to the firing squad. Count Ciano was the only one to
remain alive after two rounds were fired and had to be shot twice in
the temple until he finally died.

said. They seemed surprised. They didn't expect hospitality from a person whose home they were taking.[20]

Such a turn of events during a period of catastrophic housing shortage would have shattered anyone but my indomitable little mother who has stood up to the challenge and somehow found three rooms to rent in a large villa in a lovely residential section of the French Concession. Unfortunately, she had not reckoned with the ferocious landlady whom my sister and I quickly dubbed "The Monster." A heavy, large, vulgar, foul-mouthed woman with a jarring voice, her accent sounds like something from the East End of London. But she is obviously not a British citizen because the Japanese would have interned her, so I have no idea what her nationality might be. She carries a huge bundle of keys at her waist which jangle as she moves, sneaking about the house snooping on her tenants and checking her secret hoards of food. She consumes huge cakes with her pallid husband at her side and throws her three Scotch terriers boiled potato peels which keep the miserable dogs on the edge of constant starvation. Whenever the poor animals come within her range she yells and kicks them away sharply while my sister and I—both passionate animal lovers—quiver with fury. My sister's normally sparkling, mischievous hazel eyes fill with tears and I have to control myself from physically attacking The Monster.

The other tenants in the house, a Filipino lady, her teen-age daughter, and crippled nephew (his foot is so bent in under his ankle he walks with a very bad limp) live in a large room on the ground floor. The landlady constantly screams curses at them, threatening them with eviction. They submit to her abuse in timid silence since they are in dire financial straits and have no money to move. The Filipino lady seeks respite in occasional visits to us. She was married to an American who was murdered in Manila—I don't know for what rea-

---

[20]When we finally returned to our apartment after the War the young Japanese couple had had it entirely cleaned and repainted for us, perhaps in appreciation of my mother's kind welcome.

son—and is having a very difficult time trying to survive in occupied Shanghai. She also worries about the situation in her homeland. Last night, she showed us a newspaper item she had clipped:

In 10 years Filipinos will be a Japanese speaking nation. People will learn with enthusiasm. Japanese will become the lingua franca of Greater East Asia, a fundamental condition for binding the people and for propagating the Japanese spirit and the Japanese way of life.

Her visit was cut short by shouts and oaths emerging from the downstairs kitchen, all directed at the two unfortunate Filipino youngsters who, apparently, had wanted to warm up some food. There is only one kitchen in the house. My family, at least, has the privilege of being able to use a separate stove, but the Filipinos have to share one with The Monster, which leads to continuous harassment.

Peace descends upon our house only on the rare occasion when the landlady goes out, dressed in her best finery, with a black hat at an angle on her ugly head. How my sister and I hate her! A few nights ago when we heard her leave with her slavelike husband, we heaved sighs of relief and played records loud on our gramophone. It was like a celebration! We talked and laughed with our parents and made fun of the latest Japanese propaganda effort:

A month ago 9 WAACS [U.S. Women's Army Auxiliary Corps] were ordered to leave their homes to take barrack quarters at the one-time Syracuse University Dormitory. All 9 demurred because the barracks were unsanitary and also because the building had a latrine for men which did not belong in the women's establishment.

August 1943.

During the last semester at Aurora University we would often find on the campus grounds bodies of tiny Chinese babies wrapped in straw mattings, rags, and occasionally a red blanket. Sometimes a slippered little foot protruded from the gruesome parcel, sometimes a miniature hand rested stiffly on the earth. Most probably there is a public detail that collects such babies' corpses—probably left dead or exposed to die in the darkness of the night—from parks and open spaces, since they always disappear rather quickly.

Before the War, the American Red Cross had initiated the successful China Famine Relief Work Project. The plan's objective was to save from starvation the families of hungry laborers in return for work. To ensure that only the truly destitute be helped, wages were intentionally kept below average rates so that anyone managing to survive otherwise would not seek such poorly paid employment. Hunger in China was always endemic and now, under the Japanese Occupation, conditions have worsened. Gloom ... gloom . . . gloom. Nobody was surprised to read in today's paper an article headlined

MAN GIVES CHILD TO HAWKER
FOR ONE SACK OF RICE

My mood improved when Serge dropped in suggesting we escape the heat and spend some hours in the Public Garden. As usual, he looked—as the Russians say—"fresh as a cucumber" dressed in a neatly ironed light blue shirt. Somehow the humidity and oppression of Shanghai's summer never affect his appearance. We rode a tram where we met A.R., a "Free Australian" who greeted us in a friendly manner to which Serge responded and I haughtily ignored since A.R. writes pro-Axis articles in the Japanese-controlled press and occasionally attacks the Allies on the radio. At the same time A.R. attends the St. John's University, where he no doubt spies on the students for the Japanese authorities. Hateful creature! I was furious with Serge for being polite to him.[21]

---

[21]I was wrong. We found out after the War that A.R. had been a courageous Allied agent. I felt guilty and ashamed of my behavior towards him.

The Public Garden, an acre of reclaimed foreshore overlooking the Whangpoo River, is my favorite park in Shanghai. Its grounds were landscaped by a Scottish gardener who attempted to reproduce a British ambiance: lawns, flowers such as hollyhocks and roses, blooming bushes, and pebble-covered walks. Before the War, the British Army Band would play waltzes, polkas, jigs in the elegant iron pavilion gracing the park and on Sundays "Scotties" (the affectionate name given to the Seaforth Highlanders) would march cockily, tartans and tassels asway to the exotic sounds of their bagpipes. During summer months, open air concerts were occasionally given by the Shanghai Symphony Orchestra under the baton of our fiery-tempered Italian conductor, Maestro Mario Paci. The orchestra, established in 1870, had no Chinese musicians.[22]

A rather unusual event takes place at the Public Garden on Yom Kippur (the Jewish Day of Atonement—the most solemn holiday of the year for my people). Religious Jews who pray at the nearby Museum Road Synagogue and spend 24 hours fasting, walk to the park during breaks in the services and stroll along its paths in small groups, wearing prayer shawls and skull-caps that attract curious glances.

Under British control a sign at the park gate listed all regulations governing the Public Garden. One specified that entrance was forbidden to Chinese although it was understood that amahs watching foreign children and Chinese gardeners and cleaners were exempt. Another rule banned dogs, leading the Japanese to extrapolate these two rules from the rest, claiming that the sign had read

CHINESE AND DOGS NOT ALLOWED

In fact, I have seen photo-montages of this supposed

---

[22]By 1955, after the establishment of the People's Republic of China, the Shanghai Symphony Orchestra featured only Chinese musicians.

sign displayed by Japanese propagandists. Be that as it may, I find it scandalous that Chinese be excluded from a public park in their own country. All the more unjust because expenses to maintain the grounds were paid by municipal taxes levied not only on foreigners but also on the International Settlement's Chinese population. In the past, I remember reading newspaper articles describing the outrage of the Chinese at this unfair humiliation, their strong protests, and their success in obtaining a relaxation of park regulations. The British finally agreed, albeit reluctantly, to admit a number of "well dressed Chinese" on their hallowed grounds! To ensure that only "approved visitors" entered, a tall pink-turbaned Indian Sikh bearing a wooden truncheon stood regally at the iron gate of the Public Garden. He towered over the short Chinese who loathed this fellow-Asian, this minion of a foreign power, who arrogantly and menacingly lorded over them.

Now the Japanese have opened the Public Garden to all, perhaps as a propaganda measure to indicate their brotherhood with the Chinese. Nevertheless, this is one of the few decisions of our Imperial Occupiers that I cannot but applaud. As Serge and I sat on a bench, we saw many Chinese enjoying the cool river breeze (which also brought wafts of bad odor!) while their charming, rollicking children tumbled on the lawns. No beggars or vagrants were present, so some method must have been devised to keep out these unwanted elements. I believe the Japanese have retained the park's pre-War Chinese gardeners, because the character of the landscaping has been left intact: leafy plants and flowers the British so fancy continue to be carefully nurtured. Serge and I rambled along the paths and lanes gazing at the Whangpoo river traffic and mass of humanity living on the water. We talked about the past, the future. The present is best forgotten. A lovely morning whose memory I will treasure.

In the evening a Chinese dressed in a dark blue gown and wearing spectacles rang our doorbell and asked for me. Without a word, he handed me a letter and left. It was from my American boy friend, Bob, interned by the Japanese in Pootung Camp. Before his incarceration I promised him I would call our weekly radio "Music Request Program" and ask them to play for him "Blueberry Hill" (his favorite) if I still cared for him, or "Stormy Weather" in the contrary case. Of course, we had no idea whether he would have access to a radio but I kept my word—in a way. Even though my romantic interest in him had faded, I couldn't ask them to play "Stormy Weather" because I didn't want to hurt his feelings. So it was "Blueberry Hill."

Bob's letter informed me that he was indeed able to hear radio broadcasts but said nothing about conditions in the Japanese camp. When I showed his letter to my parents, convinced they would share my excitement, they reacted with savage anger, accusing me of total irresponsibility that endangered the entire family. They insisted that I destroy the smuggled letter and never communicate illegally with Bob. Supressing my fiery temper, I handed them Bob's message with its unconcealed words of affection and left the room secretly determined to reply should the mysterious Chinese ever reappear.

The last time I had seen Bob was when he stood together with a large group of "number one enemy nationals" assembled upon the "Order of the Japanese Command" in front of the Cathedral Church. All wore the bright red arm-bands they had been given by the Japanese "Enemy Aliens Office" in Hamilton House shortly after Pearl Harbor. The arm-bands were four inches wide and originally stamped A for American, B for British, N for Netherlands as well as with an individual "registration number." Now however, the lettering has been replaced with Chinese characters (for easier identification, I suppose). The wearing of these red arm-bands was compulsory outside the house and, in addition, all persons thus identified (British, American and Dutch nationals) were forbidden entry into certain stores and public places. Bob and all the others gathered by the Japanese now waited in total silence for transfer to internment camps at an unknown destination.

I stood fearfully some 15 yards away with a number of Chinese and stateless people who hoped to wave surreptitious farewells and wished to indicate support by their mere presence. Bob's lanky frame loomed over a group of men and he wiped his glasses in the absent-minded manner that I found endearing. When he caught sight of me an expression of pleased surprise crossed his face, he nodded discreetly and turned away. Khaki-clad Japanese soldiers grunted and the entire motley group moved towards open army trucks. An incongruous moment in history: the once all-powerful foreigners who had reigned supreme in Shanghai, reduced to impotent prisoners without rights, each carrying the single small suitcase allowed by the Occupation authorities and some bearing bedding slung over their shoulder.

September 1943

Genny and I often "talk about school," about pre-War times at the College Municipal Français that for more than a decade was the center of our entire lives. We loved the U-shaped cream-colored building, the large windows, the graceful stairways leading to an elegant Salle des Fêtes (hall for celebrations) with its ornate ceiling and to the silent library with its smell of paper, of books, of print. We enjoyed gossiping about our teachers, those miraculous, unapproachable creatures to whom we attributed qualities they probably never possessed and romances they never suspected! We both had an undying crush on our physics teacher repeating all his *bons mots* (mostly dirty!) and adored everything connected with France—its principles of liberty, equality and fraternity, its literature, its history, its art. In short, the French colonial educational system had successfully converted us into real *aficionadas* of France, into patriots without a *patrie* (fatherland).

Oh, many were the arguments I had with my cousins who attended the British schools in the International Settlement. We pitched Corneille against Shakespeare, de Vigny against Shelley, Napoleon against Nelson,

Paris (which we had never seen) against London (equally unknown to them!). We stared at maps of the world with British colonies indicated in pink and French colonies in burgundy, arguing as to which country had more territory and which colonized states were most important—in my "objective" opinion, of course, those under French domination! We all lived in the French Concession, but my cousins' loyalties were British—an act smacking of treachery in my mind.

One year after the Treaty of Nanking, the British Settlement was officially established on November 17, 1843. Six years later the Chinese government was forced to cede to France territory situated between the Chinese city and the British Settlement. In the late 1850s the United States leased land north of the British areas, although this area was never formally taken over by the United States. Eventually the British and Americans combined the territories occupied by them into an International Settlement, while the French, ever the individualists, remained separate. Thus, Shanghai was divided into three distinct parts: the French Concession, the International Settlement, and the Chinese Municipality of Greater Shanghai (including the cities of Nantao and Chapei). Streets in the French Concession are named after French World War I heroes: Avenue Pétain, Avenue Joffre, Avenue Foch; or priests: Rue Stanislas Chevalier; or diplomats: Rue Pichon, Rue Chapsal; or writers: Rue Corneille, Rue Molière.[23] The street we took every day when we walked to school, Route Vallon, honored the first French aviator to reach Shanghai flying a plane.[24] There was, of course, no airport at the time, so he had to land and take off from the Race Course, a procedure that ended in a fatal but glorious crash.

---

[23]Dr. Sun Yat-sen later lived on 29 Rue Molière, where my father met him.
[24]Mao Zedong worked on Route Vallon from 1924–1926. Zhou En-lai also lived in the French Concession in the first part of the 1940s. Today, of course, all street names have been changed to Chinese: Molière—Xiang Shan Road; Vallon—Nanchang Road, etc.

Shanghailanders call the French Concession "French-town." On Bastille Day, the 14th of July, the tricolor used to be displayed in lights and bunting on all the streets, the French Army Band would parade playing the Marseillaise with great gusto, and elaborate parties were the order of the day. Schools, offices, even banks were closed.

The rapid defeat of France's "unconquerable" army by the Germans was a great blow to the French but perhaps even more so to people like Genny and I who observed with horror how quickly the Concession authorities gave allegiance to the Vichy government. Where had French heroism gone? What had happened to the ideals of the French Revolution? How could they so quickly adopt Fascism? Of course, not all the French in Shanghai are "Pétainistes" but this does appear to be true, alas, of the great majority.

When I was in the second year of my baccalaureate, these opposing views surfaced clearly: our professors of philosophy and psychology held diametrically opposite political views. When Pétain established his govern-ment and started enforcing a series of anti-Semitic laws, the philosophy professor referred to Jews as *grossiers et sensuels* (coarse and sensual)—terms I could in no way reconcile with any of the Jews I had ever met in my par-ents' home and which I resented to the depth of my soul. The psychology professor, on the other hand, never alluded to his pro-De Gaulle leanings in class but was known to participate in anti-Vichy activities.

One morning before starting his lecture our philoso-phy professor addressed us from the *estrade* (the teacher's platform) in a voice trembling with indignation. His bushy eyebrows askew, his pallid hands gripping the sides of his table, he ranted against our De Gaulliste psy-chology professor:[25]

"He is an enemy of France, a traitor to Maréchal Pétain! You MUST boycott his classes!"

---

[25]Several days after this incident our psychology professor secretly left Shanghai and joined the pro-De Gaulle troops in Indochina.

News of this diatribe must have reached our principal who, the following day entered our classroom before we had sat down and without preliminaries rapped out an order:

"Political discussions will not be tolerated in our college. *Vous comprenez?*"

The French students who had listened just a day before with rapt attention and apparent approval to the philosophy professor now nodded, chorusing a meek *oui monsieur*, while I, the outsider and the only Jew in class, remained silent, overcome with disgust.

In spite of all these painful disappointments, I continued to study hard with the vague hope of winning the coveted Gold Medal of Honor which was presented every year on Prize Giving Day in the Salle des Fêtes. The ceremony was graced by the presence of French officers in resplendent gold-braided uniforms, high officials of the Municipality, and members of the teaching staff sitting on the stage. In the audience were excited parents, guests, and pupils. The French Army Band would play a triumphant fanfare each time the winner of some prize mounted the steps leading to the stage to receive a prize. The high point of the afternoon was the announcement of the name of the student who had earned the greatest academic distinction offered in the French Concession: the Medal of Honor. A truly splendid affair!

In the summer of 1940, when I passed the baccalaureate written and oral examinations, no medal was awarded, a fact we attributed to France's fiasco in the War and the general mood of dejection.

A week later, I received a phone call from the college instructing me (we were never "requested") to visit the principal's office. The principal, a very short man with cornflower blue eyes, sat behind a huge desk. He addressed me as "Mademoiselle"—not by my name—no doubt a sign of my new graduate status—and signed me to sit down. I sank into a large dark green leather armchair, gazed at the ugly metal studs hammered along its sides, and rather fearfully waited to hear the reason for my unusual summons.

"Why do you think I called you?"

"I don't know, Monsieur."

"You are a *bachelière* and you don't know!"

Silence.

"Well, congratulations! You won the Médaille d'Honneur." He rose slightly, stretched his arm across the desk and handed me a small flat leather box ordering me to open it. There in a bed of silk lay a large round gold medal with my name clearly engraved on its polished surface. The principal then muttered something about the Vichy government, about the impossibility of awarding the prize publicly to me for reasons I surely understood. He repeated twice that he had personally (he stressed the word *per-so-nelle-ment*) insisted that I receive "the distinction I deserved."

Tame, despondent, I nodded. His words floated by, a shapeless mass, settling in my heart, inflicting a permanent wound. The coveted Medal, far from being a triumph, was an affront. I never told my proud parents of my pain in accepting this surreptitious distinction . . . it would hurt them perhaps even more than it did me.[26]

October 1943

On the seventh of this month, Domei News Agency published a short report about the death of Ignacz Trebitsch-Lincoln, who had succumbed the previous day at St. Mary's Hospital (where I was born) after an intestinal operation. According to the newspaper, he was 64 years old. Who was this mysterious man? A spy? For the Japanese? The Germans? The Chinese? The Allies? A Double Spy? Did he die a natural death?[27]

Last year when my cousin Isa (daughter of my father's twin brother) and I were walking down Avenue du Roi

[26]It was stolen years later when someone broke into our home.

[27]In their biography, *Trebitsch-Lincoln: The Self-Made Villain* (London: Cassell, 1961), David Lampe and Laszlo Szenasi report that they had learned in London that the complete Foreign Office dossier on Trebitsch-Lincoln would be open to the public in 1993. In the latest book on this intriguing individual, *The Secret Lives of Trebitsch-Lincoln* (London: Penguin, 1989), Bernard Wasserstein discloses some hitherto unpublished information.

Albert just outside her home, we suddenly came upon Trebitsch-Lincoln, or Abbot Chao-Kung as he now calls himself. He wore a long black Buddhist monastic gown, a stiff Chinese skull cap topped by an oversized translucent bead, and a long neclace of amber beads that reached down to his waist. He cast a quick glance at us and we both later agreed that his piercing eyes had sent a chill down our spines! A friend of mine who often goes to the Public Garden, told me that he frequently sees Trebitsch-Lincoln there walking round and round the paths, apparently deep in thought and oblivious to his surroundings.

Papa dislikes "Abbot Chao-Kung" and considers him dangerous. He told me that the Abbot was born a Hungarian Jew, converted to Christianity (changing denominations several times), then to Buddhism. Nobody really knows the full story about him nor how he survives. Anna Ginsbourg, who collaborates with Papa on *Nasha Jizn* (*Our Life*), interviewed him only last summer.[28] Anna is a creamy skinned, dark-eyed young woman whom I like, much admiring the vigor and enthusiasm with which she approaches every subject. She appears to share my father's liberal ideals but often stands up to him with gumption when he tries to thwart what he claims is her hot-headedness. As far as Trebitsch-Lincoln is concerned, Papa was not too thrilled about publishing an interview about this *podletz* (scoundrel).

"Do you know who one of Trebitsch-Lincoln's supporters is?"

"Yes, Mrs. Hardoon." (She is the wealthy Chinese widow of Iraqi Jewish businessman, Silas Hardoon.)

"And who else?"

"Well . . ."

"Walter Fuchs, that traitor!"[29]

---

[28]Her story was published on July 9, 1943 in *Nasha Jizn*.

[29]Fuchs, a Jewish lawyer, had worked in the German embassy and was eventually fired. It was rumored that he still maintained contact with his previous bosses. The Jewish Community loathed him.

Anna was not to be moved, stating that many readers would be very interested to know more about a figure as controversial as Trebitsch-Lincoln, and I agreed with her although, of course, nobody asked me for my opinion!

After the interview, Anna returned glowing. She had met Trebitsch-Lincoln at the small cafe downstairs at the Y.M.C.A. (where my older cousin Essie had once treated me to the first "pie à la mode" in my life!). Upstairs there were rooms rented to gentlemen only. The "Y" also had a large modern pool where mixed swimming was occasionally permitted but—so I was told—when men swam alone they were not supposed to wear bathing trunks, and entered the water stark naked. Of course, it would have been impossible for me to verify that!

Women always considered Trebitsch-Lincoln fascinating and Anna was no exception. She found him charismatic, attractive, and not at all frightening, contrary to Isa and me. He told her about his life, his conversion to Buddhism, his philosophy. Zionism did not merit his serious interest. Somehow even this last point did not antagonize Anna, a person devoted to the cause of Jewish independence. She wrote a good story and it evoked much interest.

In a way, one could understand Trebitsch-Lincoln's well-known hatred for Great Britain in view of his personal experience. His favorite son, "Natzl," was executed by hanging in England before Trebitsch-Lincoln could reach him: he had been abroad and his ship did not make it in time. Natzl (pet name for Ignatius), a Royal Horse Artillery bombardier, had broken into a home in Trowbridge (Wiltshire) together with a buddy after hours of heavy drinking to which neither young man was accustomed. When a member of the household surprised them, the intruders panicked and Natzl fired a shot that proved to be fatal. Natzl was sentenced to death, while his partner was condemned to 14 years of hard labor. Both were 20 years old. Thousands of signatures were collected in a plea for mercy—to no avail. Trebitsch-Lincoln could never forgive the British for what he considered an injustice. He was wont to rant against England's hypocrisy, colonial exploitation, arrogance, and narrow-mindedness.

Before he died, Trebitsch-Lincoln's main occupation was "The League of Truth," his own creation. The visiting card he handed Anna stated in French:

Ligue de la Vérité
Fondée par l'Abbé Chao-Kung

pour:	*contre:*
LA VERITÉ	LE MENSONGE
LA JUSTICE	LA INJUSTICE
LA BONTÉ	LA HAINE

PARTOUT ET TOUJOURS

[League for the Truth
Founded by Abbot Chao-Kung

for:	*against:*
TRUTH	LIES
JUSTICE	INJUSTICE
KINDNESS	HATRED

EVERYWHERE AND ALWAYS]

He had a devoted group of disciples. Towards the end of his life he did appear to sincerely adopt the teachings of Buddha. His intelligence, his memory, and his exceptional ability to concentrate for long periods of time facilitated his learning the very complex Pali scriptures of Hinayana Buddhism (a small, conservative branch of the religion). The depth of his knowledge astounded experts.

Many Shanghailanders suspect Abbot Chao-Kung of having been a Fifth Columnist, an assumption strengthened by the fact that for a long time the Japanese did not appear to interfere with his activities. It was even whispered that he broadcast pro-Japanese and pro-German propaganda from a secret radio station located in a Buddhist monastery. People said he was slippery like a snake and changed colors like a chameleon. Perfect material for a double or triple spy! Who knows?

On the day that Domei announced the death of
Trebitsch-Lincoln, I questioned Papa about something
that had puzzled me for a long time. "Why on earth did
Mrs. Hardoon help Trebitsch-Lincoln?"

"Well, you know," Papa replied, "she was a staunch
Buddhist and generously supported Buddhist causes.
She probably considered Abbot Chao-Kung to be just an-
other needy monk."

What a strange man, Trebitsch-Lincoln. He will always mystify me. I am certain he purposely hid the truth
about himself in his impenetrable web of deceit.

This year the Chinese did not celebrate Double Ten—
the 10th day of the 10th month. It used to be a red-letter
day in modern Chinese history and commemorated
October 10, 1911 when the Chinese Revolution broke
out, resulting in the end of the Manchu dynasty. Before
the Japanese Occupation, Shanghai always marked
Double Ten with public ceremonies honoring the
"Father of the Chinese Revolution," Dr. Sun Yat-sen.
Dr. Sun had dedicated 30 years of his life to rebuilding
China based on "The Three Principles of the People":
Nationalism, Democracy, and the People's Livelihood.[30]

Papa met Dr. Sun Yat-sen shortly after Papa arrived in
Shanghai from Vladivostok at the age of 21 without a
penny to his name. Desperate to make a living, Papa
managed to find some Chinese students to whom he
taught Russian for a small fee. He soon formed ties of
friendship with them and they all would passionately
discuss their dreams of universal equality and justice.

The Russian classes were held at the home of a
Chinese general whose daughter, a bright, sweet girl,
was the only female in the group. Dr. Sun Yat-sen,
whom most of these youngsters idolized, was a frequent
subject of conversation. One day, Papa's girl student
asked him whether he would be interested in meeting
the great hero personally since she believed her father

---

[30]"Nationalism" called for unification and a sense of national pride;
"Democracy" meant the participation of the Chinese people in the
government of their country; "People's Livelihood" laid the
foundation of a mild form of socialism.

might be able to arrange such an introduction. My father, of course, eagerly accepted the offer.

At that time, Dr. Sun was closely watched by the Shanghai authorities, who mistrusted his ideals of freedom and independence. The colonial powers, in particular, feared that the unification of China and a genuine revolutionary movement would imperil their hold on territories that yielded enormous economic and political advantages. Dr. Sun was forbidden to take up residence in the International Settlement—which was mainly under British control—but the French, ever eager to counteract their English rivals, permitted him to settle in the French Concession. Nevertheless, his every movement was carefully scrutinized.

Papa's appointment with Dr. Sun was set for 5:00 p.m. but he arrived half an hour earlier filled with nervous anticipation. He says he was shown to a rather small hall, where 15 Chinese gentlemen, all wearing modest cotton gowns, sat waiting. They communicated in almost inaudible whispers and as the moment of the audience approached all conversation ceased entirely.

At exactly five o'clock, Dr. Sun Yat-sen came in. In spite of the fact that Papa had seen many of photographs of him, the great leader appeared rather different from what Papa had imagined. He thought Dr. Sun's expression would reflect sharp traces of his harrowing experiences, that his stride would be determined and energetic. Quite the contrary, according to Papa, who said his face, with its rounded broad cheeks and a moustache that turned softly downward, mirrored patience and repose. His movements were gentle and unhurried. He fixed his gaze kindly upon his visitors, like a loving teacher, a friend.

Dr. Sun spoke individually to each person in the room. He seemed to listen carefully to what they would say and ponder his response, displaying a sincere interest in the individual asking a question. Perhaps because Papa was the only foreigner in the room, or perhaps because his pupil's father had kindly recommended him, Dr. Sun spent more time with him than with the others. He asked him how long he had been in China and stated that he was following the development of the Russian Revolution with great interest. Stammering with embarrassment (he would always rather write than speak!) Papa expressed admiration for the national movement in China and his hopes for the future of the Chinese people. When he mentioned that he was a Jew, Dr. Sun responded that he had long admired the perseverance and courage of the Jewish people during centuries of persecution. He then made a sign to an assistant who handed him a copy of one of his books, which he autographed for Papa. Unfortunately, this precious memento disappeared during Papa's move to a new room, a fact that saddens him even today.

Shortly after Papa's unforgettable meeting with Dr. Sun Yat-sen, one of his Chinese students came to the boarding house where he lived and told him in confidence that his group was being shadowed. After much discussion, he and his friends had arrived at the conclusion that their political activities were endangering all those with whom they had contacts. They knew Papa was stateless and had no government to protect him in case of serious trouble, so they decided to stop meeting him. All Papa's protests were useless and he never met any of his young Chinese friends again.

November 1943

Prices keep rising:
    1 lb. of bread $10.50—
    1 ton of coal $7,500.

A family of four living modestly needs a monthly income of about $15,000. How do the Chinese survive in their hovels? Many don't. As a child, my schoolmates and I would buy peanuts in tightly rolled patches of newspaper on the way to school. The price: one copper (there were 300 coppers to the dollar). Today, the same horn of peanuts costs $2.00 and the street vendors' business is on the decline.

Our power rations have been slashed again by 20% with warnings of further limitations. In the streets, all

lights have been dimmed in accordance with new rulings. Often when we return home in the evening we
find our rooms in total darkness: our landlady, The
Monster, unscrews all our bulbs so as to use the entire
power allocation herself!

"You can light candles!" she screams when my
mother protests.

My sister and I vent our fury by composing poems
about The Monster:

Oh whom oh whom do we desire
Upon some distant distant isle
That monstrous, ugly creature vile
Our landlady . . .

Such lyrical creations help us let off steam as we giggle
behind her back.

Due to poor visibility at night, traffic accidents are on
the rise, leading to new Japanese instructions. Today's
paper warned:

PEDESTRIANS ARE URGED TO KEEP OFF ROADS
AT NIGHT TO CHECK ACCIDENT TOLL
Walkers must keep to the pavement on the left side of
the roads and where there is no pavement, as far as
possible in the roads, in accordance with traffic rulings.
Motorcar drivers under the present conditions at night
are often unable to spot pedestrians walking on the
streets and consequently it is essential that the public
obey.[31]

Who knows what they mean by "as far as possible in
the roads"? Whatever the case may be, Shanghailanders
avoid going out after dark, contrary to pre-War days.

The situation in Japan also appears to be deteriorating.
In spite of tough news censorship, information contin-
ues flowing into Shanghai through mysterious channels
and, although not always reliable, enables us to discern
general trends. We have learnt that in Japan all male

---

[31]Traffic in Shanghai, as in England, circulated on the left side of
the road.

university students above the drafting age (it has been lowered from 20 to 19) have been ordered to return to their hometowns for physical check-ups.[32] Mobilization starts on December 1. A Women's Volunteer Corps has been formed and women now replace men as train and bus conductors, ticket inspectors, waiters, cooks, street sweepers.

Nevertheless, the Japanese bombard us with bombastic slogans underlining their unwavering determination and unbeatable might. Shanghailanders respond with morose skepticism to *Hakko Ichiu* ("Bringing Eight Corners of the World Under One Roof" with Japan serving as "Head of the Family") and to similar declarations.

The *Mainichi* reported today that "an historic meeting" took place this November 5 in the Imperial Diet Building, Tokyo, under the chairmanship of General Hideki Tojo.[33]

Present at the meeting were "leaders" (i.e., Japanese puppets) of five Asian countries: Wang Ching-Wei, President of Nationalist China, Prince Wan Waithayakon of Thailand, Chang Ching-hui of Manchukuo, Dr. José P. Laurel of the Philippines, and U Ba Maw of Burma. Subhas Chandra Bose of the "Provisional Government of Free India" served as observer. All pledged to prosecute the War "until final victory" and to strengthen the Greater East Asia Co-Prosperity Sphere "under the leadership of Japan." This bodes no good! A particularly disturbing piece of news, especially for the Jews in Shanghai, is that the keynote speaker at the "momentous event" was a sinister figure well known here: German Ambassador Heinrich Stahmer. He was sent to Japan in 1940 by the Nazi gov-

---

[32]Less than a year later the draft age was lowered to 18. After the War, a former Japanese officer explained to me that the boys were in reality sent home to give them a chance to pay homage—perhaps for the last time—at the graves of their ancestors.

[33]General Hideki Tojo was executed by hanging on December 23, 1948 for war crimes. Before his death, Tojo led three other Japanese sentenced to die with him in cries of: "Long live the emperor! Long live the great emperor of Japan!"

ernment to forge the Tripartite Pact (Berlin-Rome-Tokyo Axis) defined as a "united front against the evil forces of democracy and communism." Having brought his mission to a successful conclusion after only 18 days of negotiation, Stahmer was rewarded with an ambassadorship to China, where he served in 1941 and 1942. Shanghai Jews feared his nefarious anti-Semitic influence on the Japanese.[34]

In a typically long and circumvoluted German sentence, Stahmer told his docile, cheering audience, "You have built a peaceful temple of a New Order based on moral foundation and the solid ground of common conviction among the allied races by expelling forever the selfish influence of the Anglo-Americans who were solely intent on exploiting various countries of Greater East Asia for their own convenient purposes, and by achieving the historical task of freedom and emancipation."

In his address, "Kamisori" (the Razor) Tojo, so nicknamed because of his razor-sharp demands for administrative perfection, aroused enthusiastic response as he declared, "We see positively nothing to prevent us from winning ultimate victory . . ."

At breakfast, as my father angrily read to us the *Mainichi* report from Tokyo, he slammed it on the table saying:"One day all these so-called Asian leaders will be branded as traitors by their countrymen! No matter what Tojo says, the fact is that the tide of war has turned and Japan will be defeated. I am sure of that!"[35]

December 1943

Our landlady The Monster was gone for the day and my sister and I took advantage of her absence to play on the

---

[34]Rightly so. The segregation of European Jewish refugees in a closed area (ghetto) was the direct result of German pressure on Japan.

[35]At the same time as the five Asian representatives left Tokyo for their home countries carrying copies of the Greater East Asia Declaration, Roosevelt, Churchill, and Chiang Kai-shek met in Cairo and pledged to continue the War until Japan accepted unconditional surrender, gave up all territories conquered from the Chinese, and freed Korea.

lawn with her much abused Scotch terriers. In our neighbors' yard (the villa has been taken over by the Japanese Navy), two officers who looked like teenagers were reclining on canvas chairs, their shirt collars open to the unexpectedly warm winter sun. As we romped with the dogs, they approached the bamboo fence separating our properties and peered at us between the sticks, smiling broadly. After some discussion between themselves in Japanese, they started picking faggots off a pile of firewood and flinging them over to our side, in a generous effort to help us overcome the general fuel shortage. My sister and I quickly gathered the wood, waved at our benefactors shouting the words we remembered from our vacations in Japan: *"Domo arigato!"* ("Thank you very much!") A happy moment of spontaneous friendship between young people. I HATE HATE HATE this War!

That evening, sitting around the dinner table with our parents, we talked about the officers' kindness, our wonderful summers in Japan, the hospitality of the Japanese people, the delicate landscape of the country. My mother explained that in spite of financial difficulties she had always made a point to take us to the mountains or to the sea in summer. She had not been as lucky when she was a child. Her father died at the age of 42 in a cholera epidemic in Shanghai and her mother was left alone to support seven children.[36] The poor woman, who had married at the age of 15 (her husband was only six months older!), had no skills and in order to survive took in boarders to whom she served meals. In the meantime, my mother was sent for a year to a convent boarding school—probably because it was practically free and provided adequate education. There were two other Jewish girls there whose parents lived in Harbin. All the students regardless of their religion were required to pray in the chapel and learn catechism. Caught up by her

---

[36]My grandfather may have contracted cholera because he had picked up an old Chinese man who collapsed from cholera on the street and taken him to the hospital. The man, aged over 70, survived, while my grandfather died within three days at the early age of 42.

memories, Mama started to recite questions and answers she had studied by rote decades ago:

"Why did God make you?"

"God made me to know Him, to love Him, to serve Him, and to be happy with him forever in Heaven."

As usual in our family's conversations, we wandered from subject to subject and my sister and I now begged Mama to tell us more about her experiences at the convent. We enjoy very much listening to her since she is a lively, humorous storyteller who never fails to captivate her audience.

Mama described the very restricted life at the convent and the severity of the nuns. Punishments were frequent and the food dreadful.

"There were maggots in our rice!" she exclaimed, indignant even today at the memory.

Still, Mama remembered one very exciting day, a break in their dull routine. On that particular morning, a great commotion in the street penetrated through the thick convent walls: shouting, clanging of metal on metal, policemen's whistles, loud ringing of fire engine bells. The girls could see nothing since closed shutters always protected them from "the evils of the outside world." Unable to restrain their curiosity, my mother and her best friend, whom she described as "another naughty girl," crept to a forbidden upstairs room and peeked outside through the window. Their daring was awarded by a most unusual sight: a green alligator was crawling on the street followed by excited Chinese banging pots and pans together. A frightened policeman was frantically trying to regulate the traffic and a red fire engine was attempting to weave through the crowd. My mother and her friend dared not tarry in fear of being caught, but the next day a young nun who had befriended them and whom they adored succumbed to their pleas and clarified the mystery. It appeared that the red brick building across the street from the convent was a *godown* (warehouse) owned by a British firm that imported opium. The alligator must have crept into one of the crates during the packing procedure in some tropical country and, when the case was opened in Shanghai, the animal wiggled out to the horror of the coolies who thought . . . it was a dragon!

The strange (and probably terrified) creature then ambled into the street where it was pursued by a clamorous mob. Finally, the Shanghai Fire Brigade captured it, killed it, and ordered it to be stuffed.

"It was exhibited in the museum," Mama said, "but we never got to see it. I wonder if it is still there today."

While my mother was telling the story, my friend Sidney, an "Overseas Chinese" from Java, dropped in. He is a student of dentistry at St. John's University and loves tennis, which he plays with remarkable precision and grace. His skin is a different color from that of most Chinese: it has bronze tints that make him look like a living statue—a very handsome one at that. Sidney is very idealistic, very nationalistic, and resents every form of foreign dominance. He laughed with us at my mother's account but could not restrain himself from commenting:

"Whenever I hear about foreigners bringing opium into my country I feel ready to explode with fury! All they want is to gain wealth and power at our expense. The Japanese are no better than the Europeans. They are probably much worse."

The history of opium trade in China goes back several centuries. The West had always coveted Chinese goods such as silk, tea, porcelains (dubbed "Chinaware"), spices, and indigo while the Chinese, convinced of their own superiority, had no desire for imported goods. As a result of this attitude, barter with China was out of question and foreigners had to pay for Chinese merchandise in silver bullion. How could one overcome this poor balance of trade? The British finally hit upon a solution: to sell high quality opium (not grown in China) produced in their newly conquered Indian territories. A fleet of British ships began to transport the drug from Bengal to Canton and later to Shanghai when the headquarters of great trading companies moved there. Other foreigners—Americans, French, Germans, Italians, Iraqis—soon joined the fray, piling up immense fortunes.

The Chinese had long used opium for a variety of ailments and were slow to recognize its pernicious long-range effects. As the drug started flooding into China in an ever-increasing stream, the Chinese discovered its narcotic effects and millions eventually became addicted. They called it "foreign smoke."

To the great satisfaction of Queen Victoria, Britain's balance of trade shifted and by 1825 it was the Chinese merchants who had to pay the difference in silver. As addic-tion to opium increased throughout China, the Chinese government became alarmed and outlawed the opium trade, but to no avail, since foreign merchants continued to smuggle the drug into China, bribing corrupt officials with *cumsha* (golden sand) and working hand in hand with murderous pirates.

In 1839, in despair, the Chinese ordered a shipment of opium to be confiscated and thrown into the sea. Britain fumed at "this infringement of the right of free trade" and sent warships to the China coast. Thus started the Opium War, which ended with Britain's total victory and China's total humiliation. It led to the establishment of settlements with extraterritorial rights, among which those in Shanghai.

"Opium enriched the foreigners and weakened my country," Sidney said. "The Japanese today continue this murderous tradition. The devils! Do you know that the sale of narcotics is forbidden in Japan but encouraged in China by the Japanese Occupying Forces here? It is the Japanese who are the real owners of factories producing morphine and heroin. In fact, according to my Chinese friends who know what they are talking about, these factories are actually operated by the S.S.S. (Special Service Sector of the Army)."[37]

---

[37]John B. Powell, in his book *My Twenty-Five Years in China* (New York: MacMillan, 1945) writes: "The first (of these) Japanese 'institutions of culture' which sprang up within a few weeks after the Japanese Occupation were gambling houses with opium dens attached. . . . The Japanese military police who patrolled the area at first made efforts to close the dens, but the S.S.S. quickly stepped in and created a so-called 'Shanghai Supervised Amusement Department.' "

According to Sidney, opium plays as important a part in Japanese aggression as armament, and is probably an even deadlier weapon. I myself have seen early in the morning truckers openly loading corpses of drug victims in front of alleys where opium dens are situated.

"Today, even coolies can afford opium," Sidney told us, his voice trembling with anger. "They shake out the tobacco of ordinary cigarettes and refill them with the drug—a white powder. If you see someone smoking a cigarette and holding it up at a 45 degree angle, you can be sure it is opium since they are worried to drop out even a tiny bit. The Japanese, who are very inventive, are now selling special cigarette holders which the coolies call 'airplane smoke.' There is a bowl on the stem which holds the cigarette in a perpendicular position and prevents the drug from spilling out."

We all remained silent as Sidney sadly said, "Once you get hooked on this habit it is the end, the end!"

A mournful end to our day that had started in such a jolly manner. My parents and sister went to bed and I remained talking with Sidney. Since I begged him to turn to a "pleasant" subject he spoke of his forthcoming tennis tournament and teased me about the way I rush all over the court trying—unsuccessfully—not to miss a ball. Well, sports were never my forte!

1944

It is hard to believe that the Bund was once a muddy, flat bank upon which the yellow Whangpoo River always tried to encroach. To check the overflow, the British piled stones and earth on the embankment in a process called "bunding." Hence the name "Bund."[1] Originally a narrow footpath, it developed into a magnificent thoroughfare, the hub of Shanghai's international power.

I love to walk along the Bund, gazing at our filthy Whangpoo River with its sampans, fishing trawlers, awkward cargo junks, and small night-soil boats that ply their way in the dense traffic with their stenchful loads. Thousands of Chinese live on the Whangpoo, a floating, colorful slum.

Facing the teeming waters, Shanghai's great buildings rise like giants: The Hongkong & Shanghai Banking Corporation (the second largest in the world today), The Oriental Bank, the Agra Bank, the Mercantile Bank, the Comptoir d'Escompte . . . Built of granite, marble, cement, they were symbols of imperial glory. Before Pearl Harbor, some 21 flags of different countries graced Shanghai's skyline, fluttering in the river breeze. Today they have been replaced by the stark white and red Rising Sun of Japan.

Before the Occupation, two bronze lions had crouched in front of the Hongkong & Shanghai Bank building, their metal teeth gleaming ferociously in the sun. Thousands and thousands of Chinese had stroked their paws in the belief that some of Great Britain's power and wealth might rub off on them. Once when I was a little girl, Mama lifted me up so that I too could touch the fearsome animals. Now the lions have vanished and we assume that the Japanese melted them down for the war industry.

My favorite building on the Bund is the Sassoon House, whose pointed roof awed me when it went up in 1929, piercing the sky in graceful splendor—the tallest building in Shanghai. Not to be outdone, the Bank of

---

[1]In the Far East there are various thoroughfares along rivers called "Bund." However, the Shanghai Bund is the most famous one.

China, right next to it, put up a long flag-pole whose tip reached slightly higher than that of the Sassoon House tower. The cost of building the Sassoon House came to the astronomical sum of more than one million pounds sterling. It quickly became a Bund landmark, encompassing a luxurious shopping arcade, banks, offices, the American Women's Club of China, and the splendid Cathay Hotel—second to none in China.[2] I once was taken to dinner in its main ballroom and danced on the white maple floor that had been placed on springs to give the dancers' movements a gentle flow.

One memorable day when wandering in the Cathay Hotel lobby, mainly to gawk, I caught a glimpse of the famous playwright Noel Coward. He was tall, elegant and quite obviously made up. His eyebrows had been plucked to a thin line. Eventually, the Cathay management honored Coward by naming their most prestigious suite after him. Little wonder, since this is where he had written *Private Lives* in a record four days!

Last Sunday, I managed to persuade my friend Fira to ride the tram to the Bund and "roam around" in spite of the cold. Fira is a girl with whom I spend most of the time giggling. When we are together everything appears hilarious to us, with the exception of drunkards, for whom Fira has a pathological fear—she starts screaming and running away. Fortunately, she does not react that way to Japanese soldiers. On the Bund, Japanese guards were stationed in front of the main buildings and we did not dare even step into the Cathay Hotel. Ah! How painful this would have been for Sir Victor Sassoon, the "father" of this magnificent construction.[3] Sir Victor's parties at the Cathay before the War had become legendary, not only in Shanghai but abroad. He loved to select specific themes for each grand occasion one of which was a sensational "circus." "Tout Shanghai" had attended dressed as clowns, acrobats, and tigers, while Sir Victor himself led the ceremonies a very elegant ringmaster swinging a leather whip. Since he favored

---

[2]Cathay Hotel: today the Peace Hotel.
[3]Sir Victor was the son of Elias Sassoon. See pp. 62–63.

My parents' wedding picture, Shanghai, November 8, 1921.

My parents, Aunt Rosetta, and Uncle Gava at a New Year's party at the Jewish Club.

My mother's sister Lena and her friends transported by wheelbarrow in early 1920s.

The author walking down Nanking Road in 1941.

My Japanese student friend, Yorifumi Enoki, in 1938.

My father at his favorite activity, writing.

Excerpts from *Nash Put* (Our Way). An anti-Semitic Russian newspaper in Harbin. Written on the serpent is the term "Judocommunism."

Coded announcement of Mussolini's resignation. When read downwards, the initial letters of each line of the poem read in Russian, "Mussolini Resigned."

Boris Topas, prominent member of the Jewish community who was tortured by the Japanese military in the infamous Bridge House.

The Palace Hotel, where Shanghai's society met at elegant tea dances.

View of the muddy Whangpoo River, gateway to China

Bet Aharon, the Sephardi synagogue built by Silas Hardoon.

Cathay Hotel, built by Sir Victor Sassoon. Noel Coward wrote *Private Lives* there.

Cathedral Church, in front of which the Japanese military assembled "Enemy Nationals" before transporting them to internment camps.

廣 告 新 聞
SHIMBUN

安い買物 安い飲食 安い娯樂
の爲には此等の商店を御利用下さい

1.

1. Trade advertising sheet printed in Honkew ghetto, August 1944.

2. Shanghai Ashkenazi Jewish Communal Association Letterhead.

3. Masthead of my father's paper, *Nasha Jizn*, (Our Life), with Russian, Yiddish (in Hebrew lettering), Chinese, and French (the street name)—a reflection of Shanghai's multicultural community.

What shall I do with that
which does not give me immortality?

From the unreal lead me to Reality,
From darkness lead me to Light.
From death lead me to the Immortal.

Rabindranath Tagore

June 28
1924

4.

4. Dedication written by the Indian author Rabindranath Tagore in Kadoorie guest book in June 1924.

5. First page of bylaws of Shanghai Ashkenazi Jewish Communal Association.

My parents' permits for immigration to Israel, December 21, 1948.

Max Scheidlinger (center) and his friend (left) who beat Ghoya, "The King of the Jews," after the war.

Board of the Shanghai Jewish Club. My father, David Rabinovich is at the extreme left. Second to the far right is his twin brother Gava.

Shanghai's famous waterfront, The Bund. In foreground the Winged Victory cenotaph erected after World War I. The Japanese military forces melted it down for weapons, forgetting that it honored their own dead who had fought on the Allied side in the first war.

beautiful women , no matter their reputation, many gorgeous but socially unaccepted creatures graced the proceedings.

Fortunately for Sir Victor, he was in Bombay on the day of Pearl Harbor and thus escaped certain incarceration by the Japanese as a British national.

A friend of mine who worked at the Sassoon offices told me that on the day of Pearl Harbor, he and other employees rushed to their place of work to destroy documents. While they were doing so, a group of Japanese "Blue Jackets" marched in. They ordered everyone into the boardroom and commanded them to stop destroying the files and continue working as they would normally. The daily routine was maintained for a while until the Japanese, who belonged to the *Izumo Maru* landing party, finally took over the business completely and interned all employees who were "enemy nationals." The others were curtly dismissed.[4]

Fira and I rambled along determined to have a good time anyway. In spite of our parents' severe warnings about buying "dirty, contaminated" food on the street, we purchased pickled plums from a vendor and sucked on them, enjoying the sweet-sour taste. However, when we reached the Garden Bridge prudence prevailed over our sense of adventure and we turned quickly back. Everyone crossing the Garden Bridge is compelled to remove their hat and bow in front of the Japanese sentinels who stand there 24 hours a day. Subservience is demanded of all civilians, high and low, Chinese, foreign, and even Japanese. The Japanese guards brutalize anyone not bowing fast enough or low enough for their satisfaction. A friend of mine witnessed the merciless beating of a Japanese dressed in a smart business suit who had failed to remove a cigaret from his mouth when bowing. Apparently, this was interpreted as a sign of disrespect by the uniformed Japanese who pummelled and slapped him until he collapsed. Of all people

---

[4]My friend praised the generosity of the Sassoon Company after the War. He was given back-pay for the War years as well as six months home leave with expenses.

the Chinese fare worst at the hands of the Japanese. A number of them have been sadistically bayoneted and thrown into the Whangpoo to drown in its swift currents. Shanghailanders have learned never, never to react to Japanese mistreatment since any show of pain or anger is regarded as cowardly or insolent, arousing murderous responses.

The Garden Bridge is an admirable engineering feat: two graceful arches, each measuring 171 feet long and 60 feet wide. Before the War, on special occasions such as the Coronation of King Edward VIII in 1936, it was brilliantly illuminated—in this particular case gigantic crowns reflected their lights in the murky Whangpoo waters.

Old China hands love to tell the amusing story of how the Garden Bridge had started in 1856 as a rickety wooden structure built by a shrewd Englishman who exacted a hefty toll from all who crossed it. He quickly became rich, but the grumbling of the Chinese rose to a roar since they were forced to pay in cash while foreigners' credit was accepted. Finally, in 1906, the Shanghai Municipal Council was compelled to intervene and solved the problem by building a modern bridge at a stone's throw away from the simple wooden one. Since the authorities charged no toll, the disappointed Englishman soon lost all his customers and eventually dismantled his structure. Today, the Garden Bridge is a revamped version of the first Municipal Council bridge.

Our cheeks red from the cold and our stomachs far from full from the pickles, we returned to Fira's house where her grandmother had prepared a most delicious borscht. We then sat in the closed "garden" veranda talking about our plans after the War, giggling about boys we "liked" and chattering non-stop until my mother called, insisting I get home before dark. Not even the Japanese Occupation can stop girls from having fun!

My sister and I were a block away from Mama's store, Peter Pan Shop, when the sirens sounded. As the first wail was heard, people stopped and looked up at the sky wondering if it was "the real thing" or a false alarm, but even before the seventh warning blast ended, the bombing began. Grabbing each other, my sister and I moved swiftly towards the fronts of buildings as we had been instructed to do in such events. Boom! Boom! The explosions were unusually loud for Avenue Joffre since the outskirts of Shanghai, the factories, the outlying warehouses, and the railways have been till now the most common objectives of the Americans.

"Should we go into Mama's shop?" my sister asked. "If we do, she will make us stay there a long time."

"Yes," I agreed. "She will be afraid to let us out because of the bombing."

Neither one of us wanted to be stuck in the store and "miss all the fun." The bombing grew heavier, people started rushing into buildings and *Pao Chia* from the Japanese "self-policing plan" yelled at everyone to clear the streets. Willy-nilly we had to take shelter at Peter Pan Shop. As we ran toward it an old woman grabbed my arm and clung to me sobbing. She kept moaning in terror, *"Boje! Boje! Boje!"* ("God! God! God!" in Russian). I had no choice but to drag her along and the three of us plummeted clumsily into Mama's shop.

Mama and some of her customers were huddled behind the counter and Mama motioned us to join her:

"Quick! Quick!"

At the same time she consoled the hysterical old woman:

"Nichevo! Nichevo! Vse budet horosho!" ("It's all right! It's all right! Everything will be O.K.!")

In all this turmoil five good-looking Italian soccer players came in for shelter—adding to my sister's and my excitement. Bombs! Wailing woman! Handsome athletes! Wow! When the bombing ended about half an hour later everyone scattered. In spite of Mama's misgivings that the bombers might return, my sister and I stubbornly insisted that all was over and went out to continue our interrupted walk. Five minutes later the sirens wailed again and bombs started falling in the distance. We went into a corner grocery store for shelter and phoned Mama to reassure her. She was furious with us.

In spite of all Japanese propaganda, it seems that the tide is turning in favor of the Allies. There are rumors of victories for the Allies in Europe and Asia.[5] People speak of powerful American counterattacks in the Pacific. I often think of my Japanese friend Yorifumi. He had spoken to me about the way the Japanese feel about war, about their sense of patriotism and honor, their code of behavior demanding death rather than submission. Yorifumi explained to me that he would never allow himself to be taken prisoner, he would rather die like a Samurai as prescribed by the Japanese Field Service Code. Whether Japan won or lost a war, how could a Japanese prisoner go back to his country in disgrace? He would be ostracized by everyone, he would bring shame to his entire family.

"If a large-scale war breaks out," Yorifumi had said, "we will have to fight to the death or commit suicide. That is the Japanese way."

It saddened me to remember our conversations because Yorifumi had such a gentle poetic nature. He loved so much his village, the beach with its small island to which we swam, the pine trees and the changing colors of the sky. It must have been so difficult for him to endure harsh Japanese military discipline, as he once hinted to me. I worry that the War has brutalized him, has broken his spirit, has perhaps maimed or even killed him. There is no doubt in my mind that Japan will lose the War. What will happen then to people like Yorifumi?

In the evening several members of Papa's paper had a meeting. A large stack of back copies of *Israel's Messenger* was piled on our dining-room table and they were leafing through them to collect material for an article on the

---

[5]On January 22, 1944 the Allies landed in Anzio.

history of Zionists in Shanghai. *Israel's Messenger* was founded in 1904 by an acquaintance of Papa's, a Sephardi Jew named Nissim Ezra Benjamin Ezra—usually called N.E.B. for short. Although my father did not much admire Ezra's literary talents, he did appreciate the man's total dedication to his publication, which he edited and wrote virtually single-handed from cover to cover. Ezra, like so many Sephardi Jews, had originally come to Shanghai to work for the Sassoon Company but later decided it was his mission to publish an English-language newspaper for the Shanghai Sephardi Community. Since he was a dedicated Zionist, one of the main aims of *Israel's Messenger* became the promotion of the Zionist cause. In due course Ezra's paper became known as an international Jewish monthly, the official organ of the Shanghai Zionist Association and the National Fund Commission of Shanghai. Until his death in 1937, Ezra dedicated his entire life to his publication. After he died in 1937, his wife took over and the front cover began to state rather quaintly:

"Israel's Messenger
The Organ of Jewry in the Far East
Founded by the late N.E.B. Ezra
Proprietress and
Editress Mrs. K. Ezra."

Although Ezra may not have been a great journalist, he was a very likable, charitable and hard-working man, who Papa and others say possessed an indomitable will, energy, and enthusiasm, as well as supreme faith in God.

Israel's Messenger folded up three years ago at an appropriate date: October 17, the day of the Balfour Declaration, an event with which Ezra was to become closely involved and which would lead to Dr. Sun Yat-sen's interest in Zionism.

On October 17, 1917 (a date to be celebrated thereafter by generations of Jews) Arthur James Balfour, Britain's foreign secretary, issued an official statement declaring that his government favored "the establishment in Palestine of a National Home for the Jewish People . . ." Immediately after publication of this historic declara-

tion, Sir Elly Kadoorie (founder of the Zionist movement in Shanghai), supported by Ezra sought the en-
dorsement of this policy by the Chinese government. To
strengthen their hand they decided to try and obtain the
support of Dr. Sun Yat-sen who had emerged as a great
Chinese leader. Ezra once told Papa how they had approached Morris "Two-Gun" Cohen to arrange an appointment for them. Not only did Cohen set up an audience, but he also spoke to Dr. Sun about the Jewish
struggle for a homeland, a fight with which he knew Dr.
Sun could sympathize. When Elly Kadoorie and Ezra
met Dr. Sun at his home on Rue Molière, Ezra managed
to persuade the Chinese leader to send him an open letter for publication in *Israel's Messenger* endorsing the establishment of a Jewish National Home in Palestine.[6]
On July 14, 1922, the Palestine Mandate was approved by
the Council of the League of Nations, of which China
was a member. I find it quite amusing that when China
made its first transcontinental radio contact with the
United States in 1931, among the messages broadcast was
the blessing of the Zionists of Shanghai to the Zionists
of America.

Papa's meeting, as usual, was a friendly but stormy
one. There were heated discussions about what would

---

[6]Sun Yat-sen's letter read:

Dear Mr. Ezra:

I have read your letter and the copy of *Israel's Messenger* with much
interest, and wish to assure you of my sympathy for this
movement—which is one of the greatest movements of the present
time.

All lovers of democracy cannot but support wholeheartedly and
welcome with enthusiasm the movement to restore your wonderful
and historic nation, which has contributed so much to the
civilization of the world and which rightfully deserves an
honorable place in the family of nations.

I am,

Yours very truly
Sgd: Sun Yat-sen

or would not pass the Japanese censors, who often acted in mysterious and—in our eyes—illogical ways.

All in all a most exciting day!

March 1944

Shanghailanders fear that as the situation deteriorates, the Occupying Army will take it out on the local population. A small item appeared in the papers about the *Amerika-Maru* having had an "accident." We surmise that it has been torpedoed or bombed by the United States. Hideki Tojo has made himself army chief of staff—he is already prime minister and war minister![7]

As tension increases in our city and food becomes scarcer the Chinese seem to become more bitter and antagonistic towards foreigners (i.e., whites). Rickshaw coolies are insolent, aggressive, almost threatening, knowing full well that foreign customers are powerless today. The few that still lord it over the rest—the Germans and other Axis members—are usually sufficiently well off to use chauffeured motorcars. In any case, after years on the streets the coolies can quickly differentiate between foreigners, knowing almost instinctively whom they can harass without fear of retribution. As to the Japanese, the poor coolies must contain their anger and submit to abuse—another reason, perhaps why they vent their frustration on helpless passengers. Last week I saw a Japanese dressed in a dark business suit kick a rickshaw puller to speed him on, and then get off at his destination a block away flinging coins disdainfully on the pavement. The poor coolie humbly picked up the money and wiped his sweating face while I watched tears of fury rising in my eyes. I have such mixed and contradictory feelings about the Chinese!

Before the War, rickshaw men often laughed, joked, and dashed like marathon runners, surging forward

---

[7]John Toland in his *The Rising Sun* writes: "Orders came to repatriate old people, women and children (from Saipan). On March 3, Amerika-Maru sailed with seventeen hundred passengers, most of them families of officials of the South Sea Development Co. or influential citizens. It never reached the homeland. Three days later torpedoes sent it to the bottom."

when the traffic light turned green. They had fun trying
to outwit bicycles, motorcycles, and carriages and concentrated their strength upon moving swiftly forward,
weaving cunningly through Shanghai's disorganized
traffic. Once I asked Ah Kwei:

"How rickshawman run so quick-ee?"

She replied:

"He takee red-ee medicine." This referred to tiny red
sugar-coated pills containing minute doses of narcotics
(opium or something else?) which the coolies could buy
for a few coppers.

Be that as it may, so exceptional is their velocity and
endurance, that Carroll Alcott,[8] the popular U.S. broadcaster, mocked retreating Italian troops in Libya claiming
they could run "almost as far and as fast" as Chinese
rickshaw coolies! Indeed, before the Japanese
Occupation, rickshaw coolies had appeared to me as a
noble breed: uncowed, independent, deriding Fate with
gumption.

But I know the truth is different from this. Actually,
some years ago an official "Rickshaw Report"was published in the papers that clearly brought to light the
abuses of the system governing rickshaws. Only 144
people owned the total of 68,000 rickshaw licenses issued
in Shanghai, and they reaped fat profits renting the vehicles to coolies for a monthly fee that devoured most of
the poor fellows' hard-earned money, leaving them and
their families on the edge of constant starvation.

My parents could never afford a "private rickshaw"
paid on a monthly basis, which was considered a luxury
at the time, at least among our circle of acquaintances.
These shiny black vehicles—contrary to shabby public
rickshaws—sport a spotless white upholstered double
seat, a clean plaid for one's lap, and a wide protective
tarpaulin to protect the passenger (or passengers, since

---

[8]"Jello" was one of his radio sponsors. He would start his daily
program with a cheery "Jello! Jello! Jello!" in a deep voice
Shanghailanders loved. Before Pearl Harbor, Shanghai's
International Settlement and the Philippines were the only two
spots in the Far East where commercial radio had penetrated.

sometimes up to three people rode together) against the rain. Of course, nobody gives a thought to the poor coolie rushing forward as water runs down his entire body and he tries to see his way through drops hammering on his face. What a cruel world!

When my sister was little, she and her friend would ride the same rickshaw every day to school. The coolie, an exuberant, long-legged youth with calves as hard as iron would prance all the way and make them giggle at his antics. The two girls loved him.

Before the War, we could see an extraordinary parade in the International Settlement on Saturday mornings: some 50 rickshaw pullers racing ahead carrying religious Jews wearing skull caps and prayer shawls. Since Orthodox Jews do not drive or handle money on the Sabbath, they paid the coolies in advance. During High Holidays the rickshawmen, having learnt in some uncanny way about the festival, would appear promptly in front of their Jewish clients' homes to take them to the synagogue. They then ran jauntily to the services exchanging hoots and pleasantries with each other. Having delivered their passengers, the coolies would wait patiently, crouching on the footrests of their carts, all the while chatting and spitting on the ground, according to Chinese custom. They cheerfully accepted payment after the holidays, showing understanding for the Jewish tradition of not touching money on specific days.

There are no such pleasant interludes in the lives of coolies today. This morning's paper published statistics indicating that the "professional" life of a riskshawman does not last over five years. After that time he succumbs to tuberculosis and other illnesses resulting from undernourishment and contagious diseases.

Considering the miserable life of rickshaw coolies, whom I see as a symbol of "man's inhumanity to man," it is remarkable that before the War both the United States and France claimed the dubious distinction for having introduced rickshaws into the Far East! According to the Americans, it was a U.S. missionary in Yokohama—a certain Reverend Globe—who converted a baby carriage to drag about his invalid wife in 1869 and thus produced a prototype of what soon became the popular rickshaw named in Japan *jin-rick-sha* (*jin* meaning "power," *riki* "man" and *sha* "vehicle"). Not to be outdone, the French declared that it was a Frenchman named Menard who brought the rickshaw to China when he arrived in Shanghai in 1873 from Japan.[9] Menard submitted to the French Municipal Council a project "for the establishment of a service of small hand carts for passenger traffic in the Concessions" demanding a 10-year monopoly for himself. Sensing the prospect of high profits, the French Council welcomed the introduction of rickshaws but would not accede to Menard's wish for sole rights. They said that agreement had first to be sought from the British in accordance with treaty regulations between the Colonial Powers. After lengthy negotiations and postponements the French Council grabbed most of the profits; the British received a piece of the pie, Menard was pacified, and a new class of exploited Chinese was created.

April 1944

Today is Genny's birthday. Ever since I can remember this is a date I always celebrate, just as she never forgets mine. Genny had a small tea party for a group of six girls. Her mother, a regal woman with velvety brown eyes, generously served us, displaying—consciously or unconsciously—her beautiful slim hands with tapered fingers. Genny's mother is famous in Shanghai for her cooking, in particular, her fluffy meat and cabbage *piroshki* (individual yeast dough pies), her fish *pirog* (large, rectangular pie) and her 14-layer "Mikado" cake, a delectable creation of thin sheets of pastry and chocolate filling one could die for!

We chattered, laughed, gossiped, and devoured every morsel. How Genny's mother managed to provide all these goodies in these difficult times remains a mystery,

---

[9]For more on the rickshaw, see Ch. B. Maybon and Jean Fredet, *Histoire de la Concession Française* (Paris: Libraire Plon, 1929).

but we certainly did justice to her cuisine, devouring every crumb.

Our fun, however, was tempered by the presence of Genny's father, Boris Topas, former president of the Shanghai Ashkenazi Jewish Community and a Zionist leader of outstanding intelligence, charm, and integrity. After having been held for many months by the Japanese in the notorious Bridge House prison he is a mental and physical wreck. Before his incarceration he was one of those rare people whose dynamic presence was felt the moment he entered a room. He had always seemed tall to me, perhaps because his dignity added to his physical stature. His features were handsome, he would stride resolutely, sometimes carrying a walking stick that gave a certain jaunty air to his rather intimidating (to me) appearance. Ah! how he has changed! Old, twisted, crippled, his face distorted in a grimace.

The very words "Bridge House" elicit a shuddering response from Shanghailanders. In this place of misery and torture, men and women are herded together in tiny cells with one single container that serves as communal toilet. Rats and bugs spread typhus, while starvation and lack of vitamins cause beriberi. Added to all this, sadistic guards beat and torment the powerless captives. How do we know? Somehow information always filters through in spite of threats by the Japanese to severely punish "rumor-mongers." There is a rumor that American airmen captured in Japan were shipped to Bridge House, tortured, and executed there.[10]

As Genny, his dearly loved daughter, blew out her birthday candles, Mr. Topas sat hunched in an armchair mumbling incomprehensible words and bursting into fits of soft weeping.

Upon my return home found my father reading the paper alone at the dining-room table—a rare opportunity for conversation. I pleaded with him to explain the reason for Mr. Topas' arrest together with other Jewish

---

[10]It was confirmed after the war that these airmen were part of General Doolittle's raid on Tokyo. They were forced to dig their own graves before being shot in the head and falling into the graves.

Community leaders and why he alone had been selected for such long incarceration and torture. After some reflection, my father said:

"I suspect many reasons for poor Mr. Topas' arrest, some of which I cannot speak about and may tell you after this *prokliataya* (cursed) War is over. However, I think I can confide to you why he fell victim to inhuman treatment by the Japanese. You understand, of course, that you should NEVER, NEVER discuss this subject with anyone. In general, avoid speaking about the Japanese. There are many spies all around, willing to report to the Japanese in return for payment. *Stid i sram!* (Shame and disgrace!) So, I beg of you, Irochka, you who so thoughtlessly and passionately express your opinion, please control yourself and think many times before you speak!"

I am always surprised how fluently Papa speaks English, considering he has never really learned the language. His business letters are also very well formulated. Of course Papa's spoken English does reflect a Russian background, but almost all Shanghailanders have some particular accent and syntax so that nobody really pays any attention to it. Apart from certain mistakes Papa makes repeatedly (such as "What's news?" instead of "What's new?"), his grammar and construction are usually correct.

I heard Papa's little sermon, deciding not to irritate him with arguments and hoping he would make some interesting disclosures. My unaccustomed patience was rewarded. Papa continued his revelations, saying he was convinced that the main cause for Mr. Topas' torture went back to 1933 when Mr. Topas had initiated and organized a protest against the mistreatment of Harbin Jews by the Japanese. Tonight, as my sister sleeps, I make a point to write in my journal while Papa's words are still etched in my mind.

"You were too young to understand and Mama and I always tried to avoid telling you details of rabid anti-Semitic acts—very frightening for a small impressionable child. Now, of course, you are old enough and, un-

fortunately, the situation of Jews today is as desperate as
during the Inquisition or the Russian pogroms. In fact, it
is even worse, far worse. *Ach! Kakoe neschastie!* (Oh!
What a misfortune!)"

My father sighed, remained silent, and I dared not
prod him. After a while he spoke again, his voice sometimes rising in anger, sometimes down to a soft sad
whisper.

According to Papa, what happened to our good friend
Mr. Topas is the result of horrifying events in recent
Jewish history. When the Japanese occupied Harbin
more than 10 years ago, it soon became obvious that certain Japanese circles—the Kempeitai and other rapacious
army and civilian groups—bent on enriching themselves would pursue a regime of terror, blackmail, theft,
and kidnapping.[11] All these abuses were welcomed in
Harbin by the self-proclaimed "Russian Fascist Party," a
gang of stateless White Russians whose "Fuehrer" was a
violent young anti-Semite Konstantin Vladimirovich
Rodzaevsky. Rodzaevsky and his "Russian Patriots" offered the Kempeitai their services for "special assign-
ments": informing, stealing, vandalizing, kidnapping,
killing.[12] Rodzaevsky's mouthpiece was the Russian
newspaper *Nash Put* (*Our Way*), whose masthead figured
a framed swastika surmounted by the imperial Russian
double-headed eagle. The paper repeatedly refered to
"Judocommunism," or rather, as they expressed it,
"Kike-communism" (*Jidovski comunism*), claimed Lenin
had a Jewish mother, and published cartoons lifted directly from Julius Streicher's *Der Stürmer*. This is the
background of the drama that was to take place.

In 1933, a brilliant 24-year old Jewish pianist, Simon
Kaspe, graduated with high honors from the Paris
Conservatoire de Musique and after a successful tour of
recitals in Tokyo, Manila, and Shanghai returned to
Harbin where his parents lived. His father, Joseph, one

---

[11]The Kempeitai were the military police founded in 1881, notorious
for acts of torture and terror, and dismantled by the Allied
Occupation authorities on October 4, 1945.

[12]Today we would probably call them "hit men."

of Harbin's wealthiest Jews, owned Harbin's finest hotel,
the Moderne, as well as an exclusive jewelry store and
several theaters. He was a French citizen and since
France was one of the world's most powerful nations,
Kaspe firmly believed that French passports provided
him and his family ample protection against Japanese
and White Russian hoodlums.

On the night of August 24, 1933, several Russian
Fascists, tacitly supported by Japanese criminals,
snatched young Simon Kaspe when his car stopped at
the doorstep of a young Jewish girl whom he was seeing
home. The next day Joseph Kaspe received a ransom
note demanding the enormous sum of $300,000 for the
release of his son. The elder Kaspe immediately rushed
to the French Consulate pleading for urgent assistance,
but the French consul merely confined himself to sending an official note to the Japanese authorities requesting clarification. Luckily, at the French Consulate there
was at that time an idealistic young man, Vice-Consul
Chambon, whose outrage at the wave of terrorism para-
lyzing Harbin propelled him to strong action. Realizing
the haughty apathy of his superior, on his own initiative
Chambon hired private detectives to investigate the
case.

As soon as Chambon's intervention became public
knowledge, several Russian anti-Semitic papers, in particular *Nash Put*, retaliated. They launched a propaganda
blast against Vice-Consul Chambon, vilifying him and
claiming, with no basis of truth, that he was a
"Communist Jew." The campaign of slander peaked
when a member of the Russian Fascist Party challenged
Chambon to a duel.

Vice-Consul Chambon advised Joseph Kaspe not to
pay the ransom, since experience in Harbin had shown
that yielding to kidnappers' demands resulted only in
further pressure and not in release of the victim.
Meanwhile the gang, fearing discovery, moved their
victim from place to place, tortured him diabolically, cut
off his ears—which they sent in a package to his father—
and eventually shot him. His mangled body was
dumped in a gutter, where it was soon discovered.

Anger and revulsion shook every ethnic group in Harbin. It seems that the entire city attended Simon Kaspe's funeral: White Russians, Chinese, Koreans, Japanese and, of course, the entire Jewish Community. In spite of strict orders from the Japanese authorities restricting the cortege to narrow side streets, and in spite of threats and the presence of armed police and military, thousands of sympathizers followed the coffin as it wended its way to the Jewish cemetery.

Joseph Kaspe hysterically insisted on seeing his son's face for the last time and when his wish was reluctantly granted he let out a blood-curdling scream and became insane, never again to regain his mind. Simon had lost his ears, the cold (25 to 30 degrees below zero) had frozen part of his face, the flesh had loosened, and gangrene had eaten at it. During the 95 days of his martyrdom he had never been given a chance to wash or change his clothing.

For a while Papa could not continue, and I sat frightened and mute envisioning the horrible images. When he regained his composure, Papa went on: "I remember it was December 4, your birthday, *Dochinka*, when I read in the *North China Daily News* the terrible report on the Kaspe murder. Dr. Kaufman, the brave president of the Harbin Jewish Community, strongly denounced the atrocity in his funeral oration.[13] The result of this daring action was an immediate summons of Dr. Kaufman to the Japanese Military Mission where he was threatened with imprisonment and deportation for being an 'agent provocateur.' That same day Rodzaevsky wrote one of his disgusting articles in *Nash Put* demanding the arrest of Dr. Kaufman, whose father, so the author claimed, had been an agent of the Communist Third International.

---

[13]In addition to his widespread duties in the Jewish Community, Dr. Abraham Kaufman (see p. 53) was responsible for the Jewish Hospital in Harbin. He was known for treating needy patients free of charge and was venerated both by Jews and non-Jews in Harbin, and indeed throughout China.

"In spite of nonstop pressures, French Vice-Consul Chambon persisted in his efforts to bring justice, and eventually the White Russian Fascists who plotted Simon Kaspe's kidnapping—but not their Japanese supporters—were apprehended. The Japanese military authorities refused to hand them over to a Chinese court and the men were detained for 15 months in a jail of the Japanese criminal police. There they lived in comfort, eating first-class meals specially delivered by one of Harbin's best Russian restaurants and entertaining family and friends!

"In the meantime, Vice-Consul Chambon was declared 'persona non grata' by the Japanese and transferred to the Tientsin Consulate by the French government. Still, his daring actions had aroused the foreign press, and the entire foreign consular body in Harbin expressed outrage. Fearing international repercussions, the Japanese reluctantly brought the gangsters to a Chinese court. Heavy-handed threats failed to intimidate the courageous Chinese judge who passed sentence in June of that year: four White Russian Fascists were sentenced to death and two to life imprisonment. Harbin's relief at this denouement was short lived. Two days later the Japanese gendarmerie arrested the Chinese judge. Six months later three Japanese judges declared the sentence null and void and dismissed the case entirely. They claimed that the criminals had 'acted from patriotic motives' and released the kidnappers. *Nash Put* published a jubilant article stating that the kidnappers were 'honest and excellent citizens,' real Russian patriots who had acted not from motives of personal gain but purely for the purpose of obtaining funds for anticommunist organizations and to continue their fight against Bolshevism."

Papa took a sip of tea.

"I read and re-read that damn article so much," he said. "I think I remember it by heart! I had the clipping for a long time in my desk but now that the Japanese may decide to suddenly search my office, I thought it best to destroy it. Any reference to the Kaspe case is very dangerous. You know, two British papers that criticized the Japanese court action were confiscated immediately by the Japanese in Harbin at the time and their editors expelled from Manchukuo.

"One can imagine the despair of the Jewish Community as attacks on Jews in Harbin now officially got the green light. Little wonder many Harbin Jews began to flee to the safety of International Shanghai. When news of these dreadful developments reached us here in the Shanghai Jewish Community, Boris Topas, backed by the entire Ashkenazi congregation, initiated and organized a formal demonstration of protest which he personally led to the Japanese Consulate. He thus succeeded in bringing the attention of representatives of the Great Powers in our city to the atrocities in Harbin and his demands for a change in Japanese attitude and policy. He also circulated a written statement strongly protesting Japanese brutality."

So Papa was convinced the Japanese never forgave Topas and now took an opportunity for cruel revenge.[14]

Before we went to bed Papa consoled me:

"In spite of all the drivel the Japanese publish in the papers, the War is going very badly for them. All this horror will soon be over and you will still have time for a happy youth."

May 1944

My sister and I have completely different characters. She is restless, cannot sit still for long periods of time and likes constant action and movement, while I can spend hours studying and reading. Also, I enjoy food which my sister consumes reluctantly. When she was a small child I remember my mother constantly pursuing her and imploring, *"Kushai! Kushai!"* ("Eat! Eat!" in Russian). However, now that my sister is growing older, the five years difference in age seems to narrow and we often

---

[14]My father was correct. It was later discovered that one of the guards at Bridge House had participated in the Kaspe kidnapping. Mr. Topas was singled out for inhumanly cruel treatment by this sadist.

have a good time together. One thing both of us enjoy is dancing and riding around on our bicycles.

Of course, cycling these days is rather adventurous. Bumps, potholes, loose stones cause the rapid erosion of tires which—according to the Japanese authorities—will soon be completely unavailable when the present supply runs out. The officially recommended alternative: metal wheels![15] Many Shanghailanders walk longer and longer distances to try and preserve their bicycle tires.

Last week, disregarding the dark "tire prognosis," my sister and I decided to take advantage of a sunny day and ride around the former International Settlement. I say "former" because last August, according to Domei News Agency reports, Britain, the United States, and France "relinquished their Extraterritorial Rights leading to the retrocession of the Concessions." As we pedaled at a leisurely pace, we saw Japanese bolting street sign replacements to metal supports—a change of names meant to obliterate from our memories foreign heroes. Among the first signs to be removed were Ward Road, Gordon Road, and Hart Road, all situated fairly close to each other.

Well, I often wonder if those "immortalized" citizens of the colonial powers were in reality the heroes we have been taught to admire. I remember reading when I was about 10 a poem that so shocked me it remains engraved in my mind. The verse was printed under a pastel-shaded illustration of an ethereal child in a field of lavender and pink flowers. Entitled "Thoughts of an English Girl," it read:

> *Little Indian Sioux or Crow,*
> *Little frosty Eskimo,*
> *Little Turk or Japanee,*
> *Oh don't you wish that you were me?*

The smug arrogance of the words struck me as a direct insult to anyone non-British and I yelled at my aston-

---

[15]This proposal never materialized since the Japanese began to requisition metals of all sorts, nor did the supply of tires run out.

ished cousin, a pupil at the English Public School, and thus became a traitor, "I hate those stuck up English people!"

She replied in Russian a cool *"Sumashedshaya!"* ("Crazy!") and I held back from punching her.

Is it possible that anyone brought up like the little girl in the poem with such certainty of her superiority could ever write history as it happened? I doubt that the French or Americans were any better than the British in their overblown self-esteem.

A good example is the case of the man that gave Ward Road its name. Frederick Townsend Ward was a U.S. citizen born in Massachusets in 1831. He attended a military school in Vermont, served as a Texas Ranger, and fought in Mexico, in Central America, and in Crimea (in the latter case as an officer in the French Army!). He arrived in Shanghai in 1859 as first mate on a clipper ship, at a time when our city was bracing itself for an attack by fanatic Taiping rebels who had infiltrated its outskirts.[16]

Although the Shanghai history books have enshrined him as a hero, Ward seems to have been more a shrewd adventurer, a buccaneer who knew how to plot and intrigue among corrupt Chinese officials, greedy foreign merchants, and ambitious representatives of colonial powers.[17] He soon realized the value of the then-despised Asian mercenaries, incorporating them within his armed forces that declared war on "bandits," "rebels," and "insurgents," in China. His first "army" was composed of British deserters (mostly sailors who had abandoned ship), a handful of other Europeans, and

---

[16]The Taiping Rebellion (1849–1864) was a major revolutionary civil war in China. Influenced by Christian ideas of egalitarianism, the revolution was a attempt to overthrow the oppressive hierarchical system of the Manchu dynasty. Most foreigners in China opposed the Taipings because they feared the loss of commercial privileges granted in treaties with the Manchu dynasty. The foreign powers collaborated with the dynasty to crush the revolution.

[17]Richard Deacon, in his *A History of the Chinese Secret Service* (London: Frederic Muller, 1974), describes Ward as a "buccaneering American adventurer who stamped his personality on the Western incursions into China."

a couple hundred Filipinos. The latter—not surprisingly, in view of the standard of the Europeans who had joined Ward—proved to be the only reliable soldiers; the others spent most of their time guzzling beer and gin and generally causing havoc. Later, in spite of prevailing Western views that "two dozen Chinese are worth one European," Ward successfully trained and incorporated Chinese men within his troops.

At first the Americans, British, and French scorned Ward, but when in the winter he cleared all the Taiping rebels from a 30-mile radius around Shanghai, they began to lionize him. Ward had quickly developed a plan to safeguard the interests of Shanghai merchants threatened by growing disorder: the organization of a privately financed army under his own command! The weak Chinese government of the time appointed him brigadier general and admiral and later awarded his troops by imperial decree the title "Ever Victorious Army."

At first Ward's battles ended in fiascos, increasing the contempt in which Shanghai's foreigners held him. This too, he disregarded. Failure did not frighten him and he regrouped his forces again and again. Realizing that Chinese recruits could respond superbly to military training if they were decently treated, fed and dressed, Ward lured capable British drill masters from the Imperial Navy (promising money and adventure) to train his Chinese soldiers. The results were astonishingly successful. It was now Ward's turn to smile at the fulminations of the British naval commander, who had lost some of his best men!

Many Shanghailanders are not aware of the fact that in March 1862 Ward renounced his American citizenship and became a naturalized Chinese. He later married a Chinese woman. A complicated personality and certainly a man of courage, true, but not the Knight in White Armor local history would have us believe. He never stopped chasing rebels, wearing only simple civilian clothes, unarmed and carrying a riding crop in his hand. He was never known to show fear. When he died on September 21, 1862, hit in the stomach by an enemy bullet, he was only 30 years old. A romantic hero in my mind! My sister—a great animal lover—particularly enjoys the touching epilogue to his story: his dog, whom he loved dearly, died a few days after Ward was killed, supposedly of grief, and was buried near his master.

Ward's grave is at Sungkiang—25 miles southwest of Shanghai. A tablet on his tomb reads:

"An illustrious man from beyond the seas, he came 6,000 li [a li equals 2/5 of a mile] to accomplish great deeds and acquire an immortal fame by shedding his noble blood. Because of him Sungkiang shall be a happy land for a thousand autumns. This temple and statue shall bear witness to his generous spirit."[18]

Several days after Ward's death a Britisher, Charles George Gordon, arrived in Shanghai and eventually took over command of the Ever Victorious Army. Gordon a true Victorian, believed his sole mission was to protect his queen's interests. Like Ward, he enjoyed the support of the colonial powers and the Chinese imperial government for defending their interests through warfare against native rebels.

When in Shanghai, he stayed at the home of the British Consul, strictly avoiding any socializing. But he, too, slowly began changing his attitude towards "the natives," i.e., the Chinese. Eventually, he went even further than Ward since he came to believe that Chinese soldiers would function better when instructed and led by officers of their own race.

He was a strange introverted man, some say a *pédé*,[19] deeply devoted to his mother in England, with whom he corresponded constantly. What amazes me in particular is that this Christian fundamentalist became fascinated with Hasidism—a Jewish socio-religious movement—after meeting a Lithuanian Jewish trader in Shanghai. Gordon began to fancy himself as a *tzaddik*, a

---

[18]This sentiment is not shared by most Chinese today, who look upon Ward with contempt for supporting what they regard as foreign exploiters and a degenerate Chinese regime.

[19]The somewhat derogatory *pédé* (*pédéraste*) was the only term for homosexual that we French College students used at the time.

righteous man endowed with mysterious powers. He so pleased the Chinese government that it awarded him by special edict China's highest decoration, "The Order of the Yellow Jacket." From then on he became known as "Chinese Gordon."[20]

The third foreigner who played a crucial role in China's history and whose name the Japanese are taking off our streets was Robert Hart, inspector-general of the Imperial Customs Service. He was once the most powerful foreigner in China. Hart too was to appreciate more and more the Chinese people. Born in Ireland in 1835, Hart was inspired to go to China when, as an adolescent, he heard a talk given by a missionary who had returned home on leave from the Far East. After completing his studies at the University of Belfast, he managed to get a post in the British Consular Service in China. He started to devote all his free time to study of the Chinese language and finally was put in charge of the Chinese Maritime Customs based in Shanghai (its authority later extended to all the treaty ports).

By 1898, as a direct result of Hart's reforms and efficient administration, the customs services produced a third of the entire revenue of the Chinese government. It was widely claimed that if not for Hart, China would have been bankrupt!

The Maritime Customs were Hart's entire life. He only took two vacations during his long stay (till 1906)— once to attend his daughter's wedding in London and once to visit the 1878 Paris World Exhibition as president of the Chinese government's commission.

Believe it or not, even in those early days Hart worried about ever-growing Japanese ambitions. He said, "Japan wants to lead the East in war, commerce and manufactures, and the next century will be a hard one

---

[20]Gordon later left China to become the "fabulous hero of Sudan." He spent a year's furlough studying the history of the Bible and archeology in Jerusalem. He rented a house in Ein Kerem (a picturesque village outside Jerusalem believed to be the birthplace of John the Baptist), and was often seen riding a white donkey in the Judean Hills.

for the West." The Japanese must have unscrewed *his* road sign with glee!

As my sister and I reached Hart Road, air-raid sirens started to whine repeatedly and even before they fell silent bombs began exploding not too far away. We dismounted our bikes and dragged them to the threshold of a brick building. The raid lasted longer than usual and we pedaled home quickly to reassure our parents of our well-being. Although we were not near enough to the bombs to see actual destruction, speeding ambulances, fire engines and military vehicles attested to serious damage. This, of course, was denied by the newspapers the following day. They carried a short item about "Americans' unsuccessful attempt to destroy Shanghai." To stress U.S. inferiority the following few lines were printed on the same page:

U.S. GUNNERS SHOOT 20 OF THEIR OWN PLANES
American inefficiency is becoming clearer every day. Sergeant Fosie stated that U.S. gunners shot down 20 of their own planes. He explained that the incidence is due to inexperience.

No details were given as to who Sergeant Fosie was nor where the incident had occurred.

June 1944

The day started off badly. Last night's bitterness was hard to dispel. While we were away our landlady, The Monster, had unscrewed all our bulbs, and as we furiously fumbled for candles, she howled, "You use too much electricity, you bloody lumps of shit!" We had never heard such language, but it was useless to respond since no civil conversation is possible with this creature. To add to this aggravation, Mama caught her sneaking around our dining room searching for who knows what. Oh how sick we all are of this endless War!

The morning newspaper did nothing to lighten our spirits. Mumbling *"Chepuha! chepuha!"* ("Nonsense! nonsense!" in Russian) Papa read out aloud two reports which I later cut out to keep in my diary. The shorter one is incomprehensible to me:

ROOSEVELT IS UNDER STALIN'S THUMB
SAYS JEWISH BARRISTER

(Domei) The sensational statement that President Roosevelt is under the absolute control of Stalin and he is on the brink of Communism was made by a Jewish Barrister, when he acted as Defense Counsel in a mass trial of persons charged with inciting anti-Semitism, according to a Western report quoted by Transocean.

Mr. Klein further reported that the trial was only arranged to protect Communism in the United States.

Why should a Jewish lawyer defend anti-Semites? How does Communism come into the picture? Could this be German propaganda garbled by the Japanese? Whatever it is, its effect is worrying and unpleasant.

The purpose of the second report is clearer but no less disagreeable:

BRITISH OFFICER TEACHES
MURDER METHODS OF U.S. KILLERS

"Give me men with the cold-blooded ruthlessness of American gangsters." This is the way the Director of a British Military School summed the prime qualities he demanded of his pupils when interviewed by the London correspondent of the New York Herald Tribune, according to Transocean. At a lecture he was allowed to attend, the American correspondent heard the School Director, who holds the rank of Major, address his class as follows:

"This is a school for murder.   Murder is my specialty. What   we are concerned with is not the simple exchange of bullets between soldiers who do not know each other but rather cold-blooded murder. It is an art that calls for steady practice and perfection."

The major told the correspondent that judging by the observations he had made in the United States, he was convinced that American gangsters would make good military instructors. Elucidating his training method, the British instructor declared:

"My pupils are taught to shoot from under the table, behind washstands and up or down the staircase."

He then expressed regret at having no living targets available for shooting practice, for, he said: "It is essential to lose the dread of murder."

As we listened glumly, we (at least I) were pleasantly surprised by Sidney's unexpected visit, all the more so because he was in excellent spirits.

"The Americans are giving the Japanese a licking!" he cried joyfully. "Their B-29 'Superfortresses' are bombing Kyushu! Americans are landing in Saipan!"[21] Sidney also told us that the Japanese no longer feel safe in their cities and that thousands of youngsters are being evacuated to the countryside.[22] All restaurants in Japan have been shut down and female employees are forced to work in war production factories.

"Things are really bad for the Japanese," Sidney said.

"How do you know?" we asked.

"I have my sources," he replied.

Although Sidney would give no further clarification, he had once told me in great confidence that he had access to a short-wave radio—an offense severely punishable by the Japanese Occupying Forces. After a short stay which brought us, according to Mama, "a ray of sunshine," Sidney left. My parents also went on their way, and my sister and I decided to take a walk. It was hot but pleasant. Bees were buzzing around the flowering bushes (we actually live in a very good residential district) and there was an atmosphere of pleasant laziness in the air. My sister and I meandered around chatting about this and that, finally reverting to earlier times and the various governesses in our family. I personally— praise the Lord!—had never had a governess but some of my cousins and my sister did. In all cases, these governesses were single White Russian women who tried

---

[21]On June 15, 1944, U.S. troops landed on the island of Saipan, where there was a Japanese Army and Navy garrison of 32,000, as well as 10,000 civilians. As the battle became desperate, thousands (among them women with children strapped to their backs) leapt off cliffs into the sea, committing mass suicide. In the following days B-29s bombed northern Kyushu's industrial complex.

[22]Over 250,000 were evacuated from Tokyo alone.

to earn a living by educating children in the family of their employers (both academically and morally). Some remained for years ruling their young "subjects" (and their parents!) with a hand of steel.

My sister and I have never liked to submit to authority, so my sister's governesses lasted none too long in our home. There was one young, pretty and intelligent woman whom I liked but resented because I believed Papa paid her undue attention. In fact, when Mama, my sister, and I spent the summer in Japan, I must have worried a great deal subconsciously since I clearly remember having frightening dreams about my parents' impending divorce. I was much relieved when we returned to Shanghai to find that the governess was engaged to a good-looking young man with surprisingly pink cheeks. She soon disappeared from our lives forever.

Two sets of my rather numerous cousins, on the other hand, had governesses who remained forever and ever and dominated the entire household. One, Anna Stepanovna, was a woman with an ugly wrinkled face but an incredibly well-formed body which she kept in shape by watching her diet, drinking a glass of boiling hot water first thing every morning and standing up (never sitting!) after lunch, while my cousins, Essie and Abe, were forced to lie down and rest. Whenever I went to visit I had to follow the established routine, but the absolutely marvelous thing was that Anna Stepanovna told the most exciting stories, detail by detail, chapter by chapter. She was a fan of Edgar Wallace and I had never never heard such exciting, blood-curdling tales. One in particular called "The Door with the Seven Locks," made my flesh creep. I don't know whether it was in this story or another where Anna Stepanovna described a terrifying (and sensual) scene about the naked body of a woman under a sheet and a man aiming a dagger at her heart! Since, of course, I did not go every weekend to these particular cousins, I would hear bits and pieces of their governess' accounts never learning the outcome of all the deliciously frightening events.

Anna Stepanovna adored animals and when the pregnant family cat "Fluffy" died by falling off the balcony and dragging along a flower pot that killed her, the governess' grief was profound. Her love for all animals was so true and encompassing that I once found her crying when she had unwittingly drowned some ants in a bath! She really was a strange but remarkable woman. She spoke French to my cousins—I believe that was the main reason why she was hired—made the most wonderful clothes as well as masquerade costumes, and prepared certain treats like hot cocoa with "islands" of whipped egg-white floating on its surface (which I found revolting). Apart from animals, I believe she loved my cousin Abe most of all in the world. He was a naughty boy constantly getting into scrapes, and Anna Stepanovna would punish him by making him sit for long periods of time on a chair in the corner of the inside hall. Nevertheless, she adored him and I am sure he reciprocated her devotion. All in all, she was a woman of imagination and creativity but my sister and I were oh so happy she didn't live in our house.

The second governess, Varvara Nicolaevna, had been employed for many years by the family of my cousins who moved to the United States before the War started. She was an educated woman, a former teacher who specialized in Russian literature and for some time gave me private Russian lessons during which we read Turgenev's *Memoirs of a Sportsman*, a series of sketches on hunting that emphasized the human qualities of destitute peasants. According to Varvara Nicolaevna, Czar Alexander II always kept a copy of the book with him and Turgenev's work eventually influenced the emancipation the serfs. When my cousins' family left China, my mother tried to help their governess by employing her as a saleswoman in Peter Pan Shop—not a good idea since her approach to everything was critical and unfriendly. She had all her meals with us grumbling nonstop at my sister and me—our appearance, our behavior, our lack of discipline.

As we walked and talked my sister and I laughed at my sister's "revenge" on Varvara Nicolaevna. Once during *tiffin* [Shanghai term for "lunch," usually a big midday meal with several courses] my sister sat fiddling with a small monkey hand-puppet. Varvara Nicolaevna started complaining about her manners, in an irritating way I used to describe as "gobbling, gobbling like a turkey!" Finally, Mama intervened by ordering my sister to leave the table and stand in the corner—all this because of this "outsider" who had "no rights upon us." As we all sat silently, my sister made a sharp movement and her hand puppet sailed in a wide arc from her corner straight into Varvara Nicolaevna's soup. The governess fumed and spluttered but Mama had a hard time controlling her giggles. Till today, my sister and I love to talk about her moment of greatest glory!

July 1944

Papa worries very much about the nefarious influence of Nazis on the Japanese who—when it suits them—parrot the Nazis' racist ideas. Can't they realize that they themselves don't fit the Aryan pattern? This morning's paper reproduced "statistics" from an article published sometime ago:

"It is estimated that at least 75 percent of the revenues of most local commercial establishments go to the Jews . . . this is also true in the biggest cities in the world, London and New York . . . Berlin is the one exception now."[23]

The fact that the Japanese often link Roosevelt's name with Jews, referring to him as "the paid servant of Jewry," is doubtless a direct result of German propaganda. Such reports plunge our Jewish Community into a heavy cloud of foreboding as we read revolting anti-Semitic news items: "Surrounded by a group of rapa-

---

[23]John B. Powell, one of the best known American journalists in China, writes in his book *My Twenty Years in China* (New York: MacMillan, 1945): "The allegation that 75 percent of the income of local industries and business establishments went to Jews was untrue, as revenue statistics of the International Settlement showed that approximately four-fifths of the local taxes were paid by Chinese retail properties, industrial or large commercial interests."

cious financiers and money-sharks, resentful and vin-
dictive Jews, and other rogues, he (Roosevelt) sought re-
election for a third term by deliberate lying . . ." The
Japanese copied these words from a Nazi propaganda
booklet, *Two Men in a Boat* (the two men being
Roosevelt and Churchill).

When such articles appear, Papa explodes with rage,
throwing the paper away from him in a heap and shouting:

"Prokliatiye! prokliatiye!" ("Damned! damned!") or
"Damn-it-it-all! Damn-it-it-all!" (For some reason he
always adds the extra "it," and I never correct him).

His fury is frightening to behold but he soon calms
down, embarrassed at his lack of control, which he
somewhat awkwardly attempts to justify.

"You know," he said at breakfast today after one such
outburst, "the Japanese don't really hate the Jews. There
was never anti-Semitism in Japan or China before
Hitler. This *prokliati* (cursed) murderer, this crazy ma-
niac, spreads his poison throughout the world!"

According to Papa the first public anti-Jewish demonstration in Shanghai's history took place only three years
ago when more and more Nazis started pouring in. It
happened during the autumn races when Germans
threw out of their top-story Park Hotel suite anti-Semitic
leaflets written in English and Chinese.[24] The wind blew
them among the thousands watching the races, quite a
propaganda coup! With the usual German thor-
oughness they had succeeded in calculating exactly
where the leaflets would land.

We all fear that as the tide of War turns more and
more against the Japanese they will strike out in frustration at the helpless people they occupy—among which
are China's Jews. It is quite obvious, in spite of all propaganda attempts to hide the truth, that the situation in

---

[24]The Park Hotel: a 16-story building located across the street from
the race course. Powell writes in *My Twenty Years:* "The Nazi
organization which had charge of this phase of the anti-Jewish
'drive' occupied a suite in the Park Hotel Tower which it rented for
$2,500 a month."

Japan is deteriorating very seriously. Sidney brings news that Japan is close to starvation and people in cities are planting vegetables on every available empty plot. It appears that even rice has become very scarce—it is probably used to feed the military.

As a result of this new hardship, the Japanese are bringing to a crescendo their efforts at misinformation. Today, on the front page of the English language paper a report from Tokyo states:

> The American defilement of the remains of Japanese soldiers killed in action was revealed in two Domei dispatches from Zurich and was bitterly assailed by the *Yomiuri-Hochi Shimbun* in its editorial this morning. One of the dispatches reported that in the United States children were found playing with the skulls of Japanese soldiers killed in action, which American soldiers on the Pacific front had sent home as "souvenirs."[25]

Another dispatch said that a congressman had presented President Roosevelt with a letter-opener made from the forearm of a Japanese soldier who had been killed in fighting U.S. forces. The source of these acts of inhumanity, the journal pointed out

> Should be traced to the brutal nature rooted deep in the national character of the American people as well as to the superiority complex they maintain in their attitude toward East Asiatics.
>
> Similar cases of barbarism are not difficult to find in the pages of American history. The massacre of American Indians, the brutal conquest of the Philippines, the American lynching of Negroes and the maltreatment of the Chinese people are cited.
>
> In the present War, the American Forces have frequently attacked hospital ships while American soldiers on the Guadalcanal ran over wounded Japanese soldiers with their tanks and tractors. The American barbarism reached its zenith when the Americans came to regard the

---

[25]To my amazement, I later learned that this actually did happen. One can only conclude that under wartime conditions nothing is held sacred.

remains of Japanese soldiers as "souvenirs." Such cases of inevitable barbarism on the part of the American army may be almost incomprehensible to the Japanese people who cherish the spirit of Bushido or chivalry, but they reveal the true character of our enemy who talks like a gentleman but acts like a beast.

I wonder who authored this!

On another page of today's paper a photograph was printed with the caption:

The above photo reproduced from *Life Magazine* shows an American girl pictured with the skull of a slain Japanese soldier which an American soldier had sent her as a "souvenir." She is about to write a reply of thanks for the unusual gift from the front.[26]

August 1944

Last week I received a letter from Heinz, who lives in the Restricted Area (ghetto) in Honkew. I had met Heinz at a friend's party when European Jewish refugees still moved freely in Shanghai. He is a quiet, pleasant, nice-looking boy, unfortunately the only member of his family to escape the Nazis. At the time he was only 15 years old.

Heinz begged me to come and visit him since he was refused a permit to leave the area in which European Jewish refugees are confined, whereas outsiders like me are free to go in and out. I did want to see Heinz very much indeed but dreaded the demeaning experience of bowing low to Japanese sentries on Garden Bridge and, possibly, being roughed up by them. I pleaded with Mama to accompany me and after some resistance she agreed because she too is very fond of Heinz and very sorry for all the misery he has to endure. In fact, last winter she worried so much about his freezing in an

---

[26]*Life* indeed published in 1944 (as I discovered to my great shock after the War) the photograph of "A Phoenix, Arizona, War Worker" writing a "Thank you, I think" letter to her Navy boy friend for sending her the skull of a Japanese that was shown lying on her desk.

unheated room that she ferreted out an almost new leather fur-lined coat for him, which he wore during the day and used as a cover at night. He is a fine looking boy with smooth clear skin and regular features and he does look very manly in his brown coat.

Mama and I set off to Honkew carrying a paper bag full of groceries, among which was a jar of sesame-seed butter, of which Heinz is particularly fond and which many people use instead of real butter (difficult to get even in the black market).

We crossed the Garden Bridge by tram without undue incidents. The tram halted in front of the Japanese guards, all the passengers bowed and the bayonet-clasping soldiers waved us on with their free hand. Mama and I looked at each other with deep relief.

When we arrived in Hongkew, we saw that barbed wire barricades had been erected around the Restricted Area with several control points left open for entry and exit. These gates are policed by armed Japanese guards and the auxiliary force, the Pao Chia. In Honkew the responsibility of the Pao Chia is to enforce strict curfew regulations, check passes, and keep order. It is headed by a German-Jewish "director" who has some 3,500 refugees under his command but, of course, the real power is in the hands of the Japanese, who hold a very tight rein over the entire auxiliary force.

Heinz waited for us some 20 yards away from the gate. He was very excited to see us and is very attached to my mother, who always treats him with great kindness. How he must suffer to be here in such awful circumstances with no family at all. However, he never complains and always acts pleasant, smiling rather shyly. Poor, poor boy!

Heinz explained to us that within the ghetto itself people are more or less left to their own devices but serious problems arise when applications are submitted for exit permits. Although Papa had somehow managed to send Heinz the "Certificate of Employment" required by the Japanese, the response to Heinz's attempts to leave the ghetto to work outside was a resounding and humiliating slap on the face.

"I will not try again," Heinz told us. "I really cannot go through this once more!"

Mama and I sympathized with his attitude.

The refugees are segregated in 40 square blocks of crumbling buildings (some four blocks wide and 12 blocks deep). The streets—or rather narrow lanes—are strewn with rubble and refuse. Most houses have no toilets nor kitchens for families who live crowded together in single rooms. Tenants are forced to use outside toilets, buy drinking water from street vendors, go to the few public baths, and cook in the lanes or on flat roofs using Japanese "hibachi" stoves. Needless to say there is no heating in winter. In view of all this, Mama and I were not surprised that Heinz did not invite us to visit his room, which he described as "tiny, stifling in summer and freezing in winter, with missing windowpanes and a warped door that never closes." There are two canvas camp beds side by side, one for Heinz and one for an ailing old man. Fortunately, they do have a toilet in the hall (for 12 lodgers) as well as a sink with running cold water—a luxury! Both Heinz and his room-mate receive one free meal a day distributed by the Jewish "Kitchen Fund."[27] Only children are given an additional evening supper. With so many horrible diseases in Shanghai, Mama worries what will happen to the refugees who are undernourished and not resistant to illness.[28]

Still, in spite of all the tensions and insufficient resources, the refugees did succeed in organizing a functioning community—the *Gemeinde.* Committees regulate the distribution of dry foods, clothing, medical supplies (bought at black market prices from Japanese and Chinese sources). Many miniature lending libraries have been set up where books in German, Yiddish, Polish, and English are available. Three daily German

---

[27]The meal consisted of 1350 calories. The Kitchen-Fund Committee was established in August 1942.

[28]Unfortunately, Mama's worries were well grounded. Between 1939 and 1945, over 13% of the refugee community died. Few died of starvation, but many did succumb to epidemics as a result of their weak physical condition.

newspapers are published, as well one in Polish and Yiddish, on paper whose quality varies from poor to deplorable, according to what is available. An enthusiastic theater company has been formed, as well as an operetta group which plans to initiate the coming season with *The Gypsy Baron*. There is an outstanding symphony orchestra that always performs to a full house.[29] Hospitals have been set up in ramshackle buildings and refugee doctors have founded the Association of European Doctors. Every effort is being made to provide children with adequate education: English is the medium of instruction while Hebrew is taught in special classes. There is even an ORT School with pupils aged 14 to 60 who attend free-of-charge six-month courses in carpentry, electricity, and mechanics. Most of the tools they use are manufactured by the students themselves and some of their products are sold to raise funds for the school.[30] In the fall of 1943, a Berliner named W. Y. Tonn founded the "Volkshochschule," the refugee university. He is a friend of my parents, who admire him very much.

The *Jüdische Gemeinde* (Jewish Community) is a democratically-elected religious and cultural body presided over by the much-respected Leopold Steinhard. It helps govern the life of the refugees and has an arbitration board staffed by outstanding lawyers—Jews in the Diaspora have always preferred to solve their disputes themselves and not refer to the authorities. To avoid the appearance of Jewish beggars—a distressful and

---

[29]The three German language dailies were *Das Tageblatt, Die Gelbe Post,* and the *Shanghai Jewish Chronicle*. The latter, in spite of its English name, was in German. The theater company produced 60 plays in a three-year period, some of the "plays" actually being skits. The symphony's violinist, Alfred Wittenberg, soon gained the reputation of being "the best musician in China." He came to love the Chinese people and after the War refused lucrative offers abroad. He remained in Shanghai, where he died in 1953.

[30]ORT are the initials of the Russian *Obshchestvo Remeslov Truda,* or, in English, "Society for the Encouragement of Handicrafts," founded by Jews in Russia in 1880 to develop trade and agricultural skills among their youth.

shameful sight—the *Gemeinde* now issues special tickets (dubbed "beggar tickets") of various denominations to be used for the purchase of essential items, such as food and clothing, in specified stores. How can I help but be proud that I am Jewish?

Heinz led us through the "Honkew Street Bazaar" where embroidered tablecloths, wedding rings, cutlery, fine porcelain, clothing, and even gold teeth are bartered for sardines, medication, candles, and razor blades. Many of the hawkers are former academics and we heard one addressed as "Herr Professor Doktor Kohn." Without regard to their former professions and social status, architects, engineers, and teachers now accept any job available be it peddling, cleaning, dishwashing, or watchman duty.

In spite of the squalor, Honkew reflects in my eyes a *je-ne-sais-quoi* of Old World charm. There are distinctive (but tiny!) millinery shops, boutiques exclusively for blouses and skirts, a "Viennese Tailor for the Man of Taste," and a "Royal Glover" haberdashery whose sign is written in English, German, Chinese, and Japanese.

My mother invited Heinz and me for tea in a "good place" Heinz had heard of but never frequented. The three of us climbed up a narrow winding staircase to the flat roof-top of a house where several small round tables had been placed surrounded by folding chairs. Two potted plants stood in the corner, and squeezed between them a serious elderly man played romantic tunes on his violin. As we drank tea and ate a surprisingly tasty "Kuchen," Heinz spoke for the first time about his traumatic journey to Shanghai as a teenager. After the horrible ordeal of Kristallnacht (November 9–10, 1938), when the Nazis attacked Jews in a frenzy of hatred, Heinz's father was arrested together with thousands of Jews and sent to an unknown destination.[31] His mother refused to leave Germany without his father but forced her only son to escape the horrors of Nazism. Heinz never found out how she managed, but one month later

---

[31]At that time none of us knew (though many suspected) Hitler's plans for the "Final Solution" of the "Jewish Problem."

he was put on a train, rode to an Italian port, and boarded a Lloyd Triestino Line ship which reached Shanghai about six weeks later—six weeks of constant seasickness, uncertainty and sorrow at leaving his family. Nevertheless, Heinz hastened to add:

"I was one of the lucky ones. Once Italy entered the War their ports were sealed off to Jewish refugees. People had to take the very difficult overland route all the way across the U.S.S.R., going through Siberia to North China where they were packed like sardines into Chinese fishing boats and transported to Shanghai." Heinz smiled reassuringly. "Yes, I was fortunate and I am so happy to have friends like your family. . . . Of course later, when Germany attacked the Soviet Union this final road to freedom was also closed."

We sat for an hour, talked about many things, laughing and joking, and Mama and I left very regretfully since Heinz, in spite of his forced cheerfulness, looked very forlorn. Unfortunately, we could not remain any longer because returning in the dark would have been most unpleasant, if not dangerous.[32]

September 1944

Just three years ago, Shanghai's most popular radio broadcaster, the American Carroll Alcott, left our city perhaps forever. His departure marked the end of freedom of speech, courage, and humor on the air. Today, we are forced to listen to renegades like Herbert Moy, a Chinese born and educated in New York, or his assistant Robert Fockler (likewise a U.S. citizen who had come to Shanghai as the leader of a jazz band). Traitors! During his farewell broadcast, Alcott had assured Shanghailanders that he would return after a short vacation, but Pearl Harbor disrupted his plans.[33]

---

[32]Heinz survived the War but, to our great sorrow, committed suicide when he found out his entire family had been exterminated in Germany. He was 22 years old.

[33]Alcott writes in *My War with Japan* (New York: Henry Holt, 1943): "My purpose in returning to the United States was to sell Washington the idea of backing a powerful radio station somewhere

My girlfriends and I—and probably many other women in Shanghai—had had a real crush on Carroll Alcott, or rather on his voice, since we had never seen him. When he joked, his wit appeared to be directed intimately to each individual listener, creating an almost physical rapport, unlike other radio announcers who sounded distant and impersonal, almost unhuman. In our imagination, Alcott was a swashbuckling movie star, perhaps a replica of Errol Flynn or Tyrone Power, and we refused to believe he was in reality a fattish middle-aged man! We miss him so!

Alcott, a young U.S. journalist, arrived in Shanghai in 1928 for what he planned would be a brief stay. He remained 13 years. At first, he worked as a police and court reporter for the American-owned *Shanghai Evening Post & Mercury* and later for the *China Press*, which he helped found. In 1938, Alcott joined Shanghai's American radio station, XMHA, preparing, announcing, and commenting on news three or four times a day, seven days a week. Quite a feat! The Japanese officials, who had angrily read his newspaper articles attacking Japan's growing encroachment on China's territories, tried to frighten him into silence.[34] Three days before he was scheduled to go on the air for the first time, Japanese agents attempted to blow up XMHA. They succeeded in severely damaging the front office, but the studio and transmitter remained unharmed and the station started operating on both long and short-wave bands. The next tactic of the Japanese was to approach Alcott and suggest, not too subtly, that he say "something nice" about them. Little did they foresee his response.

In July 1938 Shanghailanders listened during a heavy heat wave to Alcott's first broadcast. They soon forgot all physical discomfort as Alcott's mellow voice told them in pleasant tones about the Japanese wish that he be "nice." He would gladly accede to their request, he in-

in the Orient, possibly in Manila, in order to counteract Japanese propaganda against us."

[34] After the 1937 Sino-Japanese hostilities Japan occupied a 10,000 square mile area around Shanghai.

formed his audience, provided Japanese actions warranted it. Alcott then proceeded in a friendly manner to offer the Japanese some ideas of what they could do. For a start, they could close the gambling dens that now proliferated in the areas they occupied in Shanghai, and they could stop forcing Chinese farmers to accept bogus money—the so-called military yen—which they themselves refused in payment for goods or services. After this first broadcast, or rather bombshell, the number of Alcott's listeners quickly grew to 500,000 English-speaking people (both Chinese and foreign). They began to tune in regularly to his broadcasts, laughed at his jokes and repeated his witticisms. Some, like me, took to keeping paper and pencil at hand when listening to Alcott so as to jot down his daring words verbatim.

Carroll Alcott always referred to Japan's "New Order" as "New Odor." He called for urgent international economic sanctions on Japan in punishment for that country's transgressions and drew attention to Japan's efforts to "hoodwink" the rest of the world. As the Japanese intensified their terror tactics against him, Alcott announced that he had bought a car with bulletproof windows. He hired a Danish bodyguard, Jan Egeberg, who later left Shanghai to join the Allied Air Force and was replaced by two burly White Russians. Alcott also made public the fact that he had taken to wearing a bulletproof vest and carried a pistol. Threats would not silence him, XMHA fully supported his courageous stand, and Shanghailanders held their breath in fear of his assassination. Loyal advertisers remained true to him: Maxwell House Coffee, Jello, Ovaltine, and the U.S.-owned Bakerite Bread Company.

Neither did Alcott spare German Nazis and Italian Fascists, whom he mocked in his broadcasts. As British troops overcame the Italians in Eritrea and Somaliland and expelled them from Ethiopia, restoring Emperor Haile Selassie to power (May 1941), Alcott described the fleeing Italians by claiming that only "their mules stubbornly resisted." He solemnly "quoted" Marco Polo's book claiming that according to the medieval traveler Jewish merchants in Mosul (Iraq) were called

"Mosullini" and that the name "Mussolini" was no doubt a corruption of this word. He then suggested that Il Duce visit his ancestors' grave by hiring a camel in Baghdad and riding across the desert. The Italian Fascists fumed and threatened to use their favorite weapon against him—a huge dose of castor-oil![35]

Since Alcott would not succumb to fear-inspiring tactics, the Japanese decided to drown his voice by jamming his broadcasts not only in Shanghai but in other important Chinese ports as well.[36] Angry letters of protest began to flood XMHA. My good friend Fira, who was attending the American School at the time, told me that the entire school body had signed a petition which they presented to the Japanese ambassador. To no avail. Carroll Alcott responded by opening his evening program with the words:

"This broadcast is brought to you by courtesy of the Bakerite Company, Shanghai's leading bakers and makers of better bread. The jam tonight is by courtesy of Mr. Suzuki."

At the time I had no idea who Mr. Suzuki was and thought it was merely a Japanese name Alcott had invented, but Papa later told me that a Mr. Suzuki did indeed exist: he was a member of Japanese Security who ceaselessly hounded Alcott.

Actually, Japanese efforts to jam Alcott's broadcasts in Shanghai proper did not always succeed as they did in outlying ports. The reasons were technical: while Alcott was effectively silenced in the Astor House Hotel area which the Japanese had occupied, we in the French Concession could always hear him clearly since the Japanese did not have equipment capable of creating interference in our part of the city. Because the jamming was not a total success, the Japanese finally compro-

---

[35]One Fascist method of torture was to force prisoners to take a huge dose of castor-oil, which induced very painful diarrhea. We later found out that in March 1941, at a secret meeting, the Italian Fascists voted to assassinate Alcott. An attempt on his life on March 17 failed.

[36]The jamming of coastal cities was later traced to Japanese warships anchored outside these ports.

mised and stopped jamming after diplomatic pressure
from the American and British ambassadors. Alcott on
his part agreed to stop referring to Suzuki by name. This,
of course, was only a temporary respite, and six months
before Pearl Harbor the *Central China Daily News* (organ
of Japan's puppet Wang Ching-Wei) published a "Black
List" of local newspapermen scheduled for
"deportation": seven foreigners and 80 Chinese. Among
them was Carroll Alcott. During his last broadcast, he
made clear his intention to return soon.

The ship that carried Carroll Alcott to the United
States was one of the last U.S. vessels to sail from
Shanghai. Elroy Healy, an American who succeeded
Alcott on the radio, disappeared soon after. No one
knows where he is but there is no doubt whatsoever
that he is in Japanese hands. Alas![37]

Today, the situation is grim. All we hear on the radio
is vituperative pro-Axis propaganda. The Pacific War
has been dragging on for more than three long, long
years. In spite of the radio announcing daily Japanese

------

[37]Ralph Shaw writes in *China Nights* (New York: Pinnacle Books,
1974): "The Japanese, angry that Alcott had eluded them, tortured
Healy. He went insane and died bloodied and crippled in his rat-
hole of a cell in Bridge-House." Among the foreigners on the
blacklist were Carroll Alcott, XMHA; Norwood Allan, prominent
attorney belonging to a firm that controlled the *Shunpao*, a Chinese
anti-Japanese daily that the Japanese had bombed several times;
Randall Gould, editor of the *Shanghai Evening Post & Mercury* and
China correspondent of the *Christian Science Monitor*; C. V. Starr,
owner of the *Shanghai Evening Post & Mercury*; J. B. Powell, editor of
the *China Weekly Review*, at whom a hand grenade was flung by a
would-be assassin (luckily, he forgot to remove its pin). On December
20, 1941, Powell was thrown by the Japanese into the notorious
Bridge House, tortured, and finally repatriated in shocking condition
to the United States (his weight had dropped from 145 to 70
pounds). He died as a result of his ill treatment. The Japanese at
first refused to release him, probably unwilling to allow the world
to learn of the torture he had undergone. However, the U.S.
government firmly refused to permit a prisoner exchange unless
Powell was included. Also blacklisted was Hal P. Mills, publisher
of *Hwan min wan pao*, an anti-Japanese daily. The only British
person on the list was J. A. E. Sanders-Bates, manager of the
University Press, which published several Chinese papers.

victories, this is an obvious lie. In fact, the Filipino lady living downstairs ran up excitedly to our rooms last night saying she has heard that a battle is raging in her country and that U.S. troops are fighting to liberate the Philippines. In celebration of this good news she brought us a dish of delicious noodles she calls "pansit." Yumee!

October 1944

Heavy air-raid last night. Today the sirens are shrieking off and on. False alarms. The authorities must be nervous. Mama had a bad night and looks tired and upset. She insisted we all stay at home:

"I don't want to go crazy worrying where you all are!"

To pacify her we agreed without too much protest. Papa sat at his desk preparing an agenda for this afternoon's *Nasha Jizn* meeting, Mama sorted out a pile of material samples she had discovered on one of her foraging trips downtown, my sister read a book while I half-heartedly leafed through my histology text mumbling that I was "wasting" the day.

Towards noon Jesus, my new Spanish boy-friend, phoned to find out if I was at home and asked if he could drop in. I welcomed his visit eagerly. Jesus has dark glossy hair, hazel eyes with sweeping lashes, and a lithe graceful body. He speaks broken English and we spend our time together dancing the tango to records or going for walks hand-in-hand, both activities Mama frowns upon. Although she seldom complains about my rather diverse choice of boyfriends, she did say when I mentioned Jesus, "Couldn't you choose someone with a different name!" Nevertheless, she is always kind to him.

When Jesus arrived we sat in the dining-room listening to "La Cumparasita," "Ojos verdes," and "Jealousy." I remembered how at the French college everyone snickered as soon as the strains of "Jealousy" were heard. Our school version of this tango started with the words

Je t'ai vue
seduisante et presque nue
(I saw you
seductive and almost naked)

and continued with more and more erotic—if not outright obscene—rhymes.

Since no further air-raid sirens sounded, Papa went to
his meeting, Mama—actually the most impatient one of
us all—rushed to her store, and my sister rode her bicycle to a friend's house. The weather being balmy, Jesus
and I set off for a stroll. As we passed Japanese-occupied
buildings protected by barbed wire and armed guards,
Jesus muttered angrily, "Fortaleza! Fortaleza!" Jesus is
an anti-Fascist Basque and cannot return to Spain for political reasons. He and his crew-mates as well as his captain, Antonio, abandoned their ship when it anchored
in Shanghai two years ago. I don't really know how they
survive here since there is no work to be had. Antonio,
in particular, looks very thin and haggard, making me
worry whether he gets sufficient food, but I dare not ask
for fear of offending his Basque pride. Jesus' heroine is
Dolores Ibarruri, "La Pasionaria," who defied Franco's
forces with her rallying cry, *"No pasarán!"* ("They will
not pass!").[38] To Jesus' great happiness, he too, like
Ibarruri, was born in the Basque village of Gallarta. I
understand from him that life there was—and probably
still is—very hard. But Jesus' deep love for his birthplace
is something to behold: his eyes flicker with patriotic
zeal at the very mention of its name.

When I returned home for dinner found today's
newspaper on the sofa where Papa had left it. Papa enjoys a "fresh, uncrumpled" paper and it always infuri-
ates him when someone reads it before him without
putting back the pages in correct order.

A front-page item stated:

---

[38]She died in Madrid at the age of 93, some 45 years after the War
ended.

The Shikishima Unit of the Kamikaze Special Attack Corps, at 1045 hours on 25 October 1944, succeeded in a surprise attack against the enemy task force including 4 aircraft carriers . . .

The Kamikaze Special Attack Corps? What is that? Fortunately, on page 3 an article headlined "Kamikaze—Divine Wind" supplied further information. The writer referred to 13th century battles in Japan between the Samurai and the Mongol forces of Kublai Khan when at a critical juncture Japan's prayers were answered by powerful typhoons that dispersed the would-be invaders. Hence the term "Kamikaze"—"Divine Wind." Today, the article seems to indicate that this term applies to Japanese military suicide missions. We had heard previously of such sacrifices by fanatic Japanese but this is the first time that a unit appears to have been formally organized for this specific purpose.[39]

I remember that long before Pearl Harbor, when Japan was secretly preparing for large-scale warfare, my Japanese friend Yorifumi, had tried to explain to me the Samurai Code of Honor (*Hagakure*). Its main precept was:

"A Samurai lives in such a way that he will always be prepared to die."

According to Yorifumi, the study of the *hagakure* textbook at school was compulsory. I believe, however, that Kamikaze go well beyond the Samurai Code. Although the Japanese were taught to sacrifice themselves for their country, suicide had never been an official policy. How terrifying!

November 1944

It is my younger cousin Isa's birthday and we all went to her home for a jolly—and noisy—celebration. Her father, Papa's twin, Uncle Gava, was in top form telling joke after joke in his inimitable manner. Some were slightly off color and his wife—my aunt Rosetta—kept

---

[39]The "father" of kamikaze was Vice-Admiral Tokijiro Onishi. After Japan's surrender he committed ritual suicide by disembowelment (*hara-kiri*).

reminding him, *"Deti! Deti!"* ("The children! The children!") Rosetta is a very attractive woman with creamy ivory skin and graceful legs. She is over 10 years younger than her husband, who dotes on her. Her mother—Sofia Lianovna—was widowed in her early 20s and since then all her life centered on her only daughter. Isa also adores Rosetta. Nice to be surrounded by such devoted admiration!

As usual, and in spite of current shortages, Sofia Lianovna managed to prepare a wide assortment of *zakuski* (hors d'oeuvres): stuffed mushrooms, eggplant "caviar," pickled herring, deviled eggs, pickled cucumbers and green tomatoes, potato "vinaigrette" salad. My sister and I—who both hate onions, to the annoyance of all the grown-ups in our family—inspected everything carefully before eating in order to detect the possible presence of the despised vegetable. We never trusted everyone's angry reassurance of *"Netu! Netu!"* ("There isn't any!") When the table was cleared of zakuski, came the best part: a variety of cakes—chocolate, cream, nut, banana. How on earth did they manage to get all these goodies!

After tea Isa took my sister and some younger girls to her bedroom to look once more at all the presents and to listen to records, while I remained in the dining room with the grownups. Rosetta and Sofia Lianovna talked about their escape from the "Bolsheviki," their terrifying Odyssey from Moscow to Shanghai. At the time, 1925, Rosetta was hardly 15 years old, a delicate and—I imagine very pretty—girl. They crossed Lake Baikal and reached Chita where they waited three months to make arrangements to secretly cross the Amur River from a Russian border village into China. When the awaited moment finally arrived they had to struggle through muddy paths on the Russian side—a seven mile walk—led by a handsome youth who had his arm around Rosetta pretending to be her fiancé in case they were apprehended. Romantic! On the bank of the Amur another man impatiently awaited them with several other fleeing Jews. They got quickly into a small boat and rowed away as swiftly as possible but a distance away from the shore were detected by a group of Russian soldiers who started shooting in their direction. In spite of this terrifying incident they managed to reach China unscathed and Chinese villagers generously offered them some food. After a short stay, they sailed for 13 days down the Sungari River until they finally reached Harbin. Most of their little money had been used for paying out bribes.

Back to history! Harbin in 1925 was one of 48 Treaty Ports—their number had grown quickly from the original five in 1842. The city was an important railway center located in the southern part of the Chinese Eastern Railroad that continued into Russia to join a trunk line of the Trans-Siberian Railroad. Its main industry was milling flour from North Manchurian wheat. A number of Jews had prospered in the grain business and helped their co-religionists, who usually arrived penniless after fleeing the Bolsheviks. Nevertheless, Sofia Lianovna felt uneasy in Harbin. Just a year previously, in 1924, the U.S.S.R. had signed an agreement with China for joint control and operation of the Eastern Chinese Railroad, but the Chinese angrily alleged that the Russians were not keeping up their end of the bargain. In truth, the Bolsheviks were surreptitiously sending a large number of agents to Harbin in the guise of railway experts and these people carried on an active pro-Communist campaign. Since their undesired presence was clearly felt in the Russian immigrant community, Sofia Lianovna decided to leave with her daughter for the relative safety of Shanghai's International Settlement. Another long and exhaustive trip was undertaken: by train to Mukden, from there to Dairen, and then in the hold of a ship across the Yellow Sea to Shanghai. It was summer, very hot and muggy. Mother and daughter felt miserable.

In Shanghai, Sofia Lianovna rented a room in a crowded house and cooked meals in the communal kitchen. To keep her head above water she found a housekeeper's job in a boarding house and, in addition, worked as a manicurist after hours. In the meantime, the physical suffering caused by the harrowing escape

from Russia and the constant fear and worry had taken
their toll on Rosetta's health. Thin and listless, she spent
all day in their room waiting for her mother to return.
In the evening, no matter how exhausted she was, Sofia
Lianovna would take her *donichka* (little daughter) by
rickshaw to the Public Garden to breathe some "fresh
river air." Although the Whangpoo River often smelled
very bad, Rosetta said she did enjoy the breeze and the
strolls in the beautifully landscaped park.

Towards the end of the 1920s most Russian Jews
started moving to "Frenchtown" (the French
Concession) which adjoined the International
Settlement to the south. Since most of them hardly
spoke English, they felt at home there. White Russian
immigrants had already settled in this part of Shanghai
and opened shops and restaurants. There were sign-
boards in Russian, the Russian language could be heard
everywhere, and people jokingly called the main thoroughfare "Moscow Boulevard" instead of its official
name, Avenue Joffre. Before reaching her 17th birthday,
Rosetta met and married Uncle Gava, a penniless architect, and moved with him and her mother to
Frenchtown.

The conversation then turned to one of Shanghai's
most discussed topics: the galloping inflation, the worth-
lessness of today's currency. Mama remembered how,
long before Shanghai's pompous marble and granite
banking houses were built, small exchange shops han-
dled our city's financial operations. Situated in dingy
premises in narrow lanes, they carried out important
money transactions, and their Chinese owners were
known throughout China for their strict honesty and
efficiency. At the time, the money changers had to deal
with a confusing variety of currencies and Chinese
coins, among which were the *tael* (weighing about one
ounce of silver); the Mexican dollar, which was eventually replaced by the *yuan* with the same silver content,
and cash—small brass disks with a hole in the middle
which the Chinese carried strung together with a cord,
coppers whose value diminished through the years
from 100 to the dollar, to 200, and finally to 300 just be-

fore the War. Foreigners, as well as many well-to-do Chinese, did not like to be burdened with all these heavy coins, so the "chit" system evolved. The chit was actually an I.O.U. that one signed for restaurant meals, drinks in bars, cigars, taxis, goods of any type. The only possible exception was the rickshaw coolie who had to be paid in coins. At the end of the month it was the job of a Chinese employee—the "shroff"—to collect money for the signed chits. He also checked the coins to determine if they were genuine by rubbing them between his fingers and listening to the ringing sound they made when he hit them together. He did this so rapidly that onlookers could hardly follow his movements. Mistakes never seemed to occur! In one case the alertness of a shroff led to the discovery of thousands of "three piec-ee dolla": some of the silver on the inside of the dollars had been removed and replaced by an equal weight of brass. A suspicious shroff had held one of these coins in pincers over an open fire whereupon the soldering that joined the front and back melted and the two sections of silver coating fell apart revealing the brass center. All this goes to show the ridiculously low cost of Chinese labor that made such a complicated and time-consuming falsification worthwhile!

After listening for awhile to the grownups I joined the younger girls and had a wonderful time laughing, talking, and generally acting silly.

December 1944

On the fourth anniversary of Pearl Harbor an English language newspaper published an article stating:

> Quoting evidence by army officers and hotel employees, it was learnt that Colonel Theodore Wyman spent the night of Pearl Harbor attack in a wild drinking party, that he rushed to his office in civilian clothes in a drunken condition and that he changed from his civilian clothes to uniform in the presence of hotel employees, men and women, shouting orders to everyone . . .

How does one interpret the truth from propaganda, from deliberate lies? We now hear only one version on the radio—that of the Axis powers: Domei for Japan, Transocean for Nazi Germany, Stefani for Fascist Italy, Havas for the Vichy regime.

The U.S. Air Force is intensifying raids over Shanghai, sending B-29s that disappear quickly, leaving long white trails high in the heavens. The Japanese call these planes "B-ni-ju-ku" (a literal translation of the letter and number). It is rumored that they are also attacking Japan and causing great damage.

Local papers publish frequent instructions regarding air-raids. Today there is yet another "NOTICE OF IMMEDIATE IMPORTANCE." Its mention of the curfew reminded me how before this war, many restaurants, night clubs, and even stores were open all night.

AIR-RAID SIGNALS
1. Sirens:
Precautionary period: one 2-minute blast.
Air-raid: 7 five second blasts.
All clear: 2 fifteen second blasts.

2. Flags and lamps:
Precautionary period: 2 green flags or 2 green lamps.
Air-raid: 2 red flags or 2 red lamps.
All clear: 2 yellow flags or 2 yellow lamps.

NEW LIGHT REGULATIONS
All shops must be closed by 7.00 p.m. For cinemas, cafes, hotels, night clubs, the closing time is 10.00 p.m. Should they violate the regulations, businesses will receive a warning, a second offense is to result in the cutting of power supply and a fine, a third will be punished by a 10-day business suspension and a fourth by withdrawal of business license.

After every air-raid the Japanese claim success, often using the same wording:

"Sirens sound here as U.S. planes scout around and scurry off, having sustained severe damage in frontal clashes with the Japanese Air Force" . . . or "Enemy machines beat a hasty retreat upon being detected by Japanese planes . . ."

This morning, just as I was about to leave for the university, the sirens sceamed: 1 long blast followed by 9 short ones (2 more than the prescribed 7!). A heavy raid. The entire house shook as bombs whined, catapulting downwards and exploding with fearsome bangs when they hit their targets. Nobody was at home, so—before Mama could call and stop me from leaving the house—I grabbed my bike after the all-clear and raced to Aurora University. Some 10 minutes into the lecture when Père Hernault was leisurely checking his "bone box" in search of a clavicle, the sirens went off again, and again, and again! Pandemonium broke out. Students rushed to the windows staring at the sky and cheering each loud boom, while Père Hernault gazed around with benign bewilderment. He really is a kindly old man. Loud applause clearly indicated the students' hatred for the Japanese Occupation and hope for Allied victory. For the moment, the excesses of white colonialism were forgotten, overshadowed by the horrors of the New Order.

The B-29s pierced the sky like silver darts way out of reach of Japanese anti-aircraft fire and fighter planes. Japanese shells exploded in the air metamorphosing into umbrella-like shapes which we—in our hopeful eagerness—mistook for a U.S. parachute invasion. Previous air-raids had been depressing but this time, since rumors of Allied victories circulate ceaselessly, we are all optimistic and elated by the presence of U.S. boys somewhere miles above us![40]

As the raid continued, all classes were dismissed. During a lull I decided to walk home with Lee, a Chinese student, crossing the French Park. Both our bicycles—as alas so often happens—were at the repair shop. We strode quickly past Japanese soldiers who

---

[40]A plane called *Raiden* (Thunderbolt) was specially designed by the Japanese to fight the B-29s but production was painfully slow. Japanese fighter planes were unable to reach U.S. aircraft flying at 30,000 feet in the few minutes between the time the alarm was received and the bombers left. The B-29s traveled with deadly speed and caused great destruction within one or two minutes. The Battle of Leyte had destroyed Japanese sea power, civil war raged in Greece, and Budapest was encircled by the Russians.

merely glanced at our student identifications while they were busy carrying and piling up heavy sand bags. Midway through the park the alarms shrieked again and we froze in our tracks. All around us metal shrapnel from bursting anti-aircraft shells pocked the grass and clumps of earth spurted up in the air.

A young Japanese soldier—he looked like a teenager—started waving and yelling incomprehensible commands at us. As we stood uncertain, not knowing how to respond, he crawled on his stomach very rapidly in our direction, pushed me to the ground indicating to Lee to follow, then half dragged me towards thick bushes. The three of us lay panting, flat on the ground: a Jewish girl, a Chinese boy, and a Japanese soldier of approximately the same age united in a moment of danger in a youthful spirit of spontaneous friendship. When I finally reached home, I flung myself on my bed and—to my own surprise—burst into tears! The radio was denouncing the "outrage of Americans bombing residential districts in Shanghai," which they attributed to the Allies' despair at "constant losses and defeats." Papa brought the news that on this same day the Americans bombed the Nanking-Shanghai Railway. A number of passengers were killed, among them three Jews, one of whom was a young man due to be married the following week.

Tension is mounting here. Tales of frantic Kamikaze attacks on U.S. warships persist in spite of Japanese threats against "rumor-mongers." According to Papa, nothing can now halt the power amassed by the Americans.

1945

Had a wonderful New Year's Eve party at Helen's house in the International Settlement. We were seven couples. Everyone brought their favorite records and we danced till the morning. I just KNOW the War will be over in 1945! At 6:30 a.m. Helen's mother got up—I suppose we made too much noise for her to sleep anyway—and fried a pile of golden *grenki* (French toast) for us. Although she used dried powdered eggs, the toast was delicious: crispy on the outside and soft on the inside. After breakfast Jesus and I, Riva and Jackie (a charming Sephardi Jewish boy) decided to go home. As we entered Hardoon Road, Pao Chia chased us to the side, sharply blowing whistles. A barricade! There were, however, no Japanese military in sight and very few pedestrians so we leaned on the red brick wall surrounding the Hardoon Estate and chatted.[1] I told my friends that when my mother was a child, she visited the Hardoon property together with a group of classmates. According to her there were buildings topped by Chinese curved roofs, a Buddhist temple, rockeries, and an arched bridge. Literally hundreds of servants glided about in soundless steps and silent Buddhist monks in flowing robes walked in the gardens. Mama and her friends were led to the family residence where Mrs. Hardoon, wearing a simple Chinese style dress greeted them and supervised their "tea."

Jackie laughed at this description of Hardoon generosity and told us how his friend, who went to school "with one of the Hardoon boys—an adopted son," had had a completely different experience. The young Hardoon had invited him and his brother to his "birthday party" making it very clear that the present he expected was a Kodak box camera. On the set date both brothers arrived with the desired gift, entered the huge iron gates of the estate and proceeded timidly to the main building. There they were led to their classmate, who quickly unpacked the camera. There were no other guests, no

---

[1]The Hardoon Estate is today the site of the Shanghai Industrial Exhibition Hall. Hardoon Road has been renamed Tongren Road.

treats, nothing! After a while, the two visitors, feeling very foolish, left for home.

Shanghailanders well know the story of Silas Hardoon, an Iraqi Jew who arrived in our city in the last century—1873. His first job was that of watchman in one of the cavernous waterfront godowns (warehouses) belonging to the famous Sassoon Company.[2] Being a very bright youth, Hardoon quickly familiarized himself with storage techniques, inventories, bills of lading and accounting. Unlike the majority of foreigners, he felt at ease with the Chinese, learnt the Shanghai dialect and rapidly advanced in his firm. However, to his disappointment his salary remained inadequate, at least in his own estimation.

Hardoon quickly recognized the amazingly rapid growth of Shanghai. Foreign capital was flowing into this important Treaty Port and building sites were being greedily snapped up by real estate speculators. His boss at the Sassoon Company advised him to "get into the game" and buy undeveloped land which was still available at very low cost. Hardoon wisely listened to his superior, and making do with bare necessities he began to purchase small lots with his savings. In due course he steadily acquired pieces of property which yielded him rents for reinvestment. Finally, in 1920 he left his firm to engage in large-scale real estate speculation which would make him one of the wealthiest private figures in Shanghai. An English journalist once referred to him as "the richest man East of Suez."

"Do you know how Hardoon met his wife?" Jackie asked. "They say she was a seamstress who altered and repaired clothes and that he called her from his window when he saw her in the street and needed some urgent mending. At that time he was very poor and lived in a tiny room somewhere in a Chinese lane."

"Some people claim she was Eurasian," I ventured.

---

[2]Godown: the word originates from the Malayan *gedong*, meaning "space."

But Jackie hotly denied this contention.[3]

"No! She was Chinese. They were married at the British Consulate. Hardoon claims they also had a religious Jewish ceremony, but nobody I know believes it. Although she began to call herself 'Liza' she remained a devout Buddhist all her life."

"Yes," I confirmed, "my father once told me that Liza Hardoon was totally under the influence of a Chinese monk who lived on the Estate."[4]

Since the Hardoons were childless they adopted 11 children—some of European descent, some Eurasian— and sheltered more than 100 Chinese foster sons and daughters. To find the "foreign" children, Silas Hardoon sent agents to various cities in China instructing them to give preference to Jewish youngsters. Many unpleasant rumors circulated on this subject. Some whispered that the Hardoons liked fair children and unprincipled emissaries would bleach the hair of their finds before returning to Shanghai!

The "Jewish" Hardoon children ate Chinese food at home and may have worn Chinese clothing within the estate, but they always appeared in Western dress outside. They all attended foreign schools. When the second son, Philip, died in 1939 at the age of 19, he was buried in the Jewish cemetery in strict accordance with Jewish rites. The Chinese children, on the other hand, obeyed Chinese customs and ethics. They studied in a Chinese school specially built for them on the estate. Jackie, who knew some of the "Jewish" Hardoon boys said he did not notice any real brotherly ties between them, but several of the girls did appear to be close. What he would never forget was the dramatic arrival at school of

---

[3]A Chinese professor from the People's Republic of China told me in 1990 that the Chinese today believe Mrs. Hardoon's father was an Irish policeman in Shanghai. Since in China children are accorded their father's nationality, Mrs. Hardoon is now considered an "Irish woman" by the Chinese.

[4]The monk, Huang Zong-Yang, persuaded Mrs. Hardoon to publish 8,416 rolls of Buddhist canons, which he himself edited. On the first page appeared a portrait of his benefactress, Liza Hardoon.

the Hardoon children in their antique model maroon Rolls Royce. It had shiny fittings of polished brass and its roof started behind the chauffeur who sat in the open like a coachman of former times. Next to him was the doorman whose sole function was to jump down and let the children out at their destination. When it rained, an awning was stretched over the heads of the two men.

Hardoon showed little interest in Jewish causes. When poor relatives arrived from the Middle East, the only help he profered was to pay for their third class passage back home! Papa had a disheartening personal experience with Silas Hardoon. In the mid-1920s he was persuaded by friends in the Ashkenazi Jewish community to approach him for a contribution to help a small group of destitute Zionists stranded in Shanghai on their way from Russia to Palestine. With much reluctance, Papa decided to call on Hardoon in his downtown headquarters. To his amazement he found that in spite of Hardoon's legendary wealth his office was unheated, uncarpeted, and uncurtained, like a whitewashed monk's cell. On that freezing rainy day Papa shivered in his light coat while Hardoon, a heavyset man slouched breathing heavily behind an unvarnished wooden desk. He wore a thick padded Chinese gown and hid his crossed hands in his ample sleeves. Knowing well my father's distaste for fundraising and his quick temper, I can imagine his frustration, fury, and humiliation as Hardoon listened in stony silence and then responded with a categorical "No." Never again did Papa agree to seek Hardoon's intervention.

Hardoon, however, did build a synagogue in 1927—Bet Aharon—for the Sephardi Jewish Community. The edifice, praised as an "architectural gem," was a harmony of angles and curves, and I remember my mother taking me to see its beautiful illuminations on the occasion of the coronation of King George VI (1937). Once when the Bet Aharon Synagogue Committee had financial problems and were unable to pay maintenance bills, they applied to Silas Hardoon for help. His dry reply:

"If you can't afford to take care of the building give it back to me."

The lovely new synagogue never did gain great popularity, partly because of Hardoon's attitude and also because many members of the congregation had grown accustomed to their old temple where they met with their close friends.[5] This rather desolate situation changed in 1941 when 300 religious refugees from Lithuania arrived in Shanghai and were given living and study quarters in its various office rooms—certainly a use Silas Hardoon (now long dead) could never have foreseen. This ultra-orthodox group of pallid men wearing floor-length dark coats and old-fashioned hats provoked amazed stares not only from the Chinese but from Diaspora Jews such as I, who had never seen their like.

In 1927, the year he built Bet Aharon, Hardoon must have been particularly well disposed. To Shanghailanders' surprise he welcomed the entire First Unit of Shanghai's British Defense Forces to his estate, offering free food and accommodation until permanent arrangements could be made for them. However, this may have been of diplomatic purport since it appears to have contributed to his appointment as "councillor" on the Board of the International Settlement. In due course, Silas Hardoon became one of very few Shanghailanders to serve both on the Settlement Council and on that of the French Concession.

As far as the Chinese were concerned, Hardoon, as many colonials sarcastically said, "tried to uplift the ignorant masses." No doubt pressed by his wife Liza, who exerted a strong influence on him, he supported schools and founded a college where both the ancient classics as well as modern science were taught. He contributed to the organization of an "Association for Old Men" and a "Literary Society" of which he himself was the only paying member, thus providing for its very existence. As early as October 1920, the Chinese government had awarded him the "Grand Ribbon Second Grade" in gratitude for the boarding schools he had established for 500 Chinese children in the Shanghai area. At the same

---

[5]Bet Aharon today is in part a factory. No trace remains of its original architectural beauty.

time, his wife was awarded the "Mercy and Benevolence of the First Rank of Third Class" decoration. The ceremony was held on the grounds of the Hardoon estate to background music performed by the Army Band of the Governor of Shanghai.

When famines decimated China (unfortunately a regular occurrence), Hardoon contributed millions to alleviate the disasters. In 1924, the Chinese government granted him the "Order of Chao Wu with Belt." He also became the first foreign holder of the "Military Order of the First Class with Sash" and was appointed adviser to the governors of two provinces.

In spite of all this recognition, Hardoon remained obsessed with his penny-pinching old days and rent collection. He would still visit Chinese tenements, ensuring personally that rent was paid on the due date. This characteristic gained him so many bitter enemies and so much hatred that he had to be accompanied at all times by a tough bodyguard.

"Hardoon was a man of unbelievable contradictions," Jackie said. "His office was such a miserable room, but he purchased a luxurious palace owned by a Chinese general in Peking. It had 200 rooms crowded with precious furniture and antiques. Hardoon claimed he needed a suitable residence for his visit to the northern capital on government business!"[6]

Papa once told me that Hardoon had started an amazing project: the translation into Chinese of all sacred scriptures of Judaism, Christianity, and Islam. For this purpose he had hired a young Buddhist scholar, Chi Cho-wei, who lived on the estate. The first part of the project involved the translation of the Koran and a Moslem expert was added to the staff. After three years three volumes were published (20,000 copies each) and the books were distributed free of charge to educational institutions, including the Hebrew University in

----

[6]Hardoon bought the palace from the "Kingmaker," General Sun, in 1924 for the price—astronomical at the time—of 220,000 Mexican dollars.

Jerusalem. For an unknown reason the project was then cut short.

Jackie told us how his uncle had taken him to Hardoon's funeral in 1931 when he was 11 years old. The widow Liza claimed that he had instructed her to organize two kinds of religious services when he died: the first according to Buddhist rites, to be followed by a second, traditionally Jewish one. Jackie never forgot the awe-inspiring sight of the dead Hardoon lying in state while thousands of joss sticks (incense) glowed at his sides. His adopted and foster children "kowtowed" (prostrated themselves) on the ground in front of their father's body after which two bands led the funeral procession to the burial site on the estate grounds, one band playing traditional Chinese music while the other followed with military marches. After these lengthy proceedings, a Jewish service followed at which the eldest Jewish son recited the Kaddish—the Jewish prayer for the dead.

"Can you imagine?" Jackie laughed. "The president of the Hevra Kadisha (Jewish Burial Society) later furiously declared that he had been misled into believing that only Jewish services would be held. As a result he handed in his resignation, causing a huge brouhaha!"

Thus, Hardoon died as he had lived—the object of conflicting opinions and much anger. The controversy persisted for many years. Hardoon had left the bulk of his fortune to his wife but other relatives fought the will, attempting to lay hands on his enormous fortune. Litigation dragged onuntil three years ago when Mrs. Hardoon died in 1941, at the age of 78 after many years of illness and blindness.

When the roadblock was removed—we never did find out its purpose, perhaps it had been a training exercise—we made our way to the tram and back home. Poor Jesus must have felt quite left out of our conversation—which he could not possibly understand—but after a sleepless night he seemed to be too exhausted to care.

Yes, it does seem that the War will end this year. Our Filipino neighbor happily informed us that she had heard "from friends who have a short-wave radio" that U.S. forces landed in Luzon, her country's main island, and Sidney (who also has access to forbidden information) specially came over to tell us that the Burma road had been reopened. HAPPY 1945!

February 1945

Genny phoned this morning to invite me for lunch. Her mother is preparing (the Russian expression is *lepit*, meaning "modeling") *pilimeni* (a kind of Russian ravioli), which I adore. Mama tells me that when she was a little girl in Siberia, village women would make huge numbers of pilimeni which they would freeze outside in the great cold (often 40 degrees below zero!) in batches of a hundred. Later their men would pile pilimeni-filled blocks of ice on their wagons and sell them from house to house. My grandmother, Mama Katia, competes with Genny's mother in cooking expertise and, I believe, the two women make the best pilimeni in Shanghai, perhaps even in the entire world. Once, according to Mama Katia she cooked 500 pilimeni to determine who in her family could eat most. Uncle Simon was the winner, consuming 200! Various members of the Kriger family (my mother's maiden name) told me the same story so I imagine it was not exaggerated. At normal meals, men would easily eat 50 pilimeni and one must remember that a pre-War "ordinary" dinner included hors d'oeuvres *(zakuski)*, soup (pilimeni were served in a broth), meat and vegetables, followed by dessert. In addition to copious dishes, everyone helped themselves generously to bread (black and white) that was always on the table. My father would firmly declare, "A dinner without bread is NOT a meal!" This must have been a rather common Russian saying because I often hear it repeated at my Russian friends' tables.

It was eleven o'clock and nobody was at home. As I dressed to get ready to go to Genny, I heard Vicky the Scotch terrier howl in pain. The Monster, that witch our landlady, must have kicked her. I was glad my sister—

she who loves animals so much—was not at home, since she would have been very distressed. I wished things were as before and I could call the S.S.P.C.A. (Shanghai Society for the Prevention of Cruelty to Animals). They would have helped me! I remember their crusade against plucking bristles from live pigs. At the time, complaints were registered not by animal lovers but by real estate dealers. Nobody wanted to buy land near a pig slaughterhouse where animals squealed in agony day and night as their bristles were being pulled out! Pig bristles are an important Chinese export item—supposedly the best in the world—bringing premium prices, but according to experts bristles retain the necessary stiffness only when plucked from live animals. I believe this S.S.P.C.A. case against abattoir owners dragged on for years without solution because the society was only concerned with the pain the pigs suffered and not the livelihood of the slaughterhouse proprietors and their workers. However, the S.S.P.C.A. did manage to bring to cynical Shanghailanders' consciousness the dreadful torment animals endured, and in many less complicated cases they did succeed in saving helpless animals. I am sure they would have, at the very least, found a home for poor dear Vicky.[7]

After lunch some ladies arrived at Genny's house to play cards with her mother and although it was rather chilly we decided to go for a walk and look at the—alas!—sadly depleted show-windows on Avenue Joffre. As we strolled along chatting we almost bumped into Alexander Vertinsky, Shanghai's claim to theatrical and musical fame. Looking exactly like his record covers—elongated, ghostly pallid, almost inhuman—he glided rather than walked. The White Russian Association of Writers, Artists, Actors and Musicians once honored him as "The First Knight of Shanghai Bohemia." Two years ago, in the heat of the War, Vertinsky, a Russian émigré, got permission to return to the U.S.S.R.,

---

[7]A branch of the worldwide Society of Prevention of Cruelty to Animals launched its Shanghai operation at the beginning of this century.

presumably after the personal intervention of Stalin, who is reputed to be his great fan.[8]

Genny's mother once told us that Vertinsky himself composes the words and music of his songs. She explained to us that one really had to see his performance to appreciate fully the *genre* he had created. He himself admitted to friends he had no voice but concentrated mainly on expression and gesture, "acting" rather than singing his songs. Apparently he had been in his youth the toast of pre-revolutionary Moscow and got trapped in Shanghai after a world tour that led him to Paris, New York, and Hollywood. While in the United States, he fell passionately in love with Marlene Dietrich (with whom it was rumored he had an affair) and composed a romantic poem for her which he set to music and sang. However, he eventually forgot her and at the age of 46 married a 16-year-old aristocratic Georgian girl from the famous Bagrazian clan. She became the mother of his two daughters. Mama—and many of her friends—listen ecstatically to Vertinsky's melodramatic songs of unrequited love and nostalgia rendered in what sounds, to Genny's and my ears, like a prolonged whine! What we both prefer is an old record of her mother's, Caruso's version of "Over There!" Virile, melodious, and enthusiastic!

I mentioned rather proudly that many years ago—in 1936—Mama had taken me to a concert of Fedor Ivanovich Chaliapin, the world's most powerful and pure bass. He had arrived in Shanghai with his wife, daughter, manager, pianist, secretary, and bulldog. How different our city was at that time! A multitude awaited the great singer on the wharf: the mayor of Shanghai, members of the diplomatic corps, the press, hundreds of

---

[8]Stalin is said to have played Vertinsky's records over and over, especially his famous hits "Magnolia" and "The Mad Organ Grinder." In the U.S.S.R., Vertinsky became a national idol and enjoyed honors and privileges until his death. Today his two beautiful daughters are involved in film and theater and are very popular in Russia.

White Russians, and Mei Lian-Fen, the incomparable Chinese actor.

Chaliapin gave two concerts in Shanghai's largest theater, the Grand, which seats 2,200 spectators. All tickets were snapped up in advance and I never did find out how my mother managed to obtain two, nor why she chose to have me accompany her—perhaps because at the time I was painfully struggling with piano lessons! In the darkened theater, I leaned rigidly forward in my seat, my fingers clutching the armrests as Chaliapin's giant presence overpowered the stage and his resonant voice rang through the entire building. My disembodied soul floated towards the music, the audience vanished, and there was nothing but a celestial sound . . .

Air-raid sirens put an end to our conversation and we huddled in the doorway of a building as our thoughts turned to the ever-present War. Genny and I agree on one of our greatest fears: that the Japanese may force down an American plane and take its crew prisoner. We have long heard about the execution of U.S. pilots by the Japanese and know that some were—and are—tortured in Bridge House where Genny's father suffered so dreadfully. The alarm turned out to be false and we walked back home talking about the latest "underground" news. We hear that Japan is bombed regularly and that Tokyoites call the resulting fires "Edo flowers"! More importantly, according to short-wave broadcasts, the U.S. forces have launched a tremendous invasion of Iwo Jima.[9] Genny and I hope we survive what we definitely believe are the final stages of the War.

March 1945

Went to the Jewish Club on Thursday evening with Papa and Mama. Mama wore a black dress with tiny

---

[9]The invasion of Iwo Jima (Sulphur Island) started on February 19, 1945. The Americans dispatched 495 warships including 17 aircraft carriers and 1,170 planes (an unprecedented number). It was only on March 16, when the final Japanese defenders were killed, that the Allies declared the island secure.

flowers that I like. I donned my favorite maroon sailor-
dress, tight at the waist and fitting. Père de Breuverie of
Aurora University once called me to his office and complained that this outfit was too provocative. As a result
of this conversation, I stopped wearing it to classes but
like it all the more! As Mama often says, I am *nevozmoj-
naya* (impossible).

The Jewish Club was established in 1932 in the French
Concession. It served to unite disparate Russian Jewish
refugees in Shanghai and became a center of creative
Jewish spiritual and cultural life. As Hitler gained power
in 1933 and persecution of Jews increased, a Jewish
Defense League was organized in the club premises with
the stated purpose of fighting anti-Semitism, helping
victims of discrimination, and developing friendship
between Jews of different countries.

Papa is the secretary of the Jewish Club Cultural
Committee, and Genny's father, Boris Topas, president
and founder of the Zionist *Kadima* organization, held all
his meetings there before his imprisonment in Bridge
House. In spite of the great public value of Papa's social
contributions, Mama resents the many hours he spends
at the club and for this same reason, I admit to ambiva-
lent feelings about this institution. Nevertheless, I very
much enjoy the club dances and going there for a cultural soirée with both my parents is a real—and rare!—
treat.

Cultural evenings are organized on Thursdays by the
"El Ha Ka"—Russian initials for the words *Literaturni
Hudojestveni Krujek* (Literary Artistic Circle). It was
founded 12 years ago by a small group of people—Papa
among them—who hungered for creative expression.
Their purpose: a forum for all those seeking culture in
its various forms, a stimulus for writers, artists, and
musicians to develop their talents and skills.

The initiators of the group approached the Cultural
Committee of the Jewish Club for support and received
an enthusiastic response. As a result, club premises were
opened to the El Ha Ka on Thursday evenings, in spite
of the fact that not all El Ha Ka participants were club
members and several were not Jewish. To reciprocate

the club's generosity, the El Ha Ka assist whenever possible with the decoration of the club hall and dining-room, offer entertainment for its various functions in the form of music and theatrical skits, and even helped organize the club library. This successful mutual relationship flourished throughout the years and gradually attracted some of the best professionals in Shanghai, who generously offer their repertoire free of charge.

To give the group an esprit de corps, my father wrote the "El Ha Ka Hymn," which was set to high-spirited music. It consists of four verses interspersed with a chorus. The final lines—roughly translated from the Russian—read:

Oh join us poets and musicians,
Oh join us, listen to our call.
Our arms are open to embrace
All in whose hearts creative passion beats.

Neither the Nazis in Europe, nor the Japanese in Shanghai dampen the enthusiastic ideals of the El Ha Ka!

We sat at a long table reserved for El Ha Ka members and I felt rather shy as people surrounded us to greet my parents and express delight that a member of the younger generation had come. The room allotted to the El Ha Ka is rectangular, high-ceilinged, set off by large draped windows—a harmonious setting, an oasis from Japanese uniforms and bayonets. When my father's turn came to perform he stood on a small stage and declaimed several of his poems, among which my favorite is *"Jizn Sobacha"*("A Dog's Life"). It starts:

It may be sinful
To think today
Of a dog's fate
When men
Bathe in their own
Human blood . . .

Of course, my translation does not do justice to Papa's rolling, mellifluous Russian. He describes the long, lonely howl of a dog, his suffering. The short lines are printed one under the other in a curve like a dog's tail. The poem ends:

> *And we too*
> *Like dogs*
> *Are in the hands*
> *Of fate,*
> *And fate*
> *Throws us a bone*
> *And plays*
> *With our lives.*[10]

Uncle Gava (Gabriel) read his two-act play, *In the Country of Hope.*

No twins could be more dissimilar than Papa and Uncle Gava. My father is handsome, serious, idealistic, and romantic while Gava, endowed with a large bulbous nose, regales all and sundry with hilarious—often bawdy—tales told in a wide range of accents—Georgian, Tartar, Yiddish, Chinese. Once, when I was very little—probably no more than five—I asked Gava why his nose was so big.

"It is your father's fault," he replied. "When we were born, he rushed out first and wanted me to hurry, so he grabbed me by the nose and pulled it, stretching it like a rubber band." Then he added in a conspiratorial whisper:

"I'll tell you a secret. Since I have so much space on my nose I planted a seed in it and one day you will see a tall *yelka* (pine tree) growing high from its tip."

He gently rubbed his proboscis while I gazed at it with wonder and utter belief.

---

[10]In 1938, my father published a collection of his poems in a little book entitled *Serdze Nastij (The Wide Open Heart).* He dedicated it to "My children."

In spite of his humor Gava is a very well-educated man and I learnt to appreciate his deep knowledge of history and literature.[11]

After the El Ha Ka program was over we sat for a while at the table talking. Strong hot tea was served with slices of lemon. The conversation—as always happens these days—turned to the War. It appears that Allied forces are advancing in Europe and have occupied Cologne (Germany). The Japanese are also retreating and the U.S. Air Force is savagely bombing Tokyo. How I wish all this would end soon!

When we returned home Mama seemed in a happy mood. She gave me a remnant she had found—apple-green polka-dotted cotton for a dress. She also has enough white piqué for a collar and cuffs. Tomorrow, Mama will send amah to one of the Chinese lanes to call our tailor, Woo. Woo is a thin old man with a wispy beard and a mole on his cheek from which several long black hairs grow. He wears a nondescript padded gown throughout the autumn and winter which gives out a disagreeable mouldy smell. When Woo hovers about me taking my measurements I often have to hold my breath. I wonder where he lives and where he has space to sew clothes. Woo, like other Chinese tailors, never uses a pattern. All he needs is a magazine illustration or a rough drawing. There is a funny story told in Shanghai about a French lady who insisted on ordering from Paris a Vogue pattern for a fancy evening gown. Her puzzled tailor meekly accepted the pattern and a week later delivered the dress with neatly embroidered words in fine silk thread:

"Vogue Pattern No. 2758."

Several days after I handed him the material, Woo arrived for a fitting. His mouth full of pins, he grunted understanding as I stood in front of Mama's mirror giving instructions in Pidgin English, "Sleeve mo' small-ee, skirt-ee much-ee long-ee, makee colla mo' big-ee." After Woo had stuck numerous pins into my dress I had difficulty getting out of it. He waited patiently as I struggled,

---

[11]Gava died in Israel in his early 60s.

and then gathered the dress in a heap and wrapped it into a none-too-clean cloth, muttering his understanding of what I wanted:

"Savee! Savee! Woo savee! Missee no wolly (worry)."

A Chinese female student in my class once told me that tailors who work for foreigners won't accept orders for Chinese style dresses. Making Western clothes is a different profession which, I believe, the talented Chinese learn almost by instinct. I certainly cannot imagine old Woo ever having gone to courses. Some of my Chinese classmates (we have only a handful of girls in my Aurora classes) invariably wear straight blue Chinese gowns with high collars and a short, modest side slit. They tell me they pay their tailors a pittance. I don't believe anyone buys ready-made clothes, which I understand are very popular in the United States.

Before the Japanese Occupation (which appears to have dulled even our clothing!) elegant Chinese women would achieve wonders with one basic cut of dress. Since many Chinese ladies have, I am convinced, the most beautiful legs, arms, and hands in the world, their short straight dresses with long side slits and a hint of sleeves display their natural attributes to the best advantage. While elderly ladies invariably wear dark colors (mainly black), younger and more worldly women managed to create (before Pearl Harbor) fashion miracles with the deft addition of flowers and jewelry to beautifully textured silks. Fine thin stockings outlined their lovely calves. Perhaps one reason for today's grim clothes—apart from the lack of materials and other goods—is because Chinese beauties wish to escape the attention of the occupying forces. As it is, I hear many Japanese have become enamored of Chinese women, not to speak of the rapes all Shanghai girls so dreadfully fear.

The night after Pearl Harbor, when many of us were still blissfully unaware of the perils of occupation, a Japanese guard tried to rape a very close friend of mine in front of the former American School, which was taken over by the Kempeitai (military police). First he had amused himself by forcing her and the young man who was accompanying her to stand against the bamboo fence as he lunged at them, his bayonet stopping an inch in front of their rigid bodies. After these preliminaries he dragged my friend toward some bushes, ripping off her clothes. To her remarkable good fortune, a passing Japanese army truck stopped, an officer jumped out, pushed the soldier off my friend, slapped him repeatedly, and then signaled my friend to collect her things and leave. She never told her parents about this incident, fearing they would not let her out of the house for the rest of the War.[12]

To return to a more comfortable subject, in contrast to Chinese women, many Chinese men quickly adopted Western clothing and wear suits to work in offices. Chinese tailors are known to complete suits in 24 hours: apparently the tailor does the cutting and then his entire family helps at skillfully sewing the pieces together and embroidering the customer's initials on the jacket lining, should he so require. It takes foreigners time to adjust to their Chinese tailor. One arrogant Englishman handed his tailor a piece of Irish tweed and an old suit which he commanded him to "Mak-ee same same" (copy exactly). The tailor did, including a patch in one of the knees! Good-ee for him!

One of the funniest signs in Shanghai—which I never saw but Shanghailanders swear exists—hangs in front of a tailor's shop. It states: "Ladies have fits upstairs."

April 1945

Went with a group of some 20 psychiatry students to visit two insane asylums, one private and one public. In both, as far as I could tell, the patients were Europeans. The private one is located behind Mama's shop and when we lived for a time in rooms above Peter Pan we could see its grounds from our back bedroom windows. It is well kept and the patients appear to be in good physical condition. The doctor in charge explained to us

---

[12]This incident did scar my friend psychologically, giving her a lifelong fear of crowds, claustrophobia, and acrophobia.

three fascinating cases and gave us the opportunity to speak to some of the mentally ill. The second hospital is located further downtown in the International Settlement. There are no gardens, just a gloomy red brick building that looks like a forbidding prison, depressing even from the outside. The interior is dark, doors in the corridors are locked, and strange cries can be heard through the walls. We gathered in a large room where chairs were arranged in rows for us, and two girls whose age was hard to determine were brought in. Their frightening behavior was like that of forcefully caged wild animals, snarling, lashing out, making attempts to bite and scratch the attendants who held them back. I was so upset that I could hardly concentrate on the professor's explanations. However, before two stout nurses finally led them away, his words did register:

"The patients you saw are the twin daughters of Jack Riley."

Jack Riley! All Shanghai has heard of the American escaped convict Jack Riley, who, like many other fugitives from justice, managed to build up a tidy little empire for himself here. Since Shanghai was an open Treaty Port, individuals entered our city with very little control (in the case of larger groups of refugees some nominal restraints were set mainly because of economic considerations). During 15 years Riley enriched himself operating slot machines, bars, nightclubs and restaurants. Because in Shanghai money was king—and to tell the truth people were not aware of his criminal past— the successful Riley was a much admired figure in many circles. Papa, whose firm had some dealings with him, supplying Sperry flour to his restaurants, did not like him. He classified him as "charming but dangerous—a snake!" In 1940 Riley was arrested for operating gambling dens. He escaped after the first day of his trial, hiding in the Japanese controlled area (which made everyone suspect he had been paying the Japanese protection money). In spite of efforts by the Japanese to help him, he was finally apprehended and shipped back to the United States.[13]

---

[13]Carroll Alcott in *My War with Japan* (New York: Henry Holt,

Among the bars Riley had owned, two were located in the disreputable "Blood Alley" (Rue Chu Pao San). This "center of vice"—as some journalists called it—is a short 110-yard street off Avenue Edward VII, one of Shanghai's busiest thoroughfares. Within Blood Alley's restricted space some two dozen bars were set up to which sailors of all nationalities gravitated. During the day the area was nothing more than a quiet Chinese lane with closed businesses, but at night (my friends tell me, since I never was allowed to go) it was full of rowdy people and loud music. The bars opened at six-thirty in the evening and—if a foreign ship was in port and there were sufficient customers—would stay open till eight o'-clock the following morning. I heard that a large sign in one of the bars read: "IN GOD WE TRUST—EVERYONE ELSE CASH." The area was under French control but the French police (which had obviously been paid off) closed its eyes to all the illegal activities, intervening only when violent fights broke out resulting in destroyed furniture, mirrors, glasses, and savage knifings. The "flics" ("cops") would then throw troublemakers into Shanghai's well-known Black Maria (police van) that raced wildly through the city to the nearest police station. Many murders had been committed in "Blood Alley," hence its name.[14]

Blood Alley was famous for its prostitutes, apparently of all nationalities and types to please a customer's fancy.

1943) writes: "Though he had disfigured his fingertips with acid and some self-executed surgery, he had failed to remove all the telling lines. His prints were sent to Washington, where the Federal Bureau of Investigation did a remarkable job of reconstruction. Riley's record was traced, even to the doctor who officiated at his birth, and was revealed in the United States Court for China on the first day of his trial. . . . Riley was returned to the United States to serve 18 months in the federal prison at McNeil Island and to face his uncompleted sentence in Oklahoma."

[14]Pan Ling in his *In Search of Old Shanghai* (Hongkong: Joint Publishing, 1982) writes of the present condition of Blood Alley: "The alley is now in a state of almost total dereliction, the downstairs part of once lovely buildings turned into workshops for broken down buses."

Mama once mentioned two notorious Jewish whores
who plied their trade there. "One is a tall, skinny 'gingy'
[red-haired] woman whom everyone calls 'Lisa
Mosquito.' The sailors like her a lot. The other, a huge
fat thing, is named 'Hava Ox.' They hate each other.
Still, they are good Jews and donated money to the
community for orphaned children." Mama never told
us her source of information.

All these thoughts flashed through my mind as I
cringed watching Riley's mentally disturbed daughters.
Who was their mother? When I asked a Chinese doctor's assistant at the asylum he said he did not know but
had heard that as long as Riley had been in Shanghai a
generous monthly check would arrive regularly for the
children's upkeep.

When I returned home late in the evening (we had
some lengthy laboratory work at the university) the
family looked very upset. I had been bursting to tell
them the story of the Riley twins but was stopped by
their glum expressions.

"What happened?" I asked anxiously.

"Haven't you heard the terrible news?" Mama coun-
tered. "President Roosevelt died!"

Feeling I had received a physical blow I sat down on
the sofa, as Mama murmured:

"*Chto budet? Chto budet?*" ("What will be? What will
be?")[15]

Seldom had I seen my plucky mother so distressed.

In spite of Papa's complaints that the Allies had not
done enough to save Jews from the clutches of Nazism
when their rescue was still possible, Jews in Shanghai
venerated the U.S. president for his intelligence, political boldness and honesty. They somehow felt protected
by the very existence of this powerful man. And now he
was gone. We were totally abandoned!

For years the Japanese have vilified Franklin Delano
Roosevelt. They referred to him as "a man of brutal

[15]Just as in the case of President John F. Kennedy's assassination,
most people remember exactly where they were and what they were
doing when they learnt of President Roosevelt's death. Few were
aware of the very poor state of his health.

force lusting for power" and spread the Nazi lie that he was a Dutch Jew named "Van Roosevelt." Indeed, Japan's hatred for Roosevelt can be traced all the way back to October 5, 1937 when the U.S. president delivered what was to become known here as his "Quarantine Speech," words the Japanese are unable to forget and still bring up on every possible occasion when accusing the United States of insulting the Japanese people. At that time Japanese troops were closing in on Nanking and a furious Roosevelt attacked the outbreak of what he defined as "international lawlessness." He suggested that nations contributing to the "epidemic" of anarchy be "quarantined." War, declared Roosevelt, "is a contagion whether it be declared or undeclared" and "can engulf states and people remote from the original scene of hostilities." Although Roosevelt did not mention Japan by name, the entire world understood at which country he was pointing his finger. To clarify the matter even further, the U.S. State Department issued on the following day a statement that "the action of Japan in China is inconsistent with the principles which should govern relationships between nations . . ."

We listened with mounting gloom to radio broadcaster Herbert Moy's background report on Roosevelt's "treachery to the American people" and "Jewish connections." How can the U.S.-born-and-educated Moy be such a traitor? How thrilled the Nazis and the Japanese must be at Roosevelt's death![16]

What an eventful month this April is! Gleb told me the White Russian Community is in turmoil. As the Red Army advances against the Germans, many Shanghai Russian immigrants are beginning to reexamine their position. They take natural pride in the

---

[16]According to John Toland's *The Rising Sun* (New York: Random House, 1970), I was correct in my first assumption but strangely incorrect in my second. Toland writes:"The Nazis looked upon his (Roosevelt's) death as a last-minute reprieve from defeat. 'Fate has laid low your greatest enemy,' Goebbels feverishly told Hitler over the phone. . . . Japan's new leader, on the other hand, did not rejoice. Prime Minister Suzuki broadcast his condolences to the American people, expressing his "profound sympathy" over the loss of a man who was responsible for the "Americans' advantageous

courage and victories of their countrymen and some are even considering the possibility of returning one day to their fatherland! Several of Gleb's friends have removed from the walls of their rooms photographs and paintings of the czar and his family. Other White Russians consider such actions treason, openly support the Nazis, and prefer anything to a communist victory. Yes, here in Shanghai, political passions often do heat up to the boiling point. These two opposing views have led to much friction, reaching the point of physical violence. Gleb is doubtful about the "repatriation" so many envision at the end of the War but sympathizes with their desire: people long to return to their own country, their own landscapes—especially the forests, birch trees, berries, and mushrooms all Russians seem to miss so much. Even I, who have never been in Russia feel a strange nostalgia when Papa reads descriptions by Russian writers. Moreover, many Russian immigrants in Shanghai have never really done well and their situation has deteriorated even further under Japanese Occupation.

According to Gleb, the most uncompromising anti-Soviets frequent the St. Nicolas Church on Rue Corneille in the French Concession. Hardly surprising since a large marble sign on its outer wall states in Russian, French and English:

"In Memory of Martyred Czar Emperor Nicolas II and his August Family."

The interior of St. Nicolas overwhelms the visitor with its beauty and luxury. How did the practically penniless Russian Community manage to raise enough money to complete this splendid structure in 1932, with its onion domes, precious ikons, intricate wall decorations? Gleb took me there one *Pascha* (Russian Easter) to a mass, assuring me it would be "a cultural experience." I had to agree with him. The choir really did sound to me like the voice of angels. Besides, I found it exciting to see boys and girls outside the church kiss each other on

---

position today." In a note Toland adds: "Suzuki's broadcast was not reported in the Japanese press, and even his son knew nothing of it until after the War."

either cheek saying, *"Christos voskres!"* ("Christ resur-
rected!") I imagine many older people kissed each other
too, but for some reason this escapes my memory. A
very strange feeling indeed for a Jewish girl to be in such
surroundings but the wealth of artwork and harmony of
voices made my discomfort well worthwhile. Gleb tells
me that Shanghai's Russian Bishop Ioann has a deep hatred of the Bolsheviks, whom he had fought when the
Revolution broke out.[17]

About a week before Roosevelt died, news that the
Soviet government would not renew its neutrality pact
with Japan burst like a bombshell in Shanghai's White
Russian Community, leading to passionate arguments
about the consequences of this historic act. What would
happen in case of Japan's defeat? Now the situation is
very tense, the Russians are nervous and quarreling
among themselves.

As if we had not had enough excitement, the news
reached us that Mussolini was shot and Hitler committed suicide in Berlin! Are we dreaming?[18]

May 1945

All homeowners have been ordered by the Japanese to
immediately excavate a dugout in front of their property. Uneven, neglected pavements already pitted with
multiple holes will now be further damaged, increasing
the danger of accidents in our ill-lit streets. Of what possible use can these dugouts be in case of heavy bombings

---

[17]Bishop Ioann reached Shanghai on December 4, 1934.

[18]The sudden rush of events made it seem like a dream. On April 5,
1945 Stalin announced the termination of the U.S.S.R.'s neutrality
pact with Japan. According to the terms of the pact each signatory
was obliged to give one year's notice before termination. Stalin's
decision must have been a great shock for the Japanese! On April 28
Benito Mussolini and his mistress were shot by "Colonel Valero,"
who was actually Walter Adusio, a Communist Mussolini had once
helped after receiving a heart-rending plea from Adusio's mother.
They were later publicly hanged by their heels in Milano. On April
30 as the Soviet Army advanced on Berlin, Adolph Hitler and Eva
Braun committed suicide in a Berlin bunker.

by U.S. B-29s? The Japanese seem incapable of dealing with this aircraft that flies so swiftly and so high, causing widespread destruction on the ground below. Sidney told me the B-29 "Superfortress" is more than 30 feet long and carries a crew of 11 men. Although it reaches a great altitude (more than 30,000 feet) there is no need to wear oxygen masks since the cabin is "pressurized" by a special new process simulating air pressure equal to that at 8,000 feet. The Japanese planes that once ruled the air in the Pacific War are now clearly outflown and outgunned.

"The U.S. 'Superfortresses' have almost destroyed Tokyo, Nagoya, Osaka, and Yokohama," Sidney said. "American intelligence seems to know exactly where Japanese aircraft plants are located and they keep hitting them over and over. The British radio announced that in one air-raid over Tokyo more than 130,000 people were killed![19] That is what awaits us if the Americans decide to seriously bomb Shanghai. Those stupid dugouts ordered by the Japanese are pathetic!"

I did not reply. As the end of the War approaches tension increases in Shanghai to the point that it is almost palpable. We all want Allied victory but wonder if we will live to see it. Furthermore, the anti-Soviet White Russians are afraid of revenge by the Communists and feel trapped like mice. On the whole, however, come what may, Shanghailanders await the end of the War and the defeat of Japan with great hope if not optimism.

This morning after my parents and sister had already gone, I prepared to leave for Aurora. Suddenly the sirens started to wail repeatedly, signaling the presence of "enemy" planes. Snatching my books I dashed to

---

[19]"Conventional" bombing of Tokyo actually caused more fatalities than the atomic bomb. An authoritative estimate of deaths caused by firebombings is 299,485, with 368,830 wounded and 8.75 million rendered homeless. Over 97,000 were killed in Tokyo, followed by Hiroshima Prefecture with 86,141, and Nagasaki with 26,328. See *Fifty Years of Light and Dark* (Tokyo: The Mainichi Newspapers, 1975).

huddle under the staircase where the Filipino boy and girl living on the ground floor joined me. Their mother was on her daily search for provisions. As explosions near our house rocked our walls and curtains swayed violently, I attempted to revise my notes—a persistence my mother finds annoying in times of danger. Irrational as it may appear, I steadfastly study assigned texts and pursue self-imposed goals strongly, determined to have a "normal youth," developing my potential as well as enjoying life, dancing, laughing and having fun—all this a challenge in the repressive atmosphere of occupied Shanghai. Mama is right. I am very stubborn.

Our landlady, The Monster, is dead. Some months ago she sadistically forbade the Filipinos to use the only kitchen in the house, called the lame boy "a filthy cripple," and provoked such hurt and anger that the mother of the family pronounced a solemn curse on her life. Was it mere coincidence that on the very next day The Monster's massive body doubled in pain and she howled like a wounded animal for four days until she finally passed away?

"Do you really have to study now?" the Filipino boy asked, anxious for conversation, possibly to distract himself from his fear of the falling bombs. In truth, concentration was well-nigh impossible, so I closed my notebook. The boy spoke of the death of our landlady, whose passing neither he nor any other tenant in the house regretted. He explained to me that Filipinos prize their *amor proprio* (self-esteem). To be treated as inferiors, to be disparaged and disdained in public, assaults the depth of their soul. Unfortunately, our late landlady was the very essence of what is hateful and unacceptable for his people.

"You see," he said, "pride is part of our national characteristic. It is easier for a Filipino to accept a beating by a Japanese than to be humiliated by a slap on the face!"

Since the death of our landlady, tension has eased in our house, although her shadowy widower seems to have acquired his wife's nasty attributes and slithers about like a snake. However, the dogs are no longer tormented, the Fates be praised!

The bombs whined as they sped earthwards exploding when they hit targets with loud booms. At long last the all-clear sounded. WON'T waste my life like an insect waiting to be crushed. WON'T! WON'T! WON'T!

I gathered my books and notes, stacked them in the wire basket at the back of my bike and pedaled leisurely towards the university. The day was balmy, spring buds protruded on branches, sparrows fluttered freely. Suddenly my entire being was overwhelmed with joy to be alive—a contradictory, all-encompassing change of mood. Who could possibly understand me when my own emotions puzzle me so! Cycled to the university in high spirits.

As I stopped for a red light on Avenue Joffre caught sight of Lydia, a Russian girl I know. She is three years older than I and, for as long as I can remember, has worn a spotted leopard coat throughout the autumn and winter. She is tall and slim and actually good-looking except for an disproportionately small mouth. Once when I needed to return a book I had borrowed, I dropped unexpectedly by her home. It was the first time I had gone there. The rented room Lydia and her mother occupy serves both as bedroom and dining room. It is overcrowded with furniture, lamps, and other objects. On one wall hangs an enormous oil painting of a Russian officer on horseback. Lydia pointed to it saying proudly, "My father the general." I stared with disbelief. Her mother is an unattractive, heavily made-up woman who never smiles. I felt embarrassed at having barged in uninvited and my discomfort increased when there was a knock at the door and two Japanese men in civilian clothes appeared. I mumbled something and left—probably to everyone's relief. Is Lydia a spy? Since that time I avoid her, and I rode away the moment the light turned green, feeling rather guilty since she always acts so warm and friendly.[20]

In class, it is obvious that students find concentration impossible. There is an air of feverish anticipation as War events develop in rapid succession. During the first

---

[20]I later found out she was a call girl, something that never entered my mind. Apparently, some desperately poor Russian women became prostitutes during the War.

week of this month (May 7) the Germans bowed to Allied demands for unconditional surrender. Japan is now fighting alone like a wounded beast against obviously superior forces. We hear that there is talk in Japan of using bamboo spears against invading U.S. troops, should this disaster—from their point of view—arise. Can this be true?[21]

At dinner Mama told us that she met an acquaintance, Max Scheidlinger. He is a German refugee who owned a haberdashery in the International Settlement before the Japanese arbitrarily "requisitioned" everything and forced him to move to the Restricted Area. Fortunately for Max, he had opened some time ago in Honkew a small branch of his Settlement store which is within the area the Japanese designated for the refugees Thus, he was not completely wiped out financially. However, business there today is almost non-existent since people purchase only strict necessities. Occasionally, Max manages to obtain a day pass to leave the ghetto and conduct some business outside. According to him, applying for a day pass is even more terrifying than approaching the cruel Mr. Ghoya, who issues monthly permits, because the Japanese responsible for day passes is a certain smiling, "pleasant" Mr. Okura who, for reasons known to none but himself, arbitrarily sends applicants to spend several days in typhus infested cells! Contagion means almost certain death. Max, personally, has never had to endure this terrible experience, probably due to the fact that one of his customers is a German, a certain Herr Erhardt, who lives in the Park Hotel (where some important Nazis are lodged). When Max had his store in the International Settlement, Erhardt used to buy made-to-order shirts from him and shortly after the Japanese "proclamation" regarding refugees, the German advised him to phone him from

---

[21]It was. For example, in *Mother and Son*, by Isoko and Ichiro Hatano (Boston: Houghton Mifflin, 1962), Ichiro describes the mood in Japan after Germany's capitulation: "Germany has ended by losing. . . . This means Japan will have to fight the whole world alone. And it is only a matter of time before we are defeated, isn't it? . . . When I thought that there was something splendid about our fighting, the idea of death didn't frighten me. But now it just seems absurd."

time to time to receive orders for shirts. Max has his measurements and knows his requirements, so there is no problem carrying out the request. Whenever Max gets permission to leave the Restricted Area he also contacts Chinese business friends and buys available remnants—they trust him and give him the merchandise on credit, never demanding receipts. He is really very fond of the Chinese people, who have always shown him kindness and treated him decently. Lately, Erhardt asked Max to bring him gold and precious jewelry that refugee families are selling, and with these profits Max is able to keep his family from starvation (the income from his store being so low they couldn't survive on it). Erhardt always treats Max in a civil manner when Max visits him, although he never offers him any food or drink, and Max knows the German does business with other Jews who, as a result, can sometimes leave the ghetto and earn a little money to keep their head above water.[22]

This time Max told Mama an astonishing story. Several weeks ago he sat in his haberdashery—grandly called "Royal"—idly playing cards with some friends, since he had neither merchandise nor customers. Suddenly to his horror he saw the infamous Mr. Ghoya walk in with a little child. At the sight of the hated Japanese, Max felt an uncontrolled fury overwhelm him. He greeted Ghoya crying:

"Can't you see my shelves are empty? I have no merchandise, nothing! Anyway, I don't sell to Japs."

Ghoya gave him a freezing look, probably conquering his violent feelings in front of his child, and responded, "You come to my office tomorrow."

When Ghoya left, Max's friends, who had been immobilized with fear, turned upon him: "Are you crazy? He will kill you!"

---

[22]When I met Max in San Francisco in 1991, he told me that Erhardt had had a high official position and was tried as a war criminal by the United States. The testimony of Jews whom he had treated decently during the War helped prevent his imprisonment.

The story spread like wildfire in the ghetto and Max was looked upon as a dead man. The next day, with terror in his heart, he went, as commanded, to Ghoya's office. Ghoya did not refer to the incident of the preceding day, asked him several general questions, then suddenly rushed from behind his desk and started mercilessly slapping him on the face and beating him. When he finally stopped Max looked him straight into the eyes saying, "Mr. Ghoya, the War is ending soon and I will never forget what you did."

At this point, Max told Mama, he did not care what happened to him. He lay on the floor waiting for further blows but Ghoya returned to his seat and waved him to leave.[23]

We discussed this incident, commenting on the unpredictability of the Japanese, convinced that the War is really coming to an end since, otherwise, Ghoya would surely have killed the German refugee.

June 1945

Jesus has not called me for the past two weeks. I am analyzing over and over every one of my words that may have offended him and confided my "love problems" to my sister, who has suddenly grown up. She suggested

---

[23]The story did not end then. During one of our conversations in San Francisco in 1991, Max told me that at the end of August 1945 when the War had ended, an American GI—a distant relative—dropped into his Honkew store (where he had remained for lack of money to move back to the International Concession). Max described what Ghoya had done to him and how sadistically he had treated Jewish refugees who came to him to apply for permits. Thereupon the angry GI suggested they go look for the Japanese and beat him up. At the time, all the Japanese had been placed in a camp to await repatriation and the two men found Ghoya there. When he saw them he fell on his knees and begged for mercy; he had already been beaten on the street by a group of furious refugees. Neither Max nor the GI were moved by Ghoya's entreaties. Max said: "I suppose my inhibited anger was exploding. As we hit him, Ghoya kept crying repeatedly: "I never killed anyone! I never killed anyone!" It was true. This later led Max to believe the rumor that Ghoya had been an agent for the British. Although he terrorized the Jews he had never seriously harmed anyone, in contrast to the smiling Mr. Okura.

we go past the Barcelona Bar, in front of which Jesus' captain, Antonio, sometimes hangs out.

The Barcelona Bar is frequented by Basque Hai-Alai[24] players who spend their leisure hours sipping red wine at a little round table set on the pavement. (Hai-Alai is a Basque game involving a ball, or *pelota*, hurled at lightning speed from a curved wicker basket. It is played at the auditorium—located near the Barcelona—where spectators place bets and gamblers—both Chinese and foreign—risk fortunes. Manila is the only other place in the Orient, besides Shanghai, to have Hai-Alai.) The exotic, dark-haired Basques are the closest to Hollywood glamor our wartime city can offer. As they sit in front of their cafe idly watching women saunter by, they murmur flirtatious remarks (Jesus calls them *piropo*) and cast caressing, longing glances that entrance more than a few women. In fact, a month or so ago, two well-known married women had a vicious hair-pulling fight on Avenue Joffre over the affections of a Hai-Alai hero. Their public scuffle diverted Shanghailanders from all the problems of the Occupation and was the subject of excited gossip for days.

We went by the Barcelona Bar and Antonio was indeed there. He jumped up from his chair set out on the sidewalk and greeted us very courteously. As we continued to walk he hurried after us and said to me, "Jesus will be *furioso* because I promised to keep it a secret, but he is very sick in hospital." The hospital—for charity cases—is out in the Chinese section of town, Nantao.[25] Apparently, because of his Spanish (or Basque) pride, Jesus wishes to conceal from me his deplorable physical and financial situation. In fact, he had forbidden Antonio to reveal his whereabouts to me. My heart pounded as I remembered how exhausted and drawn Jesus had looked after our New Year's Eve party.

---

[24]This is the way the word was spelled in Shanghai. The Spanish would write it "Jai-Alai." I finally saw a Hai-Alai game in Manila in 1973 but did not understand it.

[25]Nantao and Chapei, adjoining the International Settlement and the French Concession, were before the Japanese Occupation under the direct control of the central government of Nanking. The area was administered by a mayor appointed by Nanking.

The following day I skipped Biology Practical Work and set off on my bicycle to the distant site of the hospital, almost two hours of hard pedaling in the hot sun, interrupted by a luckily short air-raid. Strained leg muscles were well worth Jesus' joyful surprise at my unexpected appearance and although he repeated, "Bad bad Antonio!" his happiness shone through. A young French nun tried to chase me away:

"Mademoiselle, this is the T.B. Ward. Very very contagious, especially for young people like you! Very dangerous! *Allez, allez Mademoiselle!*"

However, since I stubbornly remained perched on Jesus' bed, she gave up and left to care for patients who urgently needed her assistance.

How handsome Jesus looked in pale blue hospital pajamas, his eyes shining and his cheeks flushed with fever. I avoided the openly curious stares of other patients, one of whom—a haggard Portuguese—was gasping for air and spitting blood. Glancing at him Jesus fell silent then said: "Soon I also." I vowed I'd visit him again, a promise that fills me with dread since I know the fear it will strike in my parents and can foresee their strong opposition.[26]

I pedaled back home feeling a deep sadness, and tears—unusual for me—welled in my eyes. To add to my distress over Jesus' condition, Nantao looked so depressing, so poor, with so many starving people. It is true food has always been China's most urgent problem. No wonder Chinese customarily greet each other asking, "Have you eaten?" (*"Chi giro-le fan?"*) Foreigners who study the Chinese language sometimes comment upon the fact that the first phrases they are taught deal with eating and money:

"The rich man has food to eat, the poor one has none."

Now things are worse than ever. Shanghai swarms with beggars whom the Chinese call *yao fan* (literally, "food wanters"), many carrying dirty pails in which they

---

[26]My parents did protest strongly but I did visit him. He died without ever seeing his beloved country again. He was 24.

collect "edible" garbage. I have seen destitute Chinese remove spilled noodles from muddy streets, wash them in the filthy waters of the Whangpoo and eat them. In a course on nutrition at Aurora, the Jesuit father explained to us that the minimum quantity of food a coolie needs to be able to carry loads of 100 catty (133 pounds) a distance of 50 li (17 miles)—the usual labor demanded of him—is at least two catties of decent nourishment. Since he also has to feed his family there is no way his earnings can cover these lowest demands.

It really pains me to see how hard the Chinese try and how frugal they are. For example, the cloth shoes they wear are made by the woman of the household who buys a pair of soles to fit the largest feet in her home, usually the father's. Then cutting rags from old unusable garments she makes the tops. When the soles wear out around the edges, the woman cuts the shoes down to fit the next size of feet in the family. This goes on until the baby gets them or, if the woman had her feet bound in childhood and they are tiny, she is the last one to finally "inherit" the shoes.

In spite of all these efforts the number of beggars in Shanghai seems to be increasing constantly. Before Pearl Harbor, a White Russian policeman working for the French Municipal Council told me that there actually was a beggars union in our city headed by a powerful and despotic leader. It was he who distributed the huge army of crippled, maimed, blind, and other miserable dregs of humanity throughout Shanghai. My Russian friend explained that this "King of the Beggars" or his representative would arrive prior to a Chinese wedding or some important celebration to negotiate payment in return for which they would not molest guests by openly displaying their horrible wounds and wailing in loud voices. I believe the Japanese have put an end to such endeavors and all that is left for the beggars is to die from starvation and disease on our streets.

Well, the War does appear to near its end. Okinawa fell after terrible battles.[27] A friend of Mama's who had visited Okinawa before the War told us that the Okinawans hate the Japanese, whom they call *yamaton-chu*—"mainlanders." He said he had seen "volunteers" (mostly elderly men) who were forced by the Japanese to do backbreaking labor for them without any payment. Last night, the Filipino lady in our house came up to inform us that her friends had heard on the short-wave radio program that a "United Nations Charter" had been signed in San Francisco on June 26. Oh to live to see the end of this torment!

July 1945

Several days ago Papa visited the Restricted Area in Honkew to interview Dr. Storfer, publisher of a German language daily, *Die Gelbe Post* (*The Yellow Post*). Dr. Storfer is a psychologist who studied in Vienna under Professor Sigmund Freud. When Freud left Austria in 1938 shortly after the "Anschluss"—Nazi annexation—Dr. Storfer followed his example. In spite of feverish efforts, however, he was unable to make the necessary arrangements to escape like his mentor to England and decided to take advantage of the only other possible haven: Shanghai. Dr. Storfer is a great admirer of Sigmund Freud and is convinced that most of Freud's detractors are, perhaps unknown to themselves, anti-Semites.

Besides the *Gelbe Post* there are two other dailies in the ghetto, *The Shanghai Echo*[28] (written in German in spite of its English name) and the evening *8-Uhr Abendblatt* (*8 o'clock Evening Paper*). Dr. Storfer also showed Papa weekly and monthly periodicals written in German, English, Polish, Russian, and Yiddish. Some publications are multilingual like the Polish *Echo Szanghaiskje* (*Shanghai Echo*) and *Der Yiddischer Almanach* (*The Yiddish*

---

[27]Okinawa fell on June 21, 1945; 12,281 U.S. soldiers perished there, including the famed war correspondent, Ernie Pyle.

[28]Published continuously until 1949.

Almanac) written in Yiddish, English, Russian and German. Several professional publications include articles and notes in Chinese.

Today, as Papa sat at the dining room table preparing his notes and I leafed through samples of newspapers he had brought from Honkew, we commented on the way Jewish refugees pursue such outstanding cultural activities in spite of Japanese restrictions, the uncertainty of their future, and almost total lack of funds. According to Papa, this reflects Jewish idealism, courage, and never-ending hope.

Suddenly the wail of sirens rent the air, accompanied by the boom of explosions. U.S. planes must have entered Shanghai's air space undetected. Our house trembled, books fell off shelves, glass tinkled and cracked. By chance my mother and sister were also at home, thus we were spared great anxiety worrying about each other. Hardly had the all-clear sounded when the phone started ringing. A member of Papa's editorial board was calling to inform my father that bombs had fallen in the Honkew ghetto.[29]

"Gospodi Boje moi!" ("The Lord my God!"), Papa exclaimed." Haven't these miserable people suffered enough?" He pushed aside his glass of tea saying, "I have to leave. Maybe something can be done to help."

"Be careful!" Mama cried. "Don't start with those Japanese!"

Without replying Papa unlocked his bike and took off for some unknown destination while Mama, my sister, and I remained nervously at home waiting for his return. We are always concerned about his quick temper which could lead to dangerous consequences. It was hot, hot, hot. Shanghai summers are always hard to endure but this July seems worse than most with temperatures reaching 104 degrees. My hair, which I insist on keeping long, sticks to my nape and when I scribble notes my sweaty hands leave marks on the paper.

---

[29]The official casualty figures later obtained were 31 refugees killed, 200 seriously wounded, and 700 rendered homeless.

We listened idly to the radio. As usual, the Japanese claimed they had crippled American planes whose pilots "aim to kill and terrorize the civilian population." Hours later Papa returned looking grey and haggard. We hardly dared question him but after a while he muttered, "Things look bad, very bad. Several dozen refugees have been killed, hundreds wounded and rendered homeless. Many Chinese have also suffered great losses."

Late at night my friend Max called from Honkew.

"I'm all right," he reassured me. "Don't worry. The air-raid was very frightening but there was no panic. Emergency dispensaries were set up at once and refugee doctors took immediate care of all the wounded without discriminating between Jews and Chinese—even beggars!"

Max described how Jewish refugees are ripping the last of their treasured table and bed linens to make bandages and how Chinese help carry the wounded through rubble. They also offered to transport heavy loads to the clinics: cots, mattresses, buckets of water.

"Now we are all brothers!" Max cried with youthful enthusiasm.

When I repeated Max's words to the family, Papa brightened visibly.

"*Zamechatelno!*" ("Wonderful!") he repeated several times. "Hitler has not been able to destroy the Jewish spirit nor have centuries of repression killed the inherent goodness of the Chinese!"

Papa later confided to us a secret that has worried him for a long time: the Japanese military had concentrated across the street from the ghetto the largest ammunition and gasoline stores in Shanghai.[30]

Early next morning my parents' refugee friend, Jack, got in touch with them from the ghetto. He described

---

[30]Some say the Japanese thought these dumps would remain untouched by U.S. bombers because "American Jewry" would prevent the U.S. government from endangering the lives of Jewish refugees. We later found out that the U.S. objective in the July 17 bombing was a Japanese naval radio station that directed warships.

how he had been lacerated by glass shards during the air-raid and had bled profusely. Fortunately, his wounds are superficial. He had had, however, the dreadful experience of seeing two Chinese crushed to death by a collapsing building. Jack, like Max, is overwhelmed by the close cooperation between Chinese and Jews—one of the positive aspects of this calamity.

"You know how poor the Chinese in Honkew are," he said, "but still they brought food and even money to the emergency clinics to show their gratitude for the indiscriminate medical care given them."

At night Sidney visited us to share the latest news he had heard on the short-wave radio: thousands of leaflets had been dropped by U.S. planes over 11 Japanese cities. The Americans threatened that Japan would be subjected to unprecedented bombardment unless Allied terms of surrender were accepted. The British also report stories that the Japanese people are being warned by propagandists that handling the leaflets would "rot the hands of those who touch them and blind the eyes of those who read them!"[31]

One of today's English newspapers reprinted statements from Tokyo's *Mainichi* reflecting Japan's determination to fight to the end (probably dragging us with them into the abyss):

> The rise in unison of the military, the officials, and the people is the very factor that will call forth the miracle of the Nippon race. . . . Now is the very time for 100 million people, whether they be military servicemen, Government officials or civilians, to join a general march forfeiting all personal profit and desire for fame.

---

[31]This rumor was true. Isoko Hatano writes in his charming book, *Mother and Son:* "The country women hereabouts are terrified of the leaflets. . . . According to most people, they were not dropped for any benevolent reason. However magnanimous a man is, he is considered a traitor if he acts against the strategic needs of his country. And at the very least, if that man's act has been approved by the military, it means that it is to America's advantage."

The *Mainichi* harps again and again on the weaknesses of the "United States, the archenemy of Nippon." Among the points cited are "the decline of the American people's morale," "anti-war sentiment" (symbolized by the "heroic American flyer, Charles Lindbergh, who campaigned actively against President Roosevelt"), "stringency of the people's life on the home front," and "mounting American casualties." According to the Japanese press, their government's attitude towards the "enemy's offer of peace" is *mokusatsu*, apparently a difficult term to translate, but approximates "ignore."[32]

Events follow so rapidly that it is hard to digest them and our expectations, hopes, and fears zig-zag up and down. For me one good piece of news is that Pétain was tried for treason and condemned to death. I think he tragically misled the French people.[33] Within the past few years the world has changed completely and I feel the very foundation of my life collapsing in myriad pieces. Roosevelt, Hitler and Mussolini are dead. Churchill has not been re-elected. Only Stalin, strong and immutable as granite, survived. What does this forebode?

Postscript to July 1945

Years after the war I found among my father's papers the following list he had compiled of the many publications of the Jewish refugee community:

Unser Wort (*Our Word*): Yiddish magazine founded in 1940 by Polish refugees.

---

[32]Although the Japanese later claimed the expression *mokusatsu* implied there was room for negotiation, the Allies interpreted it as an outright rejection of their approach for peace.

[33]His sentence was later commuted to life imprisonment.

In Weg (On the Way): Yiddish magazine published by the Association of Jewish Writers and Journalists from Poland—only one issue published in November 1941.[34]

Das Wort (The Word): publication of the Agudat Israel religious group. The first issue in English and Yiddish appeared in 1941.

Der Yiddischer Almanach (The Yiddish Almanac): magazine of religious thought. Appeared throughout the War in Yiddish, English, Russian, and German.

Yiddische Stimme von Bait Mizrah (Jewish Voice from Mizrahi House): religious publication. One issue appeared in August 1942.[35]

Davar (The Word): clandestine German monthly published by Zionists from July to October 1943.

Die Gelbe Post (The Yellow Post): founded as a weekly in 1939. Became a daily German-language paper in 1940. Main theme: culture. Some political and local news. Considered one of the best cultural papers in Asia. Publisher and editor, Dr. A. J. Storfer.

Gemeindeblatt für die Jüdische Kultus-Gemeinde (Organ of the Jewish Cultural Community): German weekly published from September 14, 1939 to January 5, 1940.

Jüdische Nachrichtenblatt (Jewish News): the continuation of the Gemeindeblatt from 1940 to 1945.

The Jewish Voice: continuation of the *Nachrichtenblatt* from 1945 to 1946.

Journal of the Association of Central European Doctors: founded in 1940. Written in English and Chinese. Later renamed Shanghai Medical Journal.

---

[34] Another weekly magazine, *Unser Welt (Our World),* was published by the Association of Jewish Writers and Journalists from Poland after the War in 1946. It appeared weekly from January 25 to August 2.

[35] Was revived as a Yiddish and Russian monthly in 1946.

Medizinische Monatshefte (*Medical Monthly Reports*): German monthly published from October 1940 to March 1941.

Shanghai Jewish Chronicle: initially a weekly but later a daily morning paper renamed *The Shanghai Echo.* Editor: Ossie Lewin.[36]

The Shanghai Post: German weekly published from 1939 to 1940.

Schanghai Woche (*Shanghai Week*): first German language daily afternoon paper that appeared from 1939–1940.

8–Uhr Abendblatt der Schanghai Woche (*The 8 o'clock Evening Paper of the Shanghai Week*): continuation of *Schanghai Woche.*

Die Tribune (*The Tribune*): German weekly, 1940.

S.Z. Mittag der Schanghai Post (*Mid-Morning Paper of the Shanghai Post*): German daily published from 1939 to 1940.

Der Querschnitt (*The Cross-Section*): German weekly, published in 1939.

Der Mitarbeiter (*The Colleague*): German weekly, 1940 to 1941.

---

[36]*The Shanghai Echo* was published until the Communist victory in China's civil war in 1949. Its competitors claimed that Lewin had cooperated too closely with the Japanese, in spite of the fact that he had been briefly incarcerated in Bridge House. According to Herman Dicker's *Wanderers and Settlers in the Far East* (New York: Twayne, 1962), Lewin later wrote about his imprisonment: "We had to live in cells with 35 persons where we were forced to sit in a squatting position all day long without being permitted to lean against the wall, or to stretch our limbs or to talk. . . . The lice alone made life almost unbearable. Without exception, every prisoner found 60 to 70 lice on his body every day." Lewin contracted typhus in Bridge House but survived. He later published a German paper, *Almanach,* from 1946 to 1947.

Polish publication—name unknown: appeared on Pearl Harbor day, December 8, 1941; four pages in Yiddish, one in Polish.
Destroyed for fear of retribution by Japanese Occupation troops.

Die Laterne (The Lantern): appeared several times in 1941.

August 9, 1945

Is summer this year hotter than previously or has war eroded our stamina? Due to power shortages, electric fans remain motionless, their green blades gathering clammy grime. Mosquitoes and flies torment Shanghailanders since "Flit"—a popular insect killer—has long disappeared from the market. In the old days while people relaxed outside during elegant garden parties white-clad Chinese "boys" would walk unobtrusively among the guests, spraying the air around their feet. Long cool drinks would be served in chilled glasses. All this today but a memory of the past!

A disturbing article was reprinted this morning from the Tokyo *Mainichi:*

ATTACHED TO PARACHUTES
A small number of enemy B-29s penetrated into Hiroshima on August 6 shortly after 8 a.m. and dropped a number of explosive bombs, as a result of which a considerable number of houses in the city were destroyed and fire broke out at various places.
It seems the enemy dropped new-type bombs attached to parachutes which exploded in the air. Although details are still under investigation, their explosive power cannot be made light of.

In another statement contradicting the implied seriousness of the first report, the paper declared that Japan's war minister, General Korikechi Anami, estimated the damage to be only "fairly great." In spite of this rather laconic statement, news spread like wildfire in Shanghai that "Hiroshima melted!" Is our city to be next of the list?[37]

Hiroshima! In the summer of 1939, my mother, my sister and I made a stopover there on our way to a seaside resort. Since during our voyage from Shanghai we had suffered rough seas and debilitating seasickness, Mama decided not to board the train immediately but rather stay overnight in a hotel. The small lobby of our Japanese-style inn had a delicate wooden bridge spanning an artificial stream where goldfish swam and pebbles glistened. Maids in their blue-and-white summer cotton kimonos called *yukaka* soundlessly slid open paper-paned doors and served sweet leaf-shaped cakes on elegant lacquer plates. Through our room window we could admire a miniature garden representing a restful bamboo grove. Lovely! This is where one day I would spend my honeymoon, I decided, in this poetic, romantic, esthetic dwelling.

After a wash and a rest the three of us set out for a walk. Fortunately for my sister and me, Mama is as curious as we are to explore new places. In front of a colorful temple, we came across a group of women holding out white cotton bands of cloth and gently requesting passing ladies to sew a stitch in red thread. Their voices were soft murmurs and they bowed gracefully when their wish was fulfilled. Nobody refused them and neither did we. Later at the hotel an English-speaking gentleman explained to us that soldiers would wear these bands around their stomachs as a talisman against enemy bullets. In 1939 the "Special Undeclared War"—the Sino-Japanese Conflict—was going full blast in China and must surely have been the reason why my parents

---

[37]The news of the atomic bomb attack was published in Japan 48 hours after the event. In Shanghai, it officially reached us a day later, although rumors of a horrifying new weapon were already circulating. The Japanese soon began to refer to the mysterious atomic bomb as *pika-don: pika* referred to the blinding light and *don* to the sound of the blast. The nuclear bombing left 118,661 dead, 79,130 injured, and 3,677 missing.

decided we would be safer in Japan. According to the Japanese gentleman, the objective of the women near the temple was to collect a thousand stitches. He proudly said that no matter how inclement the weather, many women patiently spent days out in the streets in order to reach the desired number. The Japanese name for this action was *sen-nin-bari* (literally, "a thousand people needles."[38]

At the railway station the following day a more ominous scene greeted us. Boxes containing ashes of dead soldiers were ceremoniously handed to their waiting families. Nevertheless, my sister's and my spirits were not dampened: we anticipated a lazy summer among pine trees, on sandy beaches, breathing silky air. We were not disappointed.

Two months later, bronzed by the sun and strengthened by the ocean, we were homeward bound on a French Messageries Maritime liner—*Le Chenonceaux*—when, on the second day at sea, a solemn and hushed gathering assembled before an outsized bulletin board placed on a high tripod in the main lounge. I craned my head above the crowd. Huge letters screamed the news: "WAR IN EUROPE."

It was September 3, 1939. Hostilities would spread all over the world, destroy colonial power, and strangle Shanghai. At that time, however, in spite of the concern clearly apparent on the faces of adults, my sister, me, and a jolly group of youngsters with whom we had become friends glanced at each other with excited anticipation. War!

Now all this seems part of a distant, distant past. War is ugly, humiliating, repulsive. No glory, no romance, nothing but meaningless maiming, killing, and annihilation. Our chances of survival seem dimmer and dimmer.

Tonight the radio declared that Russia is in a state of war with Japan! "Coming in for the kill," Papa said. Even the announcer who usually sounds so glib and

---

[38]Saburo Sakai in his *Samurai* (New York: Twayne, 1958) writes: "Actually few Japanese airmen held faith in the charm. . . .Of course I would wear it, and I wrapped it about my mid-section."

confident appeared shaken as he tried to control the tremble in his voice.[39]

For a short time in the early morning the Union Jack was seen fluttering on the pole of the formerly British-owned tramways offices across the Soochow creek. The Stars and Stripes and Soviet flags were hoisted over the general hospital. Soon after, these were seen being removed by Japanese soldiers.The Soviet flag was hauled down from the Soviet Consulate.

August 10, 1945

Another _pika-don_, this time in Nagasaki.[40] The radio claims that the damage is "not as serious" as in Hiroshima in spite of the fact that Japan downplayed the effect of the first new bomb. Puzzling rumors circulate: one should wear white clothing because in Hiroshima those in black were more seriously injured! As panic mounts, prices get steeper and steeper. Meat costs today $22,000 a pound and one egg $1,000.

Here we are at the very edge of long desired Allied total victory and my reaction is depression! Sat on the edge of my bed and scribbled "My Last Will and Testament." Since I have nothing material to leave, I wrote an emotional statement meant to console my family—should they survive. In spite of efforts to set down my feelings simply and honestly, my words sounded fake and insincere. Drivel! I turned to read the newspaper and clipped an item about Pétain's trial, in-

---

[39] According to John Toland, _The Rising Sun_ (New York: Random House, 1970), Molotov read to Ambassador Sato in Moscow a declaration that stated in part: "Taking into account the refusal of Japan to capitulate, the Allies approached the Soviet Government with a proposal to join the war against Japanese aggression and thus shorten the duration of the war, reduce the number of casualties and contribute toward the speedy restoration of peace. . . . The Soviet Government considers that this policy is the only means to bring peace nearer, to free the people from further sacrifice and suffering. . . . In view of the above, the Soviet Government declares that from tomorrow, that is from August 9, the Soviet Union will consider herself in a state of war against Japan."

[40] 39,000 killed, 25,000 injured.

tending to save it between the pages of my diary where I keep articles that interest me. Among them is one dating back to October 3, 1940 on the Vichy government's despicable "Jewish Laws." Article 1 stated:

"In accordance with the present law a person is considered to be a Jew if he has three grandparents of this race, or if two of his grandparents and his spouse are Jews."

The laws proceeded to enumerate in detail all government jobs forbidden to Jews, all professions they could no longer exercise (including any function remotely connected with journalism, radio, or movies). The final article stated "The present law is applicable to Algeria, to the colonies, to protectorates and to territories under French mandate." Pétain had also ordered a census of persons falling in the newly defined category of Jews. How hurtful all this is to me—a young romanticist who so admired the ideals of the French Revolution!

Today I sheepishly slipped "My Last Will and Testament" into my latest diary—an outdated memorandum book from Papa's pre-War British company.

August 11, 1945

The phone rang. Volodia, a friend of Papa's, shouted joyously in my ear:

"*Mir! Mir!*" ("Peace! Peace!")

Other calls followed. People spoke almost incoherently, delirious with relief. Jack managed to reach us from Honkew, the Restricted Area, to tell us the latest news: Jewish refugees were tearing down various ghetto signs, unmolested by Japanese guards. At night my sister and I pulled the blackout curtains apart, shrieking excitedly as we saw neighbors' windows light up for the first time in many years. In the streets people broke the curfew, strolling, speaking in loud voices (have we been whispering meekly since Pearl Harbor?) and smoking. Their cigaret tips moved like fireflies—smoking outside after nightfall had been forbidden by the Japanese in or-

der to "confuse enemy bombers" in total darkness.
Mama opened two cans of pineapple she had been keeping for a special celebration and Papa acted with somewhat restrained joviality, stressing that as yet no official
peace declaration had been publicly announced. When
we angrily accused him of undue pessimism, Papa admitted that there was indeed ground for hope because of
clear Allied military superiority. It appears that the two
pika-don in Hiroshima and Nagasaki had been totally
destructive and thick clouds of dust still blanket the
ruins of both cities. While we were talking, the Filipino
tenant in our house came up to inform us that Allied
radio stations were repeatedly broadcasting messages to
the Japanese urging them to surrender before complete
annihilation.

It is certain that the situation, from Japan's point of
view, is extremely critical, but as our first euphoria
evaporated, doubts and incertitude enveloped us once
again. Later at night the local radio reported the arrest of
six Soviet citizens by the Japanese for reasons not given.
This news was followed by a Domei report from Tokyo,
one sentence of which I managed to scribble verbatim:

"The proposal of the Japanese government to the
Soviet Union on the mediation in the War in the Far
East loses basis . . ."

What does this mean? In case of total defeat will the
Japanese seek revenge on helpless civilians? Will
Shanghailanders be smothered in a final outburst of vi-
olence?[41]

August 12, 1945

The newspaper this morning published War Minister
Anami's declaration, which fired our smoldering fears:

The Soviet Union has finally taken up arms against this
Empire. Try as she may to disguise the facts by rhetoric,
her aspirations to conquer and dominate Greater East

---

[41]This was Shanghailanders' first inkling that Japan had sought
Russia's good offices in mediating peace.

Asia are obvious. In the face of this reality we shall waste no words. The only thing for us to do is to fight doggedly to the end this holy War and for the defense of our divine land. It is our firm belief that though it may mean chewing grass, eating dirt, and sleeping in the field, a resolute fight will surely reveal a way out of a desperate situation . . .

The heat is oppressive. It permeates the walls of our house and dulls our emotions.

"Chewing grass, eating dirt, chewing grass . . ." These words importune my mind in a pernicious refrain. Undressed, uncombed, I sprawl on my bed attempting to calm myself by reading a childhood favorite—Dickens' *David Copperfield*—but I cannot concentrate. Are we to be crushed after all like helpless, meaningless bugs? Will Japanese officers ever accept defeat? Will they not fight to the death to "appease the souls" of those already killed? Everyone says the next *pika-don* will be dropped over Tokyo![42]

Japanese gendarmes are burning documents in huge bonfires outside the infamous Bridge House, probably in order to destroy evidence of the horrors they had inflicted. Sidney phoned to say that gendarmes wearing plain khaki uniforms had been seen leaving in army trucks. They had removed all their Kempeitai insignia.

August 16, 1945

Stunned Shanghailanders listened in silence to rebroadcasts of the Japanese emperor's speech delivered the previous day in Tokyo. N.H.K. (Japanese National Radio Broadcasting Station) had announced that "His Majesty the Emperor" would "read his rescript to the people of Japan." After the strains of the "Kimigayo" (Japanese national anthem), the Emperor's "good and loyal subjects" heard for the first time the Voice of the Crane [the imperial symbol]. The message was clear—an admission of Japan's defeat on the highest level:

---

[42] Admiral Onishi offered to sacrifice 20 million Japanese in Kamikaze attacks. Foreign Minister Togo rejected this offer.

After pondering deeply the general trends of the world and the actual condition in our Empire today, We have decided to effect a settlement of the present situation by resorting to an extraordinary measure . . . We have resolved to pave the way for a grand peace for all the generations to come by enduring the unendurable and suffering what is unsufferable.[43]

All local radio stations in Shanghai aired a replay of the original broadcast by the emperor, spoken in what sounded to me like a high-pitched monotone. This was followed by an official English translation which, contrary to the usual gibberish, was not only grammatically correct but elegantly phrased. I wonder if the rescript has been also broadcast in Chinese?

The emperor mentioned "a new and most cruel bomb," stressing the obligation to avoid "an ultimate collapse and obliteration of the Japanese nation" and "the total extinction of human civilization . . ."

An English version of a Tokyo *Mainichi* article appeared in today's newspaper:

Upon learning of the Imperial Rescript, we the subjects, are filled with awe and cannot help weeping in consideration of our responsibility for causing His Majesty such grave concern. We have no words to express our apologies . . .

I imagine millions of Japanese bowing to their emperor's voice in front of their radio sets mesmerized by his words, subdued by the depth of their national calamity.

After the news my sister and I excitedly put on our favorite red dresses trimmed with delicate lace and went out to investigate what was happening on our main thoroughfare, Avenue Joffre. Hundreds of Shanghailanders had had the same idea and the large

---

[43]At this point Japan was on the brink of collapse: 3 million Japanese dead (both inside and outside of Japan); 3.1 million homeless. The chaos continued for years. In 1946 there were still 10 million unemployed in Japan.

street was crowded with ecstatically happy, rowdy people. Strangers smiled at each other, shook hands, hugged, laughed. Victory for the Allies! Shanghai had survived!

Met Gleb and several of his friends, who described how they had witnessed an hour earlier the public reading of the Imperial Rescript. A small group of Japanese soldiers had prostrated themselves in rigid immobility on the hot asphalt after a sharp command from an officer mounted on a Mongolian pony. The officer then unrolled a large paper scroll and declaimed its contents in a brusk, unnatural voice, like a wooden puppet endowed with speech.

Tonight all street lights are on, firecrackers spit and crackle. After years of uncertainty and terror Shanghailanders celebrate a new concept: PEACE!

September 2, 1945

Today formal surrender ceremonies took place off Tokyo Bay aboard the powerful U.S. warship, the USS *Missouri*. Japanese Foreign Minister Shigemitsu and Chief of the Imperial Staff General Umezu signed their names on the "Instrument of Surrender" in the presence of U.S. General Douglas MacArthur. The American flag was raised over the U.S. Embassy—the very same flag that had graced the U.S. capitol on the day of the infamous Pearl Harbor attack! American soldiers have entered Tokyo and Japanese citizens are carefully reading instructions issued by the police regarding behavior towards U.S. troops.[44]

A new era is dawning.

_____

[44]These instuctions were: (1) Avoid personal contact as much as possible. (2) Should an American speak to you, answer calmly, do not escape. (3) Women should dress modestly and not respond when accosted. (4). Women should avoid going out alone as much as possible, especially at night.

Postscript to August 1945

The full text of the Imperial Rescript reads as follows:

TO OUR GOOD AND LOYAL SUBJECTS;
After pondering deeply the general trends of the world and the actual conditions in our Empire today, We have decided to effect a settlement of the present situation by resorting to an extraordinary measure.

We have ordered Our Government to communicate to the Government of the United States, Great Britain, China and the Soviet Union that Our Empire accepts the provisions of their Joint Declaration.

To strive for the common prosperity and happiness of all nations as well as the security and well-being of Our subjects is the solemn obligation which has been handed down by Our Imperial Ancestors and which lies close to Our heart.

Indeed, We declared war on America and Britain out of our sincere desire to ensure Japan's self-preservation and the stabilization of East Asia, it being far from Our thought either to infringe upon the sovereignty of other nations or to embark upon territorial aggrandizement.

But now the war has lasted for nearly four years. Despite the best that has been done by everyone—the gallant fighting of the military and naval forces, the diligence and assiduity of Our servants of the State, and the devoted service of Our one hundred million people— the war situation has developed not necessarily to Japan's advantage, while the general trends of the world have all turned against her interest.

Moreover, the enemy has begun to employ a new and most cruel bomb, the power of which to do damage is, indeed, incalculable, taking the toll of many innocent lives. Should We continue to fight, not only would it result in ultimate collapse and obliteration of the Japanese nation, but also it would lead to the total extinction of human civilization.

Such being the case, how are We to save the millions of Our subjects, or to atone Ourselves before the hallowed spirits of Our Imperial Ancestors? This is the reason why We have ordered the acceptance of the provisions of the Joint Declaration of the Powers.

We cannot but express the deepest sense of regret to Our Allied nations of East Asia, who have consistently cooperated with the Empire towards the emancipation of Asia.

The thought of those officers and men as well as others who have fallen in the fields of battle, those who died at their posts of duty, or those who met with untimely death and all their bereaved families, pains Our heart night and day.

The welfare of the wounded and the war-sufferers, and of those who have lost their homes and livelihood, are the objects of Our profound solicitude.

The hardships and sufferings to which Our nation is to be subjected hereafter will be certainly great. We are keenly aware of the inmost feelings of all of you, Our subjects. However, it is according to the dictates of time and fate that We have resolved to pave the way for a grand peace for all the generations to come by enduring the unendurable and suffering what is unsufferable.

Having been able to safeguard and maintain the structure of the Imperial State, We are always with you, Our good and loyal subjects, relying on your sincerity and integrity.

Beware most strictly of any outbursts of emotion which may engender needless complications, or any fraternal contention and strife that may create confusion, lead you astray and cause you to lose the confidence of the world.

Let the entire nation continue as one family from generation to generation, ever firm in its faith in the imperishability of its sacred land, and mindful of its heavy burden of responsibility and of the long road before it.

Unite your total strength, to be devoted to construction for the future. Cultivate the ways of rectitude, foster nobility of spirit, and work with resolution—so that you may enhance the innate glory of the Imperial State and keep pace with the progress of the world.[45]

---

[45]Official translation of the Imperial Rescript from *Japan's Longest Day*. Compiled by the Pacific war Research Society (Tokyo and Palo Alto, Calif.: Kodansha International, 1968).

Epilogue

Three days after the publication of the Imperial Rescript, Mama and I rode our bicycles to the Lunghwa Camp where some Dutch friends of ours had been interned by the Japanese for the past several years.[46] The camp, situated in the vicinity of a famous pagoda, looked from afar like a pleasant vacation site. As one came nearer, however, the impression changed entirely: the grounds were unkempt and overgrown, the buildings dilapidated. Inside, families were grouped in sections of rooms separated by sheets. In the corridors shabby trunks and old carton boxes were piled neatly along the walls. We soon found our friends—once prosperous traders—who rushed towards us with open arms. How they had changed! The dark suntan acquired while washing clothes outside in canals and digging vegetable gardens did little to hide their haggard, lined cheeks. Their clothes looked ragged even to us, who had forgotten the meaning of true elegance because of wartime privations. They told us about freezing in winter (the mother of the family had once fainted from cold), starving on *congee* (a very watery rice), and doing backbreaking labor. To our embarrassment they admired our rather worn clothing and "healthy" looks! All they wanted was to forget the War and get out of the camp.

On the following day my father, sister and I took a launch across the Woosung River to Pootung to visit another internment camp where Papa's former English boss had been imprisoned by the Japanese. In comparison, Lunghwa Camp did indeed seem like a resort. The building where Papa's superior lived was once a godown (warehouse) that now housed only bachelors—over

---

[46]Internees remained in camps for some time after the War, until the necessary arrangements for lodging could be made for them.

1,000 men. Apparently some families in the camp were lodged separately. Whereas in Lunghwa an attempt at order had been obvious, in Pootung confusion and untidiness met the eye: unmade beds, squashed cartons, pots and pans. There were no signs of happiness, only apathy, negligence and dirt. The Englishman was totally unrecognizable. Once an impeccably dressed, rather haughty gentleman, he now appeared shrunken, wore torn stained shorts and . . . worst of all . . . had lost most of his teeth!

After this shocking experience, the third camp we later visited—Chapei—was a relief. The buildings had well withstood the War. The internees had organized themselves in work teams, cultivated vegetable plots of tomatoes, cucumbers, and pumpkins, raised goats and ducks and enjoyed running water. However, they too had lost tens of pounds in weight and their facial expressions were stamped with the undefinable "camp mark" that set them apart from other Shanghailanders who had remained free.

In the once Restricted Area, Jewish refugees were now celebrating the miracle of having survived of both Nazism and Japanese Occupation. As the gates of the ghetto were thrown open, my friends and I rode the tram to Honkew to rejoice in Allied victory. What a jolly time we had at spontaneously organized dances, twisting and turning to fast music—an almost primitive salute to rebirth and freedom!

In September the first uniformed Americans appeared on the streets of Shanghai. So tall, so handsome, so vivid! Shanghailanders stared with awe at their healthy color, their ready smiles, their spotless, crisp uniforms. Their generosity was overwhelming. They regaled us with chocolates, canned goods, Coca-Cola (a drink tasting at first like medicine to us, but for which we quickly acquired an unquenchable thirst!) Chinese urchins followed them like swarms of bees, begging for money and pleading, "No Papa, no Mama, no whiskey soda."

Everyone was in love—the fun-starved girls (and many a married woman!) of Shanghai and the homesick young Americans! We learned a new vocabulary:"fresh" for the English "cheeky," GI for soldier, "swabee" for sailor, "brass" for officer, "chicken" for colonel.

We wondered at the powerful ugly car we mistakenly called "peep" only to learn the correct word was "jeep"! Girls were no longer surprised when their U.S. boyfriends told them, "Come on chicken, grab a wing," or "Now you're cooking on gas!" or made rude remarks such as, "It must be jelly 'cause jam don't shake like that!" It seemed as if all Shanghailanders, foreigners and Chinese, wanted to emigrate to the United States but the "golden land" was out of immediate reach because of affidavits and quotas.

Passport-bearing foreigners began to leave Shanghai by the thousands, repatriated by their governments to their home countries. Others—the stateless—were once again caught in a tightly closing trap. World War II was over but there was no real peace in China. The communists were pushing forward in the civil war and the future of Shanghai became once again uncertain.

For Jews, history had changed forever. On May 14, 1948 the British Mandate for Palestine ended and the new Jewish State of Israel was proclaimed. Our amah, Ah Kwei, and other Chinese asked in puzzlement, "Jewman now have countlee (country)?" Trucks rolled towards air and river ports bearing huge cases marked "Lydda" and "Haifa." Smart Chinese shopkeepers, having discovered Israel has a hot climate, displayed swimsuits, straw hats, shorts and sandals in the windows of their stores.

On Christmas Eve of 1948 an old Liberty ship, the *Wooster Victory* sailed with 924 Jews around Africa's Cape to Italy and Haifa. The voyage lasted 54 days. Overcrowded four-engine charter planes started taking off for Lydda.

At the beginning of April 1949 my parents, my sister, and I left Shanghai forever. At the airport outside Tel

Aviv we smelled for the first time the enchanting aroma of orange blossoms in bloom.

Not all the foreigners had been able to leave Shanghai when on Friday, April 27, the Chinese Communist Army entered the city. Khaki-clad soldiers, some barefoot, some wearing cotton shoes, all bearing rather old-fashioned rifles, marched single file on both sides of the streets close to buildings without disturbing the traffic. Shanghailanders offered them food, a drink of water, cigarets. They courteously refused. Radio stations interrupted musical programs at regular intervals to reassure the population: "The People's Army will take nothing from you, not even a needle!"

Yes, "old" Shanghai was gone forever. As the French say, *"Un point c'est tout!* ("A full stop—that's all!")

Index

Abbot Chao-Kung. See Trebitsch-Lincoln, Ignacz
Adusio, Walter, 177n
Ah Kwei, 57–58, 110
Ai T'ien, 22
Alcott, Carroll, 110, 139–43, 173n
Aleichem, Sholem, 5
Algiers, 40
Alexander II Czar, 129
Allan, Norwood, 142n
Allied Powers, x, 7, 31, 106, 151, 152, 169, 174, 180, 197n
Almanach, 193n
American Episcopal Church, 43n
American Red Cross, 76
American School, 170
American Women's Club of China, 102
Americans, 25, 31, 190, 207
Amerika-maru, 109
Amur River, 147
Anglican Church, 68
Anna Stepanovna, 128–29
Anschluss, 19, 187
Anti-Semitism (*see also* pogroms, Nazis, Fascists): 8–9, 17–18, 39, 82–84, 93, 115–119, 126, 130–31, 137–38, 174–75, 198
Anzio, 106n
Ashkenazi synagogues, 8, 39
Ashkenazi, Rabbi Meir, 37–40
Ashkenazis (*see also* Jewish Community): 37–38, 64, 67
Association of European Doctors, 136
Association of Jewish Writers and Journalists from Poland, 192n
Astor House Hotel, 141
Atomic bomb, 194, 195n, 197, 199
Australia, 40
Austria, 17
Avenue Dubail, 23
Avenue Foch, 81
Avenue Joffre, 11, 50, 81, 105, 163, 180, 184

Avenue Pétain, 81
Axis Powers, 51, 92, 109, 142

B-29s, 127, 150, 151n, 177–78, 194
Baghdad, 64
Bagrazian clan, 164
Baikal Road Cemetery, 38
Bakerite Bread Company, 140
"Balalaika" (restaurant), 61
Bank of China, 101
Balfour Declaration, 107
Bank of England, 26
Barcelona Bar, 183
Basques, 144, 184
Bastille Day, 81
Bataan, 52n
Bengal, 96
Berlin, 51, 130, 177
Bet Aharon, 158–59
Binyanei Hauma, 8n
Bishop Ioann, 177
Bitker, J., 56
Blinchevsky, Fira, 50, 102, 103, 104
"Blood Alley," 173
"Blueberry Hill," 77
"Blue Danube Waltz," 19
Bolsheviks, 60, 118, 147, 177
Bombay, 64–65
Bombay Cotton Exchange, 65
Bombay Jewish Community, 64
Bose, Subhas Chandra, 92
Braun, Eva, 177n
Breuverie, Père de, 24, 166
Bridge House, 113, 119n, 142n, 165, 193n, 200
Britain, 3, 4, 7, 26, 31, 61–62, 68, 86, 101, 120–22
British Army Band, 77
British, 68, 80, 86, 97
British Commonwealth, 66
British Settlement, 80–81
Buddhism, 84–87, 160
Bund, 69–70, 101–102
Burma, 40, 92, 162
Bushido, 133

Canada, 47–48
Canton, 96
Canton Road, 68
Caruso, Enrique, 164
Cathay Hotel, 102
Cathedral Church, 79
Central China Daily News, 142
Central Reserve Bank, 4
Chapei Camp, 29n, 177n,198
Chaliapin, Fedor Ivanovich, 164–65
Chambon, Vice-Consul, 116–18
Chang Ching-hui, 92
Chartered Bank, 69
Chase Manhattan Bank, 17
Chiang Kai-shek, 93n
Chicago, 30
Chi Cho-wei, 160
China; Chinese (*see also* Chinese Revolution, Extraterritoriality, Open Ports, Opium, Rickshaws, Taiping Rebellion): Christianity and, 22–23; colonialism in, x–xv, 3, 4, communists in, 207–208; Einstein and, 43; Japanese and, 51, 57, 103–4; Jews and, 47–48, 189–90; opium and, ix, 95–98; poverty of, 4, 21, 90; prejudice against, 4, 12, 68; 77–78, 104; railroads in, 8, 147; skills of, 8, 169–70; Silas Hardoon and, 159–60
China Defence League, 49n
China Famine Relief Work Project, 76
China Nights (Shaw), 142n
China Press, 139
China to Me (Hahn), 11n
China Weekly Review, 142n
Chinese Eastern Railroad, 8, 9, 147
Chinese Revolution, 48–49, 84
Chinese Rites Controversy, 23
Chinese School of Hygiene, 43n
Chita, 146
Christian Science Monitor, 142n
Christianity, 22, 85, 121n, 160

Chunking, 36
Churchill, Sir Winston, 83n, 131, 191
Ciano, Count Galeazzo, 72
Ciano, Edda. *See* Mussolini, Edda
Cimetière des Sours, 23
Coca-Cola, 206
Cohen, Morris ("Two Gun"), 47–50, 108
Collège Municipal Français. *See* French Municipal College
Cologne, 169
Colonial Powers (*see also* Extraterritoriality): 61, 88, 120
Columbia American Club, 12
Communists, 34, 116, 117, 147, 178, 200
Compradores, 70–71
Comptoir d'Escompte, 101
Confucius, 22
Conservatoire de Musique (Paris), 115
Constani, Celso, 23
Coolies, 109–11, 186
Co-Prosperity Sphere, 4, 21, 36, 92
Corneille, Pierre, 80
Corregidor, 52, 52n
Cossacks, 60–61
Coward, Noel (*Private Lives*), 102

Dairen, 147
Davar, 192
De Gaulle, Charles, 3, 82
Denikine, 39
Dicker, Herman (*Wanderers and Settlers*), 193n
Dietrich, Marlene, ix, 164
Domei News Agency, 51–52, 84, 87, 120, 126, 191
Doolittle, General James, 113n
Doumer Cinema, 51
Dreyfus Case, 31

East China Institute of Politics and Law, 43n
Echo Szanghaiskje, 187
Educational Aid Society, 14
Edward VIII, King, 104

Egeberg, Jan, 140
8-Uhr Abendblatt, 187, 193
Ein Kerem, 124n
Einstein, Albert, 42–43
"El Ha Ka" (Literaturni Hudojestveni Krujek), 166–69
English Shanghai Public School, 24, 121
Eritrea, 140
Eurasians, 12
"Ever Victorious Army," 124
Evzeroff, 8n
Extraterritoriality, x –xii, 3, 8–9, 97
Extraterritoriality in China (Fishel), x
Ezra, Nissim Benjamin, 107–8

Fairbanks, Douglas, 43
Fang Hsien, 57
Far Eastern Cossack Corps, 60
Fascists, 17, 141 (White Russian), 9, 115–117
Fest der Völker, 51
Fifty Years of Light and Dark, 178 n
Filipinos, 52, 74–75, 122
Fishel, Wesley R., (*Extraterritoriality in China*), x
Flynn, Errol, 139
Fockler, Robert, 138
Footbinding, 56–57
Formosa (Taiwan), 30, 52–53
Fosie, Sergeant, 125
France, French, 3, 31, 40, 80–83, 89, 112, 116, 120, 122
Franco, Francisco, 144
Fredet, Jean (*Histoire de la Concession Française*) 112 n
Free French Forces. 3
Free French Government, 41
French Army Band, 81, 83
French Concession, xvi, 9, 11, 18, 23, 39, 41, 80–82, 89, 142 148, 159, 166
French Municipal College, 24, 77, 143
"French" Park. *See* Koukaza
French Revolution, 198

Fresno, 40
Freud, Sigmund, 187
Fuchs, Walter, 85
Fugu Plan (Tokayer), 38n

Gallarta, 144
Garden Bridge, 103–104, 134
Gelbe Post, 136 n, 180, 187
Germans, Germany, 3, 17, 20, 21, 55, 109, 137, 180, 181
Ghoya ("King of the Jews"), 58, 181–83
Ginsbourg, Anna, 85–86
Gleboff, General T. L., 60
Globe, Reverend, 111
Goebbels, Josef, 175 n
Gold Medal of Honor, 83–84
Gordon Road, 120
Gordon, Charles George, 123–24
Gould, Randall, 142n
Governesses, 127–29
Graduate Cadres Institute of Health, 43n
Grand Theatre, 12, 166
Greater East Asia Declaration, 93n
Guadalcanal, 31, 132
Gypsy Baron, 136

Hagakure, 145
Hahn, Emily, 11–12
Haifa, 207
Haile Selassie, 141
Haimovich, 8
Hamilton House, 79
Harbin, 8, 9, 94, 114–118, 147
Harbin Jewish Community, 117–18
Hardoon Estate, 155
Hardoon, Liza (Mrs. Silas), 82, 84, 155–57
Hardoon, Philip, 151
Hardoon Road, 155
Hardoon, Silas, 156–61
Hart Road, 120
Hart, Robert, 124–25
Hatano, Ichiro and Isoko (*Mother and Son*), 181n , 190n
"Hava Ox,"174

Havas, 150
Hawaii, 34
Hayim, Ellis, 56
Healy, Elroy, 142
Hebrew University, 160
Heime, 18
Hernault, Père, 59, 151
Hevra Kadisha, 161
Hevrot kadisha, 38
Hirohito,Emperor, 16, 33, 200–204
Hiroshima, 32 n, 194–95, 197, 199
Hiroshima University, 31n
Histoire de la Concession Française, 112n
Hitler, Adolf, 3, 5, 14, 36, 53, 72, 131, 137 n, 167, 177, 189, 191
Holland, 26
Holocaust, 54n
Holy Land, 8
Hongkong, 27, 47, 49 n
Hongkong & Shanghai Bank, 69, 101
Honkew ghetto, 133–37, 171, 187
Honololu, 34
Huang Zong-Yang, 157 n
Hwan min wan pao, 136n

Ibarruri, Dolores, 144
Imperial Palace, 34
Imperial Rescript, 200–204,
In Search of Old Shanghai (Pan Ling), 173 n
In Weg, 192
India, 66
Indochina, 40, 82 n
Inokuchi, 31, 32n
Inquisition, 26, 115
International Settlement, xiv, 9, 30n, 37, 41, 53, 77–78, 80–81, 89, 110n, 111, 120, 130n, 147 155, 159, 171, 181
Iraqis, 3, 141
Islam, 160
Island Within, 6
Israel, 10n, 207
Israel's Messenger, 107–108
Iwo Jima, 165
Izumo Maru, 103

Jaca, 32 n
Japan, Japanese (*see also* Hiroshima, Tokyo, Japanese military): 18, 30, 31–32, 36, 40, 42, 57, 74, 91–92, 94, 106, 119, 127, 131, 140, 172, 174, 177, 190–91, 195–97, 198–206 passim
Japanese Imperial Family, 36
Japanese military. *See also* Bridge House, Jewish refugees, Kempetai; 3–4, 9, 28, 30, 42–43, 49, 55, 73, 77, 90, 93–94, 103, 106, 109–10, 117, 140–42, 145, 150–52, 165, 171–72, 177–78; Chinese and, 77–78, 130–104, 109–10, 186; Filipinos and, 75; Jews and, 39, 53–54, 119, 130–31; prisons of, 52, 113–15; propaganda of, 40–41, 51–52, 75, 92, 125–26, 130–31, 143, 151, 189, 190–91
Japan's Longest Day, 204n
Jello, 110n
Jerusalem, 161
Jesuits, 21–23, 30, 59
Jewish Book Publication Society, 5–7
Jewish Cemetery, 157
Jewish Club, 37, 166
Jewish Community (Ashkenazi), 6, 9–10, 37, 38–39, 53–56 passim; 67, 113–16, 119, 158
Jewish Defense League, 165
Jewish Hospital, 41
Jewish Kitchen Fund, 135
Jewish quota, 60
Jewish refugees,xiii, 6–7, 14, 17–19, 67, 93n, 133–37, 182–83, 182 n,187–94, 205–206; Einstein and, 42–43; German, 15, 137, 181; internment of, 53–56, 58–59; 133–35; Latvian, 6; Lithuanian, 6, 159; Polish, 6, 15; 59; publications of, 136, 187–88, 190–94; Russian, 9, 38–39, 59–60; U.S. Jewish aid to 18
Jewish Voice, 192

Jews (*see also* Anti-Semitism, Ashkenazi, pogrom, Sephardi; 3–10 passim; 13–14, 17, 47, 82–83, 89, 92–93, 107–108, 130–32, 159, 173–74, 198; Chinese, 22; Indian (*see* Bombay Jewish Community); in Japan, 56 n; Iraqi, 26, 156; Middle Eastern, 64–66, 64 n, 158; Orthodox, 111; Portuguese, 28; Russian, xiii, 8–10, 38–39, 59–60, 147–48; U.S., 18

Journal of the Association of Central European Doctors, 192

Judaism, 15, 39, 160

"Judocommunism," 115

Jüdische Gemeinde, 135–36

Jüdische Nachrichtenblatt, 192

Kadima, 166

Kadoorie, Eleazar, (Elly), 13, 26–29, 103

Kadoorie, Horace, 24–29

Kadoorie, Laura. *See* Mocatta, Laura

Kadoorie, Lord Lawrence, 26 n

Kaifeng, 22

Kaiser Wilhelm Schule, 3

Kamikaze, 145, 152

Karatsu, 20

Kaspe, Joseph, 115–18

Kaspe, Simon, 115–18

Kaufman, Dr. Abraham, 55, 117

"Kavkaz," 61

Keio University, 31

Kempeitai (Japanese Military Police), 34 n, 115, 192

"Kimigayo," 200

King Albert Apartments, 50

Koran, 160

Korea, 30, 117

Korikechi Anami, General, 194

Koukaza, 18, 121, 151

Kriger, Abraham (author's grandfather), 94, 94 n

Kriger, Katherine ("Mama Katia") (author's grandmother), 94, 162

Kriger, Simon (author's uncle),
162

Kristallnacht, 17, 137

Kublai Khan, 145

Kyushu, 127

Ladies' Auxiliary Committee, 25

Lake Baikal, 146

Lampe, David (*Trebitsch-Lincoln*), 84 n

Laterne, 194

Laurel, Dr. José P., 92

League of Nations, 108

League of Truth. *See* Ligue de la Verité

Lenin, Nicolai, 115

Lewin, Ossie, 193

Lewisohn, Ludwig, 6

Life, 133

Life and Death in Shanghai (Nien Cheng), xi

Ligue de la Vérité, 87

Lindbergh, Charles, 191

"Lisa Mosquito," 174

Literaturni Hudojestveni Krujek ("El Ha Ka"), 167–68

London, 26, 27, 47, 49 n, 130

Lubavicher Hassid, 37

Lunghwa Camp, 205–206

Luzon, 162

Ma Kun. *See* Cohen, Morris

MacArthur, General Douglas, 52 n, 202

Madrid, 144 n

Mainichi, 92, 93, 190, 194

Malaya, 40

Manchu dynasty, 88, 57, 121 n,

Manchukuo, 9

Manchuria, 8–9, 30, 40

Manila, 60, 74

Marble Hall, 25–28

Maritime Customs Service, 69, 124

Marseillaise, 81

Maxwell House Coffee, 140

Maybon, Ch. B. (*Histoire de la Concession Française*), 112 n

Medizinische Monatshefte, 193

Mei Lian Fen, 165

Memoirs of a Sportsman (Turgenev), 129
Menace of Japan (O'Conroy), 31
Menard, 112
Mercantile Bank, 101
Middle East, 65
Military Archives (Tel Aviv), 55
Mills, Hal P., 142 n
Mitarbeiter, 193
Mocatta & Goldsmid Ltd., 26
Mocatta, Laura, 26–27
Moderne, 116
Mohawk Road, 66
Molotov, V. M. 197 n
Moneychangers, 148–49
Mother and Son (Hatano), 181 n, 190 n
Moy, Herbert, 138, 175
"Mr. Mills,"12
Mukden, 147
Munch, Edvard, 42 n
Museum Road Synagogue, 77
Mussolini, Benito, 72, 141, 177, 191
Mussolini, Edda (Ciano), 72–73
My Truth (Edda Mussolini), 72 n
My Twenty-Five Years in China (Powell), 130 n, 131 n
My War With Japan (Alcott), 139 n, 172 n

Nagasaki, 197, 199
Nanjing Road, i x
Nanking-Shanghai Railway, 151
Nantao, 73, 184–85
Napoleon Bonaparte, 80
Nash Put (Our Way), 116, 117
Nasha Jizn (Our Life), 6–7, 64, 85, 143
National Fund Commission of Shanghai, 107
Nazis, 3, 5, 7, 13, 15–17, 20, 42, 92, 130, 133, 137, 140, 174–76, 181, 187
Nelson, Admiral Horatio, 80
Neutrality Pact, 177
New York Herald Tribune, 126
New York, xi, 40, 130
Nicolai II, Czar, 59

Nien Cheng (*Life and Death in Shanghai*), xi
North China Daily News, 12, 72, 117
Northern Construction Company of Canada, 48
Novomeysky, M. S., 8 n

Obshchestvo Remeslov Truda (ORT), 136
O'Conroy, Taid (*The Menace of Japan*), 31
Okinawa, 187
Okura, 181
Olympic Games, 51
Onishi Tokijiro,Vice-Admiral, 145 n
Open Ports, 17
Opium, 96–98
Opium War, 3
Oporto, 28
Oslo, 42 n
Ovaltine, 140
Owens, Jesse, 51

Paci, Mario, 77
Palestine, 7, 15, 16, 107, 158, 207
Palestine Mandate, 108
Pan Ling (*In Search of Old Shanghai*), 173 n
Pao Chia, 58, 105, 134, 155
Paper chase, 66
Paris, 42, 80, 169
Park Hotel, 131, 181
Patriotic Press Association, 40
Pearl Harbor, xiii, 3, 18, 28, 42, 67, 70, 79, 101, 103, 110 n, 139, 142, 145, 150, 170, 186, 198, 202
Peking University, 43
People's Liberation Army, 207–208
Perry, I. M., 13
Persian Gulf, 64
Pétain, Marshal Henri Philippe, 82, 191, 197
Pétainistes, 82
Peter Pan Shop, 11, 105, 129, 171
Petlura, Simon, 39
Philippines, 40, 60, 92, 110 n, 127,

Pickford, Mary, 43
Pidgin English, 35, 70, 68 n, 169
Pika-don. See also Atomic Bomb;
  195 n, 197, 199, 200
Pogroms,xiii,8–9, 14, 39, 115
Polo, Marco, 141
Pootung Camp, 77, 205
Pope Clement XI, 23
Portuguese, 69
Powell, John B. (*My Twenty-Five
  Years in China*), 97 n, 130n,
  131 n
Power, Tyrone, 139
Private Lives (Coward), 102
Provisional Free Government of
  India, 92
Public Garden, 76, 77
Pyle, Ernie, 187n

Quaker Oats, 16
Querschnitt, 193

Rabinovich, Aida (author's
  mother), 5–21 passim, 31–57,
  passim, 66–74 passim, 94–105
  passim, 114, 127–143 passim,
  169, 178, 195, 207; business of,
  11; refugee relief and, 50–51
Rabinovich, Alla (author's sister), 5, 10, 31–33, 61–72 passim,
  87–111 passim, 119–30 passim,
  143, 195, 205
Rabinovich, Boris (author's
  grandfather), 37, 40
Rabinovich, David (author's father), 5–11, 31–41 passim, 57–
  71 passim, 85, 89–90, 106–114
  passim, 130, 143, 156, 167–68,
  198; aid to refugees, 54–55, 56,
  180–89; Jewish Club and, 166–
  67; Morris Cohen and, 47–49;
  Silas Hardoon and 158; Sun
  Yat-sen and, 88–90
Rabinovich, Gabriel (Gava), 38,
  145–47, 168–69
Rabinovich, Isabel (Isa), 84, 146
Rabinovich, Mrs. Boris
  ("Babushka"), 37, 38, 59

Rabinovich, Rosetta, 146–47
Race Course, 67, 81
Raiden, 151 n
"Renaissance" (restaurant), 61
Ricci, Matteo, 22–23
Rickshaws, 109–12
Rising Sun (Toland), 109n, 175n,
  197 n
Riley, Jack, 172–74
Rodzaevsky, Konstantin
  Vladimirovich, 115–17
Roosevelt, Franklin D., 93n, 126,
  131, 132, 167–68, 191
Route Vallon, 81
Royal Horse Artillery, 86
Rue Chapsal, 81
Rue Corneille, 81
Rue Molière, 81, 108
Rue Pichon, 81
Rue Stanislas Chevalier, 81
Russia: Russians (*see also* White
  Russians): 3, 9, 57–63, 175–75
Russian Emigrants Association,
  62
Russian Revolution, 8, 9, 60, 86
Russian Sports Club, 57
Russo-Japanese War, 8

S.Z. Mittag der Schanghai Post,
  193
Saburo Sakai (*Samurai*), 196n
Saipan, 107n, 127
Samurai,(Saburo), 196n
Sanders-Bates, J. A. E., 142 n
Sassoon Company, 26, 156
Sassoon House, 101–103
Sassoon, David, 64–65
Sassoon, Elias, 64–65
Sassoon, Sir Victor, 102–103
Schanghai Woche, 193
Scheidlinger, Max, 181–183
Schwarzbard, Shalom, 39
Seaforth Highlanders, 77
Sephardi,xiii,13, 15, 26, 38, 64n,
  64–65, 107, 155, 158
Seattle, 69
Secret Lives of Trebitsch-Lincoln
  (Wasserstein), 84n

216 STRANGERS ALWAYS

Sfarim, Mendele Mocher, 5
Shakespeare, William, 80
Shanghai, ix
Shanghai Bank, 69
Shanghai Echo, 187, 193
*Shanghai Evening Post &
Mercury*, 139, 142n
Shanghai Fire Brigade, 96
Shanghai Industrial Exhibition
Hall, 155n
Shanghai Jewish Cemetery, 63
Shanghai Jewish Chronicle, 136n,
193
Shanghai Jewish Club, 37
Shanghai Jewish School, 13–14,
24
Shanghai Municipal Council, 10,
104
Shanghai Passage (Taussig), xi
Shanghai Post, 185
Shanghai Society for the
Prevention of Cruelty to
Animals, 163
Shanghai Symphony Orchestra,
77
Shanghai Zionist Association,
107
Shaw, Ralph, (*China Nights*),
142 n
Shelley, Percy Bysshe, 80
Shibota, 55, 56n
Shilo, Moshe, 55
Shmulevsky, Abe, 128
Shmulevsky, Essie, 53, 85, 128
Shonan, 16
Shunpao, 142n
Siberia, 8–9, 37, 138, 162
Singer, Israel Joshua, 5
Sino-Japanese War, 49, 195
Sino-Judaic Institute, xi
Society for the Rescue of Chinese
Jews, 22
"Sokol," 57
Soloveichik, Rabbi, 37
Somaliland, 140
Soong Sisters (Hahn), 11n
Soviet Union (USSR), 138, 147,
163, 177n, 197n, 199
Speelman, M., 56

SS *Empress of Asia*, 48
St. John's University, 43, 76, 96
St. Mary's Hospital, 84
St. Nicolas Church, 176
Stahmer, Heinrich, 92–93
Stalin, Joseph, 72, 126, 164, 177 n,
191
Stanley Camp, 29n
Stark, Admiral, 60
Stateless people (*see also* Jews,
White Russians) xiii, 11, 43,
53–54, 68, 90
Stefani, 150
Steinhard, Leopold, 136
Storfer, Dr. A. J., 187, 192
"Stormy Weather," 77
Streicher, Julius, 115
Stürmer, 115
Subhas Chandra Bose, 92
Sudetenland, 17
Summer Club, 25
Sun, General ("Kingmaker"),
160 n
Sun Yat-sen, 48–49, 88–90;
Zionism and, 107–108
Sun Yat-sen Hospital, 27
Sun Yat-sen, Mme., 49n
Sunkiang, 123
Sungari River, 147
Swartz, Mary (*Fugu Plan*), 38 n
Synagogue of Immigrants from
China, 38 n
Syracuse University, 75
Syrians, 3
Szechuan Road, 35
Szenasi, Laslo (*Trebitsch-
Lincoln*), 84n

Tagore, Rabindranath, 28
Tageblatt, 136n
Taiwan (Formosa), 52
Thailand, 92
Taiping Rebellion, 121
Taussig, Francizka (*Shanghai
Passage*), xi
Tel Aviv, 15, 38 n, 55, 207
Temple, Shirley, 11
The Scream (Munch), 42 n
Thought Police, 34

Tientsin, 9, 20, 118
Tojo, General Hideki, 93, 109
Tokayer, Marvin (*Fugu Plan*), 38n
Tokyo, 33, 55, 113n, 127n, 132, 165, 169, 178, 178n, 200, 202
Toland, John (*The Rising Sun*), 109n, 175n, 197n
Tonari Gumi, 34
Tongren Road, 145n
Tonn, W. Y., 136
Topas, Boris, 57, 113–115, 119, 166
Topas, Genny, 10, 41, 80, 82, 112–13, 162–66 passim
Topas, Lubov, 112
Tower Apartments, 73
Trans-Siberian Railroad, 147
Transocean, 126, 150
Treaty of Nanking, 3, 23, 81,
Treaty Ports, 64, 147
Trebitsch-Lincoln, Ignacz, 84–88
Trebitsch-Lincoln, Ignatius ("Natzl"), 86
Trebitsch-Lincoln: The Self-Made Villain (Lampe and Szenasi), 84n
Tribune, 193
Tripartite Pact, 93
Turgenev, Ivan (*Memoirs of a Sportsman*), 129
Two Men in a Boat, 131

U Ba Maw, 92
U.S. Air Force, 125, 127, 150, 151
U.S. Army, 40, 52n, 75, 132–33
U.S. Marine Corps, 31
Ukraine, 9
Undeclared War, 18
United Nations, 187
United States, 3, 4, 7, 31, 40n, 62, 70, 81, 109, 111, 120, 126, 129, 132, 139n, 142, 170–75 passim
Université de l'Aurore (Aurora, Aurora University), 21, 23, 41. 75, 151, 166, 170, 186
University Press, 142n
Unser Wort, 191
USS *Missouri*, 50n, 202

Varvara Nicolaevna , 129
Vertinsky, Alexander, 163–64
Vichy government, 82, 84, 150, 198
Victor Emmanuel, King 72n
Victoria, Queen, 93
Vienna, 18, 179
Vigny, Alfred de, 77
Vladivostok, 7, 8, 36, 38, 57, 85
Vogue patterns, 169
"Volkhochschule," 136

Wainwright, General Jonathan, 52
Wallace, Edgar, 128
Wan Waithayakon, Prince, 92
Wanderers and Settlers in the Far East (Dicker), 193n
Wang Ching-Wei, 29, 36, 42 92, 142
Ward Road, 120
Ward, Frederick Townsend, 121–23
Wasserstein, Bernard (*Secret Lives of Trebitsch-Lincoln*), 84n
Wayside (District), 9, 52
Wayside Road, 37
Whangpoo River, 19, 53, 60, 69, 76, 77, 101–104, 186
White Russians,xiii,4, 11, 20, 60–62, 127, 148, 163, 164, 176–77
Williams, Leonard, 40
Wittenberg, Alfred, 136n
Women's Volunteer Corps, 92
Wong, Anna May, 12
Woo (tailor), 169–70
Wooster Victory, 199
Woosung River, 207
World War I, 8
Wort, 192
Wyman, Colonel Theodore, 149

XMHA, 139–40

Yangtze River, 55
Yangzepoo District, 52
Yates Road, 29
Yiddischer Almanach, 187, 192

Yiddische Stimme von Bait Mizrah, 192
Yiddish, 19, 193
Yokohama, 69
Yokohama Specie Bank, 69
Yom Kippur, 15, 77
Yomiuri-Hochi Shimbun,132
Yorifumi Enoki, 31–33, 106, 145

Young Men's Christian Association (Y.M.C.A.), 85

Zi-Ka-Wei Observatory, 30
Zionists, Zionism, 7–8, 47, 86, 106–108, 113, 158, 166
Zola, Emile, 31
Zürich, 32